THE BEST BUDDHIST WRITING 2011

 A SHAMBHALA SUN BOOK

THE BEST
BUDDHIST
WRITING
2·0·1·1

Edited by Melvin McLeod
and the Editors of the *Shambhala Sun*

SHAMBHALA
Boston & London 2011

Shambhala Publications, Inc.
Horticultural Hall
300 Massachusetts Avenue
Boston, Massachusetts 02115
www.shambhala.com

9 8 7 6 5 4 3 2

Printed in the United States of America

⊗This edition is printed on acid-free paper that meets the
American National Standards Institute z39.48 Standard.
♻This book is printed on 30% postconsumer recycled paper.
For more information please visit www.shambhala.com.
Distributed in the United States by Random House, Inc.,
and in Canada by Random House of Canada Ltd

Library of Congress Cataloging-in-Publication Data

The best Buddhist writing 2011 / edited by Melvin McLeod
and the editors of the *Shambhala Sun.*—1st ed.
p. cm.
ISBN 978-1-59030-933-9 (pbk.: alk. paper)
1. Buddhism. I. McLeod, Melvin. II. Shambhala sun.
BQ4055.B475 2011
294.3—dc22
2011014494

Contents

Introduction

Two thousand five hundred years ago, an Indian prince-turned-ascetic-yogi did something simple but profoundly radical: he sat down under a tree and stopped struggling. He had long ago stopped struggling for material pleasure and success, and now he also ceased the Herculean spiritual struggle he had undertaken since he left his princely palace. He stopped, rested his mind, and looked directly at the profound nature of his own being and the world in all its brilliance. He saw that it was all perfect just as it was and that suffering came only from the unnecessary struggle, founded in ignorance, to make it something different. He awakened to his true nature, which is the true nature of all beings. He saw that he was naturally a buddha, and at that moment, he became the Buddha.

From the Buddha's world-transforming act of cessation 2,500 years ago has grown the religious tradition we know today as Buddhism. Great philosophical schools developed from his simple act of stopping. His disciples founded the Buddhist monastic sangha, the oldest continuous institution in human history. Teachers trained their students in the methods he had developed and they in turn trained new generations of students, in a living transmission of spiritual practice and realization that continues unbroken to this day. His teachings spread across Asia, taking on the flavor of each culture they entered, and now they are taking birth among us.

Buddhism began to have real impact on American culture in the 1950s, with Zen's influence on the Beat writers and other artists and intellectuals. So we are only six decades into what might be a two–hundred-year process to establish a Western Buddhism that is genuine and complete. Some say that Buddhism is still in its infancy in the West, but I think perhaps it is a little more advanced than that, a toddler now taking its first hesitant steps on its own.

This series of *The Best Buddhist Writing* anthologies, now in its seventh year, is one guide to the state of Buddhism in the West. I think the news in this year's edition is good. These writings reflect an increasingly natural integration of Buddhist practice and philosophy into modern life, while remaining true to the depth and integrity of Buddhist tradition. It is a delicate process to adapt Buddhism to a new culture and yet maintain unbroken that lineage of genuine dharma that goes back to the Buddha himself. But it has been done successfully in other cultures over the course of 2,500 years, and it will be done here too. I think it is already happening.

What is the sign that Buddhism is truly taking birth in our culture, no longer standing outside the mainstream as an exotic foreign import? I think it is when there is no separation between our practice of the dharma and our lives as modern people, when our practice blends naturally into our lives and our lives are fully integrated with our practice.

You can see this is happening in the many marvelous personal stories in this year's *The Best Buddhist Writing*. Karen Maezen Miller's memoir of new love, marriage, and the reality of dishes opens this book. Miller's Buddhist practice takes place in the kitchen-sink reality of the modern American family. She does not deny or try to escape its stresses and problems; she finds love and awareness right within them. She does not fall prey to the idealization and perfectionism that separates spiritual practice from real life.

I am grateful to these writers who open their lives to us. Misha Becker describes a bond of unconditional love between one very old and one very young. In a painful breakup, Susan Piver discovers the wisdom of a broken heart. Karen Connelly invokes ancient teachings to help her deal with her headstrong young son. Susan Moon finds there can be joy in old age, cabdriver Brian Haycock follows the dharma road, and R. J. Eskow goes home again to the gritty industrial town he grew up in. Since the practice of Buddhism is about the way we lead our lives, these honest, moving, and loving stories are great teachings in themselves. To me they are the hopeful sign of a Buddhism truly taking root in the life of America.

Yet it is not enough for practitioners to incorporate Buddhism into their personal lives. To fully take its place in our society, Buddhism also must participate in the social and political sphere, bringing its values and practices to the important questions of our times. This is a natural reflection of Buddhism's dedication to the welfare of all sentient beings, and so Buddhist practitioners, writers, and activists have passionately engaged with questions of war and peace, social justice, human rights, and the environment. Their numbers may be small, but their Buddhist philosophy and practices have been influential.

This is particularly true in the environmental movement, whose basic principles Buddhists have espoused for thousands of years. In this volume, Joanna Macy, a seminal figure in the deep ecology movement, tells a powerful story of healing in Chernobyl; Rick Bass and Wendy Johnson address our own environmental disaster, the BP oil spill in the Gulf of Mexico; and Lin Jensen tells a simple human story with global lessons. As they point out, a true commitment to the principles of non-ego, interdependence, and loving-kindness could offer us a turn back from the disastrous direction we seem to be heading in.

Like any world religion, Buddhism has vast bodies of texts, elaborate rituals, and great institutions. Yet at its heart Buddhism is about the personal relationship between teacher and student, in which the deep truths and profound methods of Buddhism are transmitted in accord with the student's individual needs. To succeed, Western Buddhism must develop its own native-born teachers who can join the honored succession that goes back to the Buddha himself. A number of fine Western-born teachers are represented in this book. What they offer is real.

Witness three sparkling teachings by contemporary American Zen teachers. Bonnie Myotai Treace is a poetic and subtle voice in American Zen. Here she joins the generations of teachers who have added their own realization to the enlightenment stories of the old Chinese masters. We can be proud that Americans like her are joining this august lineage. Enkyo Pat O'Hara leads the Village Zendo, an eclectic and progressive Zen community in New York City. She brings a modern perspective to that famous description of the enlightenment experience, "Body and mind dropped away." Joan Sutherland, one of American Buddhism's finest writers, contemplates the gateless gate where the form and formless meet.

Western teachers are taking their place in all traditions of Buddhism. Also in this volume are teachings by Jack Kornfield and Rodney Smith of the Theravada school, and Matthieu Ricard, Elizabeth Mattis-Namgyel, Ken McLeod, and Kathleen McDonald of the Vajrayana tradition. Actually, many writers in this book teach Buddhism, although they may not primarily be known as teachers. All give us hope that American Buddhism will develop the learned and realized—dare we hope, even enlightened?—teachers it will need to become a genuine and sustainable tradition.

A maturing Western Buddhism must not only be true to its ancestors but confident enough to make its own contribution to the religion. All traditions have done this in the past, enriching Buddhism through their own cultural and social values, and American Buddhists are already doing this in important ways. None has been more significant than the historic advance in gender equality that Western Buddhists have spearheaded. This book itself tells the story: excluding the contributions by male Asian teachers, more than half of the writings in this anthology are by women. This reflects the important role that women teachers, leaders, and scholars are playing in American Buddhism, making it a leader in gender equality among spiritual traditions and a positive influence on Buddhist culture globally.

This book reflects another important innovation of American Buddhism, the vital cross-fertilization taking place across Buddhist schools. While Buddhist practitioners traditionally focused exclusively on the philosophy and practices of their own school, American Buddhists, while maintaining true to their own tradition, benefit from all teachings of Buddhism. As you read this book, you will find yourself enriched by the voices of Theravada, Zen, and Vajrayana practitioners—each bringing the special genius of their tradition to bear on the issues of modern life.

I have already mentioned how many stories in this anthology are personal—memoirs of marriage, family, work, activism. These stories of life in the modern world reflect perhaps the most fundamental—and challenging—characteristic of the new Buddhism that is emerging in the West. For 2,500 years, full-time practitioners in all their variations—monks, nuns, cave-dwelling yogis, Zen hermits, forest monks—have been the heart of Buddhism. Buddhism in the West, however, has developed largely as a community of lay practitioners who aspire to find enlightenment right in the midst modern life. As Rodney Smith considers in his thoughtful essay in this book, this is leading to new approaches to Buddhist practice, and new approaches to the lay life of Buddhists.

The challenge remains to develop that cadre of full-time practitioners, scholars, and translators who can guarantee the depth and authenticity of American Buddhism long into the future. For now, we still have the good fortune of great Asian teachers to guide us. In this volume, they range from His Holiness the Dalai Lama, who is not only a teacher to Buddhists but to the world; to the great Zen master and Engaged Buddhist founder Thich Nhat Hanh; to the young Tibetan teacher Dzogchen Ponlop, with his modern take on the Vajrayana; to my own teacher, Khenpo Tsultrim Gyamtso, the Milarepa of this age. These are the parents, wise and compassionate, who hold the hand of American Buddhism as it takes its first toddling steps.

Thus my thanks go first to the teachers who have illuminated my life—the late Chögyam Trungpa Rinpoche, Khenpo Tsultrim Gyamtso, Thich Nhat Hanh, and Thinley Norbu Rinpoche—and to all the teachers past and present who offer to us the truth of suffering, the cause of suffering, the truth of the cessation of suffering, and the path to enlightenment. This book—and Buddhism itself—exists only because of them.

I would like to express my deep appreciation to my friend Peter Turner, who conceived this series and asked me to be its editor. I would like to thank Beth Frankl and all her colleagues at Shambhala Publications, with whom I share personal, professional, and dharmic bonds. I always look forward to going to my office at the Shambhala Sun Foundation because of the people I work with there. Buddhist and non-Buddhist alike, we share a deep commitment to the foundation's mission. Finally, I thank my wife, Pam Rubin, and our daughter, Pearl. Through the blessing of our teachers, we seek in our lives as a family the unique path that will come to be known as genuine Western dharma.

Melvin McLeod
Editor-in-chief
The Shambhala Sun
Buddhadharma: The Practitioner's Quarterly
Mindful: Living with Awareness and Compassion

The Best Buddhist Writing 2011

Hand Wash Cold

Karen Maezen Miller

The best Buddhist writing, like the best writing in general, is about real life. That's because Buddhist practice is about living life as it really is—without trying to transcend or escape it—and finding love and joy right in its ups and downs. It's literal kitchen-sink wisdom, and its most eloquent voice is Karen Maezen Miller, who writes of her family life as an expression of her Zen practice, and vice versa. Here's her story of love, marriage, and dishes.

Broken Glass: Cracking the Illusion of Security

Dinners were difficult. No matter what, dinners were difficult, while the days took care of themselves.

I had learned as much on the very first night, when I looked in the guidebook, called ahead, and walked a short way up a narrow Florentine street to the place where they held, ridiculously, my reserved table for one. I felt conspicuously incomplete as I entered the restaurant trailing a plume of empty space. The tables were crowded by parties of four or seven or twelve, loud and laughing groups, whole and happy families, while I sat insulated in my own dirigible of hushed air. I ate, paid, and discharged myself to bed.

This was not how it was supposed to be, this trip of a lifetime to northern Italy, the ripened hills that had awakened a thousand years of passionate appetites. I should have been accompanied. I should have been accompanied by a man, preferably younger and fashionably bohemian, someone who would stir my fearlessness. As fantasies are prone to do, my imaginary companion had failed to materialize. I had taken the trip alone, egged on by friends who believed I should do it to commemorate another milestone: my thirty-eighth lousy birthday.

Days were spent in and around famous places: the Duomo, the cathedral that swallows the city whole; the Pitti Palace, with its forsaken majesty; and the Forte di Belvedere, the southern mount from which all of time splays out in postcard panorama. One afternoon walking back toward my hotel, I stopped on the Santa Trinita Bridge to admire a blushing sunset and rainbow. Twilight traffic traced the river Arno's eternal curve. People hurried by me. I watched it all, uncertain of what to watch for. What was it, really, that brought people here? What was so special about a certain place or time? What transformed life into love? Had I missed the turn?

Soon, I would have to brave the evening meal. The book I'd borrowed from an acquaintance back home had the names of restaurants penciled inside the front cover. I chose one, Le Quattro Stagioni, eyed the map, and realized the restaurant was just a block across the bridge on which I stood. I headed on to see.

The place was tucked into a corridor of tall and darkened buildings, not a spot you could arrive at unaware. I entered its narrow and deep interior, yellow walls warmed with age, cozy and inviting to those who ventured inside. The maître d' took me into the far room and seated me against the back wall, a special spot for single diners, I gathered, because I was sitting nearly shoulder-to-shoulder with another single diner.

It was a woman. A very old and small woman, her hair wintry white, her face creased, her hands bent and bony. She was finishing her meal when she turned and smiled and spoke in a gentle accent.

"Are you Italiana?"

"No, I'm an American," I responded, pleased to have prompted a second guess.

The woman cupped her hand to her ear and leaned toward me. "I can hardly hear. I'm over eighty years old!"

"But you're so beautiful," I said. Surprisingly, I meant it.

"I was," she said. "I won prizes."

I quaked to full attention. Here I sat in a restaurant named for life's seasons, another pathetic year beyond my summer's glistening youth, entering midlife's mystery, suddenly someplace I'd never been, with no one, no hope or promise, and an oracle had spoken. When would I finally seize this fleeting life of mine like a trophy in my hands?

I ordered a plate of crostini, bite-sized toast topped with tomato relish. Skimpy fare even for someone who didn't eat.

Soon, the woman rose and hobbled on a cane to leave. Passing by, she reached down and cradled my chin in her hand.

"Sweetheart," she said, "good luck and good appetite." And she left.

Minutes later the revolving front door turned again. A dark-haired man in a white shirt entered. I watched the waiter lead him in my direction, into my room, into my corner, into the old woman's still-warm seat, eyeing me all the while, making clear to me, at least, the main course he was serving.

I was afraid I knew who this man was. I was afraid I knew who had come to have dinner beside me. I was afraid I knew, but for once I knew I wasn't afraid.

He was my future husband, of that I was scarily certain, although I knew nothing more about him than that. It would become my repeated resolution to keep it that way. To know nearly nothing of him, and to expect nothing, for the long life of our marriage.

When we think we know someone, you see, we are already halfway to disappointment, and no one needs a head start on that.

This is not how we have learned to choose our partners, is it? This is not how we greet people, is it? With an open mind? With an eager hand? Like an unopened gift? Not when we make a life's work out of finding and keeping the perfect mate, the ideal match for our economic aspirations, political views, religious preference, height, weight, taste in coffee, and wardrobe sensibility—all the ways we foolishly seek in another mere validation for ourselves. When we believe we know what's good for us, what's right, and what we're looking for—and believe me, we all do—we condemn all our current relationships and doom the ones to come.

At this moment, I had no idea what I was looking for. I wasn't even looking. For what seemed like the first time in my life, I was truly alone, no longer appending myself to a love story. No longer trying to reconstitute a partner from the past, no longer imagining a fairy-tale future. My guiding impulse, as I studied the shadowy profile in my peripheral vision, was simply this: Oh, what the hell.

From that vantage point, I can assure you, anything can happen.

"How's your crostini?" he asked.

I invited him to have a taste. And you know what happens when you have a nibble. Before long, you've cleaned the plate and gone back for seconds.

In some sense, this was the most dangerous thing I'd ever done. It wasn't the first time I'd flirted. It was the first time I'd flirted without the slightest trepidation about how it would end. I suppose that's why it hasn't—not yet, anyway. It's the things we fear that chase us down, that haunt and hobble us until they inevitably overtake us and leave us with the weary self-fulfillment we were so afraid to find. I knew this would happen.

Fear is our first and, if we're not careful, our last love. It is our most enduring relationship. It never leaves our side. It tells us where to go, what to wear, what to say, and what not to say. We surrender all other options to it. Before, after, and during most of our relationships, we are concerned above all not with the other party but with what we fear he or she will do. Let me count the ways.

I'm afraid I'll be embarrassed.

I'm afraid I'll be disappointed.

I'm afraid I'll be hurt.

I'm afraid I'll be left.

I'm afraid I'll be alone.

I'm afraid I'll be unloved.

I'm afraid I'll be taken advantage of.

I'm afraid it won't work out.

I'm afraid of change.

I'm afraid to live.

I'm afraid to die.

When I tell you that fear is the basic ground of ego, the false sense of a separate self, you might conclude what I do. We are unavailable for any truly loving and fulfilling relationship as long as we are trapped in a committed relationship with the most controlling part of our own mind—our fear. Our fear of what will happen and our fear of what will not.

Nearly everything we're afraid will happen is going to happen anyway, so what's to fear? There is no secure or unchanging ground, and we make ourselves safe only when we see and accept the way life is. Utterly spontaneous and impermanent. When it is time to laugh, we laugh. When it is time to weep, we weep. We are cheated of nothing in life except that from which we withhold ourselves by ego's narrow bounds. These bounds were made to break; indeed they must, if we ever hope to be whole again.

I'm not proposing that you play fast and loose with your self-respect, just that you abandon the lost cause of keeping yourself securely fixed in one place. It can't be accomplished while you are alive, and I can't offer an eyewitness account of what comes after.

During the dismal stretch of time I was wearing my big broken heart like a signboard, a flashing hazard light, a friend gave me a carved wooden heart. It was big, painted pink, and hewn from a single piece of pine. But the wood was too green. It was insufficiently aged, because the heart was nearly riven in two with a crack wide enough to see through.

"Is it cracked, or is it open?" she said pointedly when she gave it to me.

"How has he managed to stay alone for so long?" my teacher Maezumi Roshi asked me when he heard that I'd landed a good-looking forty-year-old American bachelor from Los Angeles on my pilgrimage to Italy.

"He wasn't alone," I said. He'd had any number of relationships that, like mine, had gone wrong.

"Oh, good, then you will heal each other," he said.

He must have meant the kind of healing that happens when a blister pops and bleeds, when skin burns and flays, or when a fracture is rebroken to set it straight again. The kind of healing that keeps hurting as we break with our fearful selves over and over again.

I have broken many things in my second marriage: plates, glassware, door hinges, a wristwatch, and a heart or two, all flung in fear and frustration at not having my way. It's a habit I keep vowing to break.

A year after that first dinner in Florence, a rabbi wrapped a goblet in a table napkin and set it on the stone floor at our feet. My new husband shattered it with one stomp.

"Mazel tov!" the crowd around us cheered. It was a fitting benediction, the starting blast, for a lifetime promise to break up with myself.

SCRAPE OR RINSE: MARRIAGE ON A PLATE

He studied the models, rated the features, and compared the prices. He did what he does best, and what I ask him to do in circumstances like this. He ran the numbers, and then he picked out the new dishwasher.

I was happy with the size (it fit), the color (it matched), and the delivery in two days.

He was happy with something else. "The best thing is, you don't have to rinse the plates," my husband said.

For the record, you have to rinse the plates. You have to scrape them to within an inch of their lives. You have to scrub them, yes, even though that constitutes a complete washing before you load the machine. And sometimes, you have to throw them. Things have to break. This is a marriage, you see. Something's got to give.

"When will you write about marriage?" I hate when people ask me that. I just don't know what to say. I've been looking at a blank page for months—all right, years—and I just don't know.

After the courtship, after the kid, after too many conflagrations to count, I just don't know how marriage is supposed to work. There are no experts in my house. More and more it seems to me that every question in life is how, and every answer is do. And do, and do, and do.

You can try tidy formulas and messy compromises. You can soak the splatters overnight and hope they loosen by morning. You can stick religiously to the nonstick surfaces, and after a while even those start to stick. You can try all the methods professionals recommend and you still have a mess on your hands.

I've never found an easier way around it, so let me save you from expecting to find it. Forget the advertised claims. Drop the romantic illusions. Let go of your cherished ideals, the hoped-for bonds held intact by lifetime glue. For a marriage to last, you have to scour it yourself every day until not a fleck of fettuccine is left behind and it gleams like a mirror beaming back your own reflection.

Then, put it in the dishwasher for good measure and go to bed.

I've noticed that how we load the dishwasher says everything about the difference between my husband and me. I have a system that I rather like. I put the plasticware and glasses on the top and the plates and bowls on the bottom. I use the prongs on the racks to prop things in place so that the blast from the sprayer arm reaches each piece. I don't put my stainless, restaurant-quality pots and pans in the machine, because the instructions said not to. So I wash them by hand. I wash a lot of things by hand. Like when my husband loads the dishwasher, I wash many things that come out of it by hand. I do it my way.

As you might have guessed, he doesn't fully rinse the dirty plates or cruddy bowls before he loads them, because the instructions said not to. He doesn't always use the prongs to prop things the way I think is right. He might squeeze a wineglass into the lower rack, crowd an oatmeal bowl beside it, and cantilever a stew pot over both. Then he might take the cutting board and put it crossways on bottom, against the door, so the blast from the spray arm bounces off, pulsing out the side of the machine and soaking the kitchen floor. He does it his way.

Miraculously, it works. In the morning, I take the dirty dishes caked with dried food out of the machine and hand wash them. The miracle does not occur in the machine. The miracle does not occur in the second wash. The miracle occurs when I don't say a word about it. It's not only what I do or don't do; without me knowing, he silently performs a million miracles himself.

Truly, the miracle of marriage lies in what we don't say, and deeper still in what we don't know. Marriage takes one dishwasher and two miracle workers.

Sometimes people think I'm telling them they have to keep a marriage together at all costs. Phooey! That's something else I never say, because nothing stays put, intact, and inert forever. I only say that you have to keep waking up and washing the dishes, rinsing away your unmet expectations and stubborn resentments.

That's what helps me see my marriage for what it is: not the roaring flame we ignited, not the seamless partnership we promised, not the friendship we fantasized, and not quite what we were thinking.

It's taken me a long time to admit that my husband and I aren't each other's best friend, although friendship has never been our lot. At the onset of our midlife, long-distance courtship, after that fling as frisky strangers on vacation in Italy, I was uncompromising about our prospects. "I don't need a friend in Los Angeles," I said on the phone from Houston, a fair warning about the biological time bomb that had sent me hurtling in his direction.

The bomb went off, and shortly after our daughter was born I spent a good bit of time assessing the collateral damage. Having a newborn is more than enough reason to break down and call it quits, but she wasn't the problem. While the baby napped, I parked myself in front of the TV to watch a hypnotic loop of *The Wedding Story*, which back then ran in repeats throughout the cable network's afternoon time slots. The episodes impaled me with doubt, because the real-life couples on the verge of their vows always had a dreamy sense of destiny, adoration, and friendship that was unlike anything I experienced in my own life. I worried myself heartsick. Did everyone marry a best friend but me?

My best friend was back in Texas, and if I called her and said I had a flat tire in the pouring rain in rush hour on the 405 freeway, she would climb on a plane with two umbrellas and a jack. My husband would more likely counsel me with a cool head while never leaving his engineering cubicle: "Call Triple A." My marriage was not the stuff of white-horse rescues. Of course, it never rains in southern California, and I didn't fall in love with a tow truck driver. You think my expectations were off course?

That was before I decided to give myself a break. It was before I decided that marriage—at least our marriage—wasn't about friendship at all. Come to think of it, why would anyone want to marry a friend? I have plenty of friends and I do not want to marry any of them. I want to go have coffee with them and talk about how my husband infuriates me. That's the place to bring it up, if at all.

No, ours is not a marriage of friends making nice. Ours is a marriage of adversaries making peace. I wonder if that's what makes this odd and uncomfortable convention so transformative: not that we marry our friends but that we marry strangers—indeed, opposites—and then remarry one another every day. Perhaps that's what creates lifetime peace, love, and harmony: the honest effort, not the butterflies and moonbeams.

"So you mean there's no reason to get married?" says a friend whose very ceremony I performed. She is stumbling, dazed and defeated, through the scorched earth of her fourth year.

"There's no good reason at all," I say. There is no good reason to make any of the promises we make, and that's where the magic occurs. Marriage is not a choice you make like picking the glass tumblers from Crate & Barrel that promise to be dishwasher safe. (Mine cracked anyway.)

Marriage shows us how flimsy and meaningless the reach of reason can be. It teaches us to go beyond what we think we can do—we can do more—and reexamine just exactly who we think is going to do it for us: each of us, by ourselves.

Truly, there is not much two people can share. My husband and I do not share the same opinion about many things, except certain U.S. presidents and Academy Award nominees. We don't share tastes in music or reading; we don't have the same habits; we don't favor the same religion; we don't have the same inclinations about money, except we'd both like the other to make more of it. It doesn't take very much self-awareness to see that it is impossible for two people to share the same point of view.

We seem to disagree just because we can. It's another mindless habit. In the split second after one of us speaks, there is a choice to be made: accord or discord? Acceptance or rejection? A nod yes or a shake no? What you do or don't do in that second is the source of all second chances.

When the going gets tough, he'll say something like: "If people could see the way you really are, they wouldn't think you were so Zen." That's one thing we instantly agree on. I remind him that I don't practice meditation because I'm someone better. I practice because I'll never be anyone else.

A marriage is a lot like a silent meditation retreat anyway. In both cases, you come face-to-face with the most unlovable aspects of yourself, your messy unpleasantness, your selfishness, and the panicked impulse to duck and run. Neither experience is anything like the honeymoon you signed up for. The point is to pitch all that out and stay put. With my meditation practice, I can see that I'm still a cranky person, but I try to be a kinder cranky person. One who says less but always says, "I'm sorry."

You know I've been married before, so you might wonder how the second time around is better than the first. Surely the first one was wrong and the second one is right? I've stopped thinking that way. It seems to me that we have the same fights, the same frustrations, the same salty tears, the same low-grade despair, and yes, even the same loneliness. I've stopped thinking that one husband is better and one is worse, or even that my husband is different from yours. Comparisons are inherently false, distorted by our own self-centeredness, and serve no one. Besides, the way we tell it, husbands can seem uncannily alike. After two, five, ten years or more of cohabitation, we still complain about the toilet seat.

In the middle of it all, I remember that my husband doesn't claim to have a spiritual practice, so how could he see things as I do? In the middle of it all, I remember that I do have a spiritual practice, so why don't I try to see things as he does? I cannot find a different husband, but I can find a different me who looks at things differently, taking more responsibility and assigning less blame, appreciating the whole instead of dividing the parts.

Two people may not share many things, but the truth of it is, they can share everything.

I share my husband's humbling and terrifying love for our child.

I share his pride and satisfaction when he fixes the sprinklers, his fuming frustration when they need fixing all over again.

I share a refuge, until one of us turns it into a war zone.

I share the unpredictable ride in this life of ours: the fits, the fights, the glide, and the cycles. There really are seasons, and they really are different. Take care that you do not measure the autumn by the spring.

I share the shortening horizon and the coming certainty that we will need each other's strength and gentleness over the steepest ground yet.

I share the blanket of calm, the dark secret of sleep's mysterious company.

I share his glance, his twinkle, his smile, and his touch.

I share the love that is quiet, patient, and kind, the love that bears all things and surrenders its way.

I share a pot of coffee in the morning and a sink of dishes at night.

"Do you want me to load the dishwasher?" he asks, because he so often aims to help me out.

"That's okay, I'll manage it," I say, and wave him off, so caught up in my own arrogance that I've overlooked the gift. I do not say what I mean, what I still mean after all these years, the declaration that serves us without either of us knowing quite how. So I say it here before the assembled guests.

I do, honey, I really do.

Pass It On

Joanna Macy

Buddhism's first noble truth is suffering, and not just because that's the basic dilemma that Buddhism seeks to solve. The truth of suffering is noble because acknowledging our suffering, as difficult as that is, is where the path to healing begins. Here's a story of how that journey works, as the renowned ecophilosopher Joanna Macy takes the people of Chernobyl, reluctantly as first, into the heart of their great suffering and onto the path of healing.

There is a circle dance we do in all of my workshops and classes, whether on systems theory, Buddhism, or deep ecology. We do it to open our minds to the wider world we live in and to strengthen our intention to take part in its healing. Each time we put on the music and link hands, I think of Novozybkov in the fall of 1992.

Our team of four—two Russians named Harasch and Yuri, my husband, Fran, and I—had been traveling from one town to another in Belarus and Ukraine, offering workshops to people living in areas contaminated by the Chernobyl disaster. Now we had come to our final stop: the town of Novozybkov, an agricultural and light industrial city of fifty thousand a hundred miles due east of Chernobyl, in the Bryansk region of Russia. Together with its surrounding villages, it is considered to be the most contaminated city of its size that is still inhabited.

Drawing on what we learned from years of leading groups in despair-and-empowerment work, we came to offer, as we put it to the authorities, "psychological tools for coping with the effects of massive, collective trauma." We had entitled the workshops "Building a Strong Post-Chernobyl Culture." The name had a nice Soviet ring to it, but I soon realized that the word "post" was wrong. It suggested that the disaster was over, but it was soon obvious that it was far from over. The radioactivity was still spreading silently through wind, water, fodder, and food, creating new toxins as it mixed with automotive and industrial pollution, and sickening bodies already weakened from previous exposures. Our workshops, we soon realized, were not so much to help people recover from a catastrophe as to help them live with an ongoing one.

We came to Novozybkov at the insistence of Harasch; he preferred to be called by his family name rather than his first name, Adolph. A Russian psychologist practicing in Moscow, he flew to Chernobyl within hours of the accident to give support to the operators of the doomed reactor. In the six years that followed, he traveled to towns throughout the region to help the survivors, but no place had touched his heart more deeply than this city and its fate.

On the train, as we headed east from Minsk toward the Russian border, Harasch pulled out the map and told us the story in greater detail. The burning reactor was a volcano of radioactivity when the winds shifted to the northeast, carrying the clouds of poisoned smoke in the direction of Moscow. To save the millions in the metropolitan area, a fast decision at the highest levels of government was taken to seed the clouds and cause them to precipitate. The towns, fields, and forests of the Bryansk region just across the Russian border from Chernobyl were soaked by an unusually heavy late April rain, bearing intense concentrations of radioactive iodine, strontium, cesium, and particles of plutonium. The highest Geiger counter readings were—and still are—around the city of Novozybkov. "The people there were not informed of their government's choice—who wants to tell people they're disposable?" said Harasch. "By now it's common knowledge that the clouds were seeded, but it is rarely mentioned, and that silence, too, is part of the tragedy for the people of Novozybkov."

In a big open room of a school for special education, fifty people of Novozybkov, mostly teachers and parents, women predominating, were seated in a large circle. Carefully, almost formally dressed, they sat upright, eyes riveted on the speaker, and stood up when they spoke, the way their children stand in school when called to recite.

As I explained the nature and purpose of the work we came to do, Yuri offered swift and cogent translations. A young physician and social activist, he had used my books extensively in Moscow and had his own things to say about how people can overcome feelings of isolation and powerlessness and reconnect to take charge of their lives. To interpret from Russian to English for me, without delaying things, Fran murmured in my ear. By mid-morning, I was glad for a respite from all the words when I put on the tape of the Elm Dance and demonstrated the simple steps. Then we all joined hands and moved together to the music.

The fifty-four of us were too many to dance in one circle, so we formed concentric rings. The movements are easy to learn, and soon the rings were slowly orbiting to the music; each time we stepped toward the middle, raising our linked hands high, it was like a giant sunflower or a many-petaled lotus.

As we danced I wondered what the mayor of Novozybkov would think to see us. Upon our arrival the previous day, our team had called on him to explain what we'd come to do. The handsome, heavyset man of about forty listened guardedly. "It is good of you to come to undertake psychological rehabilitation," he said.

That was the term now in vogue, "psychological rehabilitation." I was glad that the emotional toll of the disaster was at last acknowledged by the authorities, especially since, in the three years following the accident, doctors were ordered by the Ministry of Health to dismiss its effects. When people insisted that their sickness and exhaustion, their cancers, miscarriages, and deformed babies, had something to do with Chernobyl, they were diagnosed as afflicted with "radiophobia," an irrational fear of radiation. Still, the phrase "psychological rehabilitation" irked me; I considered it an affront to the victims of Chernobyl. It reduced their suffering to a pathology, as if it were something to be corrected.

How could we convey to the mayor the basic difference in our assumptions? "Mr. Mayor, we do not imagine that we can take away the suffering of your people," I said. "That would be presumptuous on our part. But what we can do is look together at the two main ways we respond to collective suffering. The suffering of a people can bring forth from them new strengths and solidarity. Or it can breed isolation and conflict, turning them against each other. There is always a choice."

At that the mayor's demeanor totally changed. Leaning back in his chair, he spread his hands on the table and said, "There is not a single day, not a single encounter in this office, that does not show the anger stirring just under the surface. Whatever the matter at hand, there is this anger that is barely contained, ready to explode." Then, after a pause, "What can I do to support your work here?"

On that first day of the workshop, however, it became clear that these people had no desire to talk about Chernobyl and its ongoing presence in their lives. They referred to it in passing as "the event" and went on to speak of other things. People in less contaminated towns had told us in detail of the exhaustion, the chronic infections, the emerging patterns of cancers and birth defects. Now I'd come to this most toxic place to be with these people in their suffering, and they didn't want to talk about it. Even when a married couple took turns leaving in the morning and afternoon, they said nothing about their little girl in the hospital, to whose bedside they hurried.

The group's silence seemed to say, "This we don't need to talk about. We have to deal with this nightmare all the rest of our time. Here, at last, we can think about something else. We can look together at how we can achieve some sanity and harmony in family life." On that last point, they were explicit. They wanted to know how to deal with defiant children, sullen and depressed spouses, backbiting neighbors.

Harasch leaned over to me. "It's all the same thing," he whispered. "Chernobyl. On the conscious level, Chernobyl becomes tension and strife in family relations."

So we focused on family life. It was lively, as people took partners to enact encounters between parents and children, switching roles, practicing how to listen to each other. This led them to remember their own childhoods—not only the adolescent frustrations that could help them empathize with their own offspring, but the good times, too. They shared reminiscences of harvest seasons with the grandparents, sleigh parties, and fishing outings to the Dnieper. It all felt so restorative—as if we were partaking together of an excellent and wholesome meal—that Fran set up more exercises where people could remember together the old sources of joy.

Why did this suddenly feel so important? "We're strengthening our cultural immune system," I thought to myself, then said it aloud. Just as radiation attacks the integrity of the body, breaking down its capacity for resilience and self-healing, so does it assault our society. Through physical exhaustion and moral despair, it erodes a community's sense of wholeness and continuity. To bolster our cultural immune system, we need to recall who we are and what we love; memories help us do that.

In the evening, before disbanding to go home, we circled once more to the music. A guitar was playing and a woman singing in Latvian, evoking the trees of her land and hopes for its healing. Her words, I was told, disguise other meanings as well—a call for freedom from Soviet occupation and for the will to endure and resist. It didn't matter that we don't know Latvian; it was the lilt of her voice that we danced to and the haunting melody, stately and filled with yearning.

By now the simple steps were so familiar that some people danced with eyes closed. Their faces grew still, as if they were listening for something almost out of reach. Once they had their own folk dances. When did those traditions die away, relegated to a useless past? Was it under Lenin? Stalin?

Our host family lived in a fourth-floor apartment in a cement housing block. Covering one wall of their parlor was a beautiful woodland scene: sunlight flickering through birch trees into a grassy glade. In the room crowded with overstuffed furniture, that wallpaper vista provided a refreshing sense of space and natural beauty. I commented on it that evening as I took tea with our host's father, Vladimir Ilyich, who happened to be the Novozybkov school superintendent. Sitting there with his ten-year-old grandson, Vladimir showed me the large Geiger counter he carried in his car; it indicated where the poison had newly appeared, and where to tell the children not to play.

Following my eyes, he said, "That is where the children may not go—or any of us, for that matter. You see, the trees hold the radioactivity a long time. And that is very hard for us because, you see, our ancestors were of the forest, our old stories are of the forest. During the Nazi occupation, our partisans fought from the forest. Even in the hardest times under Stalin, we went into the woodlands every holiday, every weekend—walking, picnicking, mushrooming. Yes, we were always people of the forest." Quietly he repeated, "People of the forest."

"Vladimir Ilyich," I asked him, "when will you be able to go back into the forest?" With a tired little smile, he shrugged. "Not in my lifetime," he said. Looking at his grandson, he added, "and not in his lifetime either." Then he gestured to the wallpaper: "This is our forest now."

It was the second morning of our three days together, and the people entered the school assembly room to take each other's hands and, before any words were spoken, move into the Elm Dance. Every fourth measure, between moving right or left, forward or backward, we paused for four beats, gently swaying. To my eyes that morning, we could have been trees, slender trunks swaying from firm roots, our arms, as we raised them, looking like branches meeting, interlacing. Are we dancing for the forests we can no longer enter?

As I circled in step with all the others, I recalled the connections that brought me this dance—how it came to me from Hannelore, my friend in Germany, who had received it from Anastasia, her German friend, who had created it from the Latvian song. The dance is not only for the healing of the elm, said Anastasia to Hannelore to me. It is for intention. It is to strengthen our capacity to choose a purpose, and to follow through on the resolve our hearts have made.

That afternoon the grief broke open.

It happened unexpectedly, at the close of a guided meditation in which I invited these people of Novozybkov to connect with their ancestors and harvest their strengths. Moving through the room, as on a vast wheel turning, they went backward in time through all preceding generations, with Yuri's voice guiding them. Then they stopped and moved forward, retracing their steps through time, in order to gather the gifts of the ancestors. But when we came up to the year 1986, they balked. They did not want to come any further into the present. They refused to accept the horror of what happened to them then—and that very refusal compelled them to speak of it.

Talk exploded, releasing memories of that unacceptable spring: the searing hot wind from the southwest, the white ash that fell from a clear sky, the children running and playing in it, the drenching rain that followed, the rumors, the fear. Remember how it was? Remember, remember? I saw you standing in your doorway, watching. Our team had laid out paper and colored pencils for people to draw the gifts they'd harvested from the ancestors, but now there was one theme only. A number of the drawings featured trees, and a road to the trees, and across the road a barrier, or large X, blocking the way.

When we finally reassembled in one large circle, the good feelings that had grown during the workshop shattered in anger, now directed at me. "Why have you done this to us?" a woman cried out. "What good does it do? I would be willing to feel the sorrow—all the sorrow in the world—if it could save my two little daughters from cancer. Each time I look at them I wonder about tumors growing inside them. Can my tears protect them? What good are my tears if they can't?"

Angry, puzzled statements came from all around me. Our time together had been so good until now, so welcome a respite from what their lives had become; why had I spoiled it?

Listening to them all, I felt deeply chastened and silently blamed myself for my insensitivity. What, now, could I possibly say? To lecture on the value of despair work would be obscene. When I finally broke the silence that followed the long outburst, I was surprised that the words that came were not about them or their suffering under Chernobyl, but about the people of Hannelore and Anastasia.

"I have no wisdom with which to meet your grief. But I can share this with you: After the war that almost destroyed their country, the German people determined they would do anything to spare their children the suffering they had known. They worked hard to provide them a safe, rich life. They created an economic miracle. They gave their children everything—except for one thing. They did not give them their broken hearts. And their children have never forgiven them."

The next morning, as we took our seats after the Elm Dance, I was relieved to see that all fifty had returned. Behind us, still taped to the walls, hung the drawings of the previous afternoon, the sketches of the trees, and the slashing Xs that barred the way to the trees. "It was hard yesterday," were my opening words. "How is it with you now?"

The first to rise was the woman who had expressed the greatest anger, the mother of the two daughters. "I hardly slept. It feels like my heart is breaking open. Maybe it will keep breaking again and again, I don't know. But somehow—I can't explain—it feels right. It connects me to everything and everyone, as if we were all branches of the same tree."

Of the others who spoke after her that morning, one was the man who regularly stepped out to visit his little girl in the hospital. This was the first time he had addressed the whole group, and his bearing was as stolid, his face as expressionless, as ever. "Yes, it was hard yesterday," he said. "Hard to look at the pain, hard to feel it, hard to speak it. But the way it feels today—it is like being clean, for the first time in a long time." The word he used for "clean," *chisti*, also means "uncontaminated."

At my turn, I spoke of the World Uranium Hearing that I would attend the following week in Salzburg, Austria. People from around the world were coming to testify about their experiences of nuclear contamination. Navajo and Namibian miners would come, Marshall Islanders, Kazakhs, Western Shoshone downwinders from testing sites, and many others would speak out about the disease and death that follow in the wake of nuclear power and weapons production.

I wanted these men and women of Novozybkov to know that they are not alone in their suffering, but part of a vast web of brothers and sisters who are determined to use their painful experience to help restore the health of our world. "At the hearing, I will speak of you," I said. "I will tell your story to my own people back home. I promise you."

I made that vow because I loved them now, and because I knew they felt forgotten by an outside world that prefers to think that the disaster of Chernobyl is over. As the years pass since that fateful April of 1986, the catastrophe can be wiped from our consciousness as easily as the bulldozers razed the old wooden houses of Novozybkov because, as Vladimir Ilyich said, "wood holds the radioactivity." And now, as their own government proceeds to build more reactors, it can seem to these families that nothing has been learned from all the suffering. That may be the hardest thing to bear.

I have kept the promise I made to my friends in Novozybkov. I spoke of them at the World Uranium Hearing, and then to every group I met, every class I taught. I found it easier to share their story when I shared the Elm Dance they loved. In Boston and London, in Bonn and Vancouver, in Tokyo and Sydney, and everywhere else I've led workshops, I ask people to imagine they are dancing with the men and women of Novozybkov, holding the hands of Vladimir, Elena, Olga, Igor, Misha. I want them to feel, more strongly than is possible through words alone, how their lives are interlaced with the people of Chernobyl.

Awakening the Kind Heart

Kathleen Mcdonald

To be loving and kind is our deepest aspiration, because love and kindness is the true nature of the human heart. We all love someone, and we are all often kind, but we can go much further and discover the universal love that is the ultimate goal of the world's religions. For that we need not just aspirations but methods. Here is a series of powerful loving-kindness meditations from the Tibetan tradition, as taught by the Buddhist nun Kathleen McDonald, who explains their benefits not only for others but for ourselves. Such universal love, as the Dalai Lama often points out, is the ultimate in enlightened self-interest.

Tibetan lamas often begin teaching by saying, "All beings want happiness, and do not want to suffer." Accepting this simple truth is the basis of both love and compassion. Every living being has the same essential desire: to stay alive, to feel safe, loved, and appreciated, to satisfy its need for food and shelter, and to have pleasant, positive experiences.

The desire for happiness unites all beings, human and non-human. Feeling love for others means acknowledging this desire, respecting it, and doing what we can to fulfill it. This kind of love is sometimes called "loving-kindness" to distinguish it from love that is mixed with lust or selfish attachment. Loving-kindness is pure, unselfish, and unconditional. It is best illustrated by the love of a mother for her child. Out of love she accepts the discomforts of pregnancy, endures the pain of childbirth, and devotes herself twenty-four hours a day to the care of her newborn, expecting nothing in return. But all of us, even if we are not mothers, have loving-kindness; it is a natural quality of everyone's mind. We feel it most easily and naturally for relatives, friends, small children, or pets. But we can cultivate it further and gradually extend it to more and more people and beings, including strangers and even those who harm us. The ideal in Buddhism is to develop love for *all* living beings without exception.

Immeasurable love means wishing all beings to have happiness and its causes. Such love may sound like a fantasy, but it has been attained by others, and we can do it, too. We do not have immeasurable love now because of the presence in our mind of ignorance and the other delusions. These obscure our vision, causing us to have negative rather than positive emotions toward others. As we know, however, delusions are not permanent fixtures in our mind. They are transitory and can be eliminated, and once this is done, our mind will be able to feel love for everyone. One of my teachers, Amchog Rinpoche, once said that if we could see the true nature of living beings, we would feel nothing but love and compassion for them.

You might worry that you have only enough love for your family and friends but not for every single living being. "If I try to love everyone, I'll be exhausted!" But you need not worry about that. Love is an inexhaustible energy. Learning to be more loving is like discovering a natural spring within yourself: however much love you give, more will always come bubbling up. It is habitual self-centeredness and self-limiting ways of thinking that constrict the flow of love. As you gradually lessen these, your ability to love will increase.

You will not achieve this immediately, of course. It's a long-term goal, but an attainable one. It is simply a question of making your mind familiar with loving-kindness, and de-familiarizing it with opposing attitudes. Gradually love will arise in your mind more easily and more often.

The Benefits of Cultivating Loving-Kindness

It takes time and effort to develop immeasurable loving-kindness. At times we have enthusiasm for it, but at other times we feel indifferent or just lazy: "Why bother?" Sometimes we may wonder why we should cultivate love for people we don't know, or who have negative attitudes and harm others. Some might even question the whole idea of cultivating love, thinking that it should arise all by itself.

These obstacles are easily cut through if we simply contemplate the benefits of practicing loving-kindness. When we see the benefits of growing flowers and vegetables in our garden, we are enthusiastic to do so. Similarly, by seeing the benefits of cultivating loving-kindness, we want to put our energy into it.

The main purpose of cultivating loving-kindness is not so that we will benefit. It is for others, but considering benefits that we will experience can help get us started. If in helping others, we receive benefit as well, is there anything wrong with that? Also, are you even capable of being purely altruistic right now? Can you be completely free of all wants and needs at this moment, and totally dedicate yourself to helping others? If you are honest, you will probably admit that you are not. Even if we are 100 percent committed to being unselfish and altruistic, it takes time and effort to become that way, and in the meantime, we do have our own needs to fulfill. Practicing loving-kindness and other positive attitudes is actually a way to fulfill our needs: we will be more happy, healthy, and enthusiastic, and less likely to get burned-out and depressed. The Dalai Lama calls this being "wisely selfish"; that is, using our selfish tendencies to act wisely, in ways that bring genuine happiness and benefit to ourselves as well to others. Consider these benefits of loving-kindness, which are commonly presented in Buddhist texts:

Your mind will be happy, and you will be more physically healthy. You can see this for yourself. How does it feel to be angry, hateful, jealous? Is this a pleasant experience? Is your body relaxed and comfortable? Is your mind happy? On the other hand, how does it feel to be loving and kind to others? If you have a choice, which state of mind would you rather have, an angry one or an altruistic, caring one?

You will be more loved, helped, and protected by others. When you feel love, and treat others with care and kindness, they will naturally feel the same toward you and will be there for you when you need help. This may not work in every case, of course—some people are so full of anger that they may know no other way to respond to your warmth. But if you continue to show them kindness, even they may soften and become more friendly.

You will sleep better at night, have more pleasant dreams, and wake up more refreshed. By cultivating positive, loving thoughts for others and being kind in our daily life, at the end of the day your mind will naturally be more at ease, free of stress and regrets. This will enable you to fall asleep and wake up easily, and to have pleasant, even auspicious, dreams.

Your appearance will start to be more radiant, smiling, and relaxed, and you will be able to communicate more easily with others. This is easy to see: hatred makes us ugly, and loving-kindness makes us beautiful. But again, the ideal motive for cultivating loving-kindness is not wanting such results for our own sake, but for the sake of others. If we have a pleasant appearance, people will be attracted to us and will trust us, and thus be more attentive to what we say and do. That puts us in a better position to help them.

Your mind will be more serene and easily concentrated, and you will more effortlessly accomplish your aims. Hatred, jealousy, and other negative emotions make the mind painfully disturbed, like boiling water, while positive mental states such as loving-kindness make the mind cool and calm. When we try to concentrate—while meditating, reading a book, or doing a task—if we are more habituated with anger and less with loving-kindness, we may be distracted and upset by noise, people, or other beings, so our efforts will not be very successful. By contrast, familiarity with loving-kindness enables us to remain peaceful and focused on what we are doing, no matter what is happening around us. Loving-kindness is an essential component in the cultivation of concentration, which is in turn the gateway to higher states of bliss and peace.

You will die unconfused. If you ask yourself what state of mind you would like to have at the time of death—confused, frightened, and angry, or peaceful, positive, and loving—I'm sure you would choose the latter. But in order to be in a positive mental state when you die, you need to familiarize yourself with positive thoughts during your life. And the time to start is now, because you don't know when death will happen.

According to Buddhism, our state of mind at death is a major factor determining our next rebirth: dying in a positive state leads to a fortunate rebirth, but dying in a negative state leads to an unfortunate rebirth. This is one of the main reasons why it is so important to work on our mind. But even those who do not accept rebirth would probably wish to die peacefully, painlessly, and with dignity. A nurse who worked with many dying people told me that the people who have the greatest difficulty with pain are those whose minds are negative—fearful, angry, not accepting their death—whereas those whose minds are positive have little or no pain. The way we die depends on the way we have lived.

A Basic Meditation on Loving-Kindness

This meditation utilizes the awareness that every being wants happiness, just as we do, and that all beings deserve to be happy. In that meditation, we bring to mind specific people or beings, contemplate their desire for happiness, and generate the wish for them to be happy.

People sometimes report that they do not feel anything when they try to meditate on loving-kindness. They repeat the words to themselves, but their mind feels blank, empty. This is actually normal, especially when we are new to the practice. Part of the problem is that we have expectations: in the back of our mind we are hoping for some fantastic experience. For example, we hope that our mind will be suffused with blissful love for all beings everywhere. And if that doesn't happen we feel let down, disappointed, and may even think that the practice doesn't work.

My teacher Lama Yeshe used to say to us, "Don't have any expectations when you meditate." It's quite hard to do this, because our normal tendency is to expect results from the things that we put effort into. So, when we take up meditation, we do so hoping for wonderful, blissful feelings flowing through our body and mind. The irony is that having expectations in meditations on loving-kindness meditation is counterproductive, an obstacle to attaining its results. If we grasp at wonderful experiences, we are pushing them further away. It's when we can relax and just do the practice without expecting anything that the results will come.

Try not to have expectations, as Lama Yeshe advised. Just do the practices, repeat the words of the meditation to yourself, and accept whatever happens in your mind. Of course, it is okay to try to generate the feeling of loving-kindness, but don't worry if nothing seems to happen. Expecting instant results from meditation is like expecting that flowers and vegetables will appear in your garden right after you plant the seeds. Things don't happen like that. You need to look after your garden, nurture the tiny shoots when they appear, and wait patiently. Eventually, when the time is right, the results will come.

Just so, after planting the seeds of loving thoughts in your mind for a while, you will begin to notice small, subtle positive thoughts and feelings arising spontaneously, of their own accord. If you nurture them and continue doing the practice, they will arise more frequently, both during and outside of formal meditation practice.

This meditation is divided into five parts: loving-kindness for a friend, a neutral person, an enemy, yourself, and all beings. The number of parts you meditate on in each session can vary, according to the amount of time you have and your ability to sustain your mind in a meditative state, as well as your needs at any given time.

For example, if you are having difficulty with someone at work and wish to generate loving-kindness for him or her, you might want to focus on just that person.

Also, you can sometimes alter the sequence of the parts. Some teachers recommend that you start meditating on loving-kindness for yourself, then a friend, and so on; others recommend putting yourself last. There are no hard and fast rules. Feel free to experiment with different sequences to find what works best for you.

Preparation

Sit comfortably. Relax your body and mind and let all thoughts and worries subside. Mindfully observe your breath until you are calm and your awareness is focused in the here and now.

Motivation

Think that you are doing this meditation for the benefit of yourself and others, to generate more positive, loving energy in your mind, and to send it out to others, to the world. If you are comfortable with the idea of bodhichitta, you can think you are doing the meditation in order to become enlightened, so that you can help all beings in the best way.

Main Meditation

It is helpful to begin by generating a feeling of love in your heart. You can do this by thinking of someone you find easy to love—a relative or friend, a small child, or a pet—and letting your natural good feelings for this person (or being, in the case of an animal) arise in your heart. You might like to imagine your love as a warm, bright light or energy glowing in your heart. Then bring to mind one or more of the following persons and do your best to extend this feeling of loving-kindness to them.

LOVING-KINDNESS FOR A FRIEND

A "friend" is someone we find easy to like and feel close to—it can be an acquaintance, a partner, or a family member. However, it is best initially not to think of someone for whom you have romantic love or sexual desire; otherwise, those feelings may arise and hinder your ability to distinguish love from attachment. You can visualize the person sitting in front of you, or in the place he or she is right now. Contemplate that this person has, deep in his or her heart, the wish to be happy. Feel that the person deserves to be happy. Generate the wish that this person could have the happiness he or she longs for.

If you like, you can think or say to yourself phrases such as: "May you be happy. May you be safe, free from harm and danger. May you have all that you need to be truly happy, peaceful, and satisfied. May all your thoughts and actions be positive, and all your experiences good." You can modify these phrases, using whatever words enable you to generate genuine loving-kindness.

If you imagined your loving-kindness as light or energy, you can visualize it radiating from your heart to this person. Let them become filled with it. It is also effective to imagine the person receiving what they need to be happy, such as the food they like to eat, a comfortable place to live, pleasant encounters with other people, positive thoughts and feelings in their mind, and so on.

Spend as much time as you wish meditating on loving-kindness for this person, and then you can bring to mind another friend and do the same reflection with that person. Alternatively, you can do one of the other parts of the practice below, or conclude your meditation with the dedication.

Loving-kindness for a Neutral Person

A neutral person is someone we neither like nor dislike. It could be a neighbor or someone we work with whom we are not close to. Imagine such a person in front of you, and contemplate that this person, like yourself and your friends, simply wants to be happy. Feel that this person deserves to be happy. Generate the wish that he or she could be happy.

Then you can repeat the phrases, or whatever words you find most effective: "May you be happy. May you be safe, free from harm and danger. May you have all that you need to be truly happy, peaceful, and satisfied. May all your thoughts and actions be positive, and all your experiences good."

Imagine the light or energy of your loving-kindness radiating from your heart to this person, filling him or her. And imagine the person receiving what he or she needs to be happy.

LOVING-KINDNESS FOR AN ENEMY

"Enemy" is quite a heavy word, and we may think we have no enemies because there's no one we really hate and wish to harm. But it can simply mean someone we close our heart to, someone we dislike or find irritating. Bring to mind such a person; it could be someone you know, or a public figure like a politician. If you are relatively new to this part of the practice, and if there is someone you strongly hate, it's better not to use that person. Start with someone toward whom your feelings are more low-level, and you can gradually work your way up to the more challenging people. Imagine the person in front of you, and contemplate that he or she, like yourself and your friends, simply wants to be happy. Feel that the person deserves to be happy. Generate the wish that the person could be happy.

Then you can repeat the following phrases, or whatever words you find most effective: "May you be happy. May you be safe, free from harm and danger. May you have all that you need to be truly happy, peaceful, and satisfied. May all your thoughts and actions be positive, and all your experiences good."

Imagine the light or energy of your loving-kindness radiating from your heart to this person, filling him or her. Imagine that the person receives what he or she needs to be happy.

LOVING-KINDNESS FOR ONESELF

To be able to truly love others, you need to love yourself. Loving yourself means accepting yourself as you are, with your present faults and shortcomings. It means being kind to yourself, being a friend to yourself, rather than being angry and frustrated that you aren't the person you'd like to be. It also means acknowledging your potential to change and grow, to experience greater happiness, peace, and positive qualities. And it involves giving yourself the space to fulfill that potential, and truly wishing yourself to be happy and free from problems.

Contemplate that you are a being who wishes to be happy and that you deserve to be happy. Then, really wish yourself all the happiness and goodness there is. "May I be happy. May I be safe, free from harm and danger. May I have all that I need to be truly happy, peaceful, and satisfied. May all my thoughts and actions be positive, and all my experiences good." Imagine that the warm energy of loving-kindness in your heart radiates out, gradually filling your body and mind, and you become suffused with happiness and its causes.

LOVING-KINDNESS FOR ALL BEINGS

Send loving-kindness to all other living beings—human beings and non-human beings such as animals. You may like to think especially of those who are going through extreme difficulties such as war, sickness, poverty, hunger, fear, oppression, and so forth. Think, and feel sincerely: "May all beings everywhere be happy. May they be safe, free from harm and danger. May they have all they need to be truly happy, peaceful, and satisfied. May all their thoughts and actions be positive, and all their experiences good."

Feel the gentle energy of loving-kindness radiate out from your heart to all living beings, everywhere in the universe. Imagine that it gives them comfort, relieves them of their mental and physical suffering, and helps them to experience happiness and peace of mind.

Dedication

When you are ready to conclude the meditation, dedicate the positive energy of your meditation to all beings, intently wishing that they find happiness and, ultimately, enlightenment.

Through the Dharma Gate ⏾⏾

Joan Sutherland

Buddhism is often portrayed these days as the religion of reason, the one most consistent with our modern knowledge of science and the mind. That may be true, but only as far as it goes. Reason rules only the relative world of form, while Buddhism's true province is the ultimate truth of formlessness, beyond the narrow powers of the rational mind. Here Zen teacher Joan Sutherland, one of American Buddhism's deepest and most poetic voices, takes us to the Gateless Gate, the place in our practice where the form and formless meet.

As I think about the shapes and forms that meditative practices take, I keep returning to the afternoon before the fateful night in which a man named Siddhartha would sit under a tree, and at the rising of the morning star, become the Buddha. On that long afternoon, Siddhartha took a bowl, went down to the river, and made a vow: "If this bowl floats upstream, I'll become enlightened before tomorrow dawns." He threw the bowl into the river and bent all his intention to its journey against the current, against the unceasing tumble of being and doing and becoming, making and unmaking, birth and growth and decay and death—against the unrelenting torrent of stuff and matter, of thought and feeling and sensation, to the source of it all, in its stillness and eternity.

That is the same intention we set as we take up a meditative practice: we throw our bowls into the river, hoping to find its source. And yet we set this intention as embodied beings, in an embodied world of shapes, colors, sounds, tastes, and smells. We begin practice with bodily acts—breathing, postures, gestures, sounds, offerings, rituals. These are accompanied by acts at a subtler level of embodiment, acts of the heart-mind: the stilling of thoughts, mindfulness of sensation and emotion, the contemplation of a koan, visualization, prayer. We trust that the world's radiant, eternal aspect is not outside our experience but an enlargement of it, and so it is with eyes and skin and hearts that we go out to meet it.

The bowl Siddhartha flung into the river did float upstream, but he chose to follow it by turning back toward the world. He bathed in the river, and then he went to sit under a tree. The world came to meet him, to offer its support: he encountered a grass-cutter, arms full of soft, fragrant green, who offered him some grass as a cushion.

On that first afternoon there was no formal Buddhist practice yet; there was only Siddhartha's brilliant improvisation in a landscape of river and grass and tree. But over millennia we've added a gate to the landscape: We've created an edifice of meditation, made of an architecture of methods. Rather than examine its individual stones, let's look at the gate in its original setting, there by the tree. Let's look at what it's like to sit in its shade, at the place where things come in and out, and meet each other.

There is the gate, always in the same place, enduring, unmoving, and yet with an opening that invites things to pass through it. There is the person who comes to sit at the gate, different every time, agreeing to stay put so that those things moving in and out of the gate can find her. The location of the gate—the forms of meditation—is fixed and known, but what will happen there can never be known ahead of time. The experience of sitting at the gate is made up, inseparably, of both what is repeated and what is spontaneous— what can only happen in this moment, in this place, amidst these circumstances with what we bring to the gate and what comes through it.

We sit down and gather ourselves. We are creatures of habit, using habit—a particular sitting posture, the smell of incense, the sound of a chant repeated many times—for our benefit, to bring body, heart, and mind together. In gathering ourselves we make ourselves available to be acted upon, to be marked by the worlds, visible and invisible, in which we sit. Available to what comes through the gate.

We're making an offering of ourselves. We're announcing our desire for the deepest meeting of all, the one between the vastness and the individual, between what is without form and what exists as form. We offer ourselves as the place where these two great realities might meet and mix and create something new.

Fortunately for us, people have been making this offering for thousands of years and have developed some good ways to do it. The constancy of forms and their repetition make a field that holds us until we can hold ourselves. At the very least, we can fall back on forms, just do them no matter how we're feeling, in the same way we can fall back on courtesy when our natural instincts fail us. We can consent to a form and surrender for a while. The poet Adam Zagajewski writes about how the things of the world agree to every minute of the year, every change in season or the weather, so that they can go on living. In meditation each of us acknowledges that we too are things of the world.

Just as the postures of meditation are a way of holding the body still long enough for something to happen, our consent is a way of holding the heart-mind still, creating an opportunity for something to find us and strike up a conversation. For a while, at least, we are saying that we won't turn anything away; we won't jump to categorize or assign value to things. We'll just listen. For this little while we agree not to know, and to follow where the form takes us.

Through the gate come our subjective experiences—our inner narratives, moods, and physical sensations. After a while, meditation also shows us what it's like before the shaping power of thoughts and feelings kicks in. We consent to giving the usual cognitive and emotional filters a rest, so that meditative forms can influence us at deeper levels. Over time they change how we perceive and feel about things, how our intuition works, and even how we respond somatically, before cognition. We are allowing the long, slow waveforms of tradition and practice to act upon the spiky graph of our moment-by-moment experience.

This can be hard work, and it takes some trust, so it's helpful that we discover pretty quickly how not alone we are. There's the tradition and the ancestors; we're sitting with everyone who has ever sat. The gate is an address the ancestors recognize, and through it they come, bearing their encouraging and their disorienting advice. Through the gate come intimations of the vastness and of the source of the river of being. The vastness doesn't need an address to home in on, since it's already everywhere, but we need to be able to receive it. It's one of the beautiful paradoxes of meditative practice that consenting to occupy a particular, small location in a very particular way—body arranged like this, heart-mind like that—actually opens us to the unbounded, immeasurable aspect of reality. What exists as form meets what is without form.

As these various aspects of the world begin to meet up in the field of our meditation, sometimes things flow together easily and the field effortlessly expands. We discover ways to harmonize with the rhythms of the Earth and eternity. We realize that we're becoming the place where the teachings take on actual, embodied life. When we practice together, our individual, introverted practices connect us with others and we become part of an even larger field.

Sometimes there's tension. Perhaps the most important aspect of our consent is the willingness to stay put, and even to be interested, when the things that come through the gate seem to jostle each other and argue with us, or provoke us to argue with them. Sometimes becoming intimate with the realm of thoughts and feelings is tremendously painful. Sometimes the ancestral voices seem not just inscrutable but crazy or wrong. Sometimes the vastness is overwhelming and frightening. The conversation at the gate becomes colored with complaint, mistrust, or fear.

That's when it's good to feel solid stone at your back, something you can lean against when the field starts to spin. To stay with a form when things get dicey is simply to choose the ground upon which to meet the disturbance. Since we focus so much on meditation's stilling and expansive qualities, it might seem surprising that one of the intentions of meditation is to put us in a state of tension. The steadiness of meditative forms allows apparent dualities to emerge, and the invitation is not to smooth over their differences or choose between them. Doing either is settling prematurely; it's settling before unsettling tension can become creative. For example, meditation might go along quite deeply and peacefully for awhile, and then one day it's filled with agitation and rumination. Has something gone wrong? Was there good meditation and now there's bad? Here's a tension. If we refuse to choose a label and widen the perspective a little, we might notice a couple of things. The external form remains the same; we're sitting the way we always have. Is there something internally that also remains the same, something underneath states of either peace or agitation? Perhaps we discover that the field of meditation is constant, and it's just a matter of different qualities and states arising in it. This is how a tension between apparent dualities becomes creative, pointing us to a third thing that includes both and is bigger than either. To the extent we can shift our allegiance from the transitory states to the constant field, we begin to create a new possibility, a new way of living.

If we stay put long enough, we'll confront the largest tension of all: that we and everything else are formed and formless at the same time. As we learn to see the creative potential of the smaller-scale tensions in our meditation, we experience for ourselves how the apparent tension between form and formlessness resolves itself over and over again to produce the manifest world.

All helpful forms eventually have to blow themselves up. Everything has its shadow, and the danger in having a static relationship with meditative forms is when we focus primarily on getting them right. When we do this, correct form is no longer a beautiful means of discipline and surrender, but the goal itself. Instead of providing a liberating experience of the largeness of things at the intersection of form and emptiness, the forms of practice can become constricting and self-centered affectations. Eventually we have to break free of the idea that a particular state of heart-mind is dependent on a particular meditative form. What we experience by sitting at the gate has to roll out in a kind of slow-motion explosion to affect the rest of our lives. The original form doesn't necessarily disappear; we might continue to practice it. But it becomes something less bounded and more fluid, present in more of our lives, taking the form of whatever we're doing.

This is the final tension: that which is between formal discipline and the formless permeation of meditation throughout our lives. As we hold the tension, we might notice that a remarkable transformation is taking place. The gate has begun to impress itself on us, and we are taking it in. The gate made of stones is becoming flesh and blood, hands and eyes; it is becoming a part of us wherever we are. The decision to sit down at the stone gate in that ancient landscape is made by individuals, one by one, but there are no limitations on who and what can be affected by a gate made flesh, carried into the world.

I'm Loving It

Genine Lentine

*This story by Genine Lentine was controversial when it was published in
the* Shambhala Sun. *Too honest, too sexy for some readers, maybe a little
impious in its meditative celebration of teenage lust. All that, plus it's
funny, thoughtful, and beautifully told.*

What brings you here this morning?

This is the guiding question of the "way-seeking mind talk," a
talk students at the San Francisco Zen Center are invited to offer on
Thursday mornings during intensive periods of study. On these
mornings, the regular schedule of zazen and service is abbreviated
so that a student may tell her story of how she got there—a twenty-
five-minute slice of how she came to be sitting on a cushion in the
Buddha hall at 6:45 a.m., speaking to a group of people sitting in
zazen posture, their eyes lowered to a forty-five-degree angle.

These talks chronicle an arc of awareness, an unfolding portrait
of a mind getting to know itself. They often single out specific trau-
matic events as turning points, recounting new permutations of
what other human beings and circumstance can levy onto the self.
They are tales of extremity and moments of clarity, of hunches followed, of determined recommitment to life: an emergency trache-
otomy on a premature infant, as recounted half a century later
through that blessed, resealed trachea; an encounter with a person

who sees something everyone else had missed; an offhand reference to a parent in prison, to suicide attempts. One after another, students explore the infinite ways a life cracks open and shines.

These accounts are registered by the assembly with extremely subtle facial responses, the kind Paul Ekman studies, the kind long-time meditators are said to be better than the average population at detecting. Faint variations that say, *I'm here with you,* or *that was funny,* or *that was tragic,* or *that's just like my life.* An upturned corner of the mouth, delicate nostril flare, lift of the chin. Sometimes there's outright laughter—relief at the prevailing nervous suspension—and, of course, much quiet sniffling.

A feeling of temporal dilation pervades the room, but still there's a clear boundary. At 7:20, if the talk hasn't already tapered off into, "Well, I think that's about it," or, "Does anyone else have a question?" a bell might ring to indicate the time. This audience was woken up by a different bell at 4:55 a.m., and they haven't yet eaten breakfast.

When I gave my talk a couple years ago, I focused on a cascade of revelations brought about by a string of very thorny breakups, so-called losses, and strokes of fortune. Yes, they are indistinguishable. Mostly, I gave examples of how the world makes explicit offers framed almost exactly to the specifications of one's barely registered needs, but usually the offering remains unrecognizable to the recipient. I illustrated this phenomenon by describing how one afternoon I set out on my bike down Commercial Street in Provincetown, Massachusetts, heading to the library to work at one of the spacious oak tables overlooking the harbor, and I almost rode right past a beautiful, perfectly proportioned maple writing desk a guest house had put out at the curb. I caught just in time the familiar flaw in the logic of my hurry: *Too bad I can't stop to pick up that table; I have to get to the library . . . so I can, uh, use the table there.* I turned back to get the desk and right then a gardener appeared from the adjacent yard and asked if I'd like some help carrying it home.

With so many tiny moments when an acutely relevant lesson feels fully articulated and noticed in the nick of time, it's impossible to include them all. I did not find time, for example, to speak of how, the very next day after I met Popeye—a beloved figure in Province-town who collected aluminum cans, told fabulous stories, and marched at the front of the Fourth of July parade every summer—he suffered a fatal heart attack the morning before the parade. He was found in a Porta-Potty in full sailor regalia. I took his death personally, numbering it among all the other incidents that verified my theory that if I cared about someone, that person would disap-pear immediately. But somehow this incident with Popeye, in its acute swiftness, helped me see the absurdity of my theory. And with the hairsbreadth of space that opened for me in relation to this per-son to whom I'd spoken only once, I was emboldened to entertain other, closer, losses with more space as well.

Time constraints require one to be selective, so no Popeye story—that will have to be saved for the director's cut—but still, the expectation is that the talk is going to touch on all the key points. And so, for months after the talk, whenever I mentioned a new fact about my life to my friend Stephen, his face took on a wide-eyed, genuine disappointment, confusion, and shock: *I can't believe you left that out of your way-seeking mind talk!* For him, the way-seeking mind talk is the primary point of reference, the hegemonic text for knowing anyone, as if you are supposed to include every pivotal in-cident, overshot gesture and course correction, relationship, and part-time job in your life.

Though I mentioned only briefly the profound and abundant gifts of working for six years with the poet Stanley Kunitz, Stephen remembers my talk as being very "heavy on Stanley" and yet consid-ers grave the following omissions: (1) My brother is a magician. (2) My first job was as a hostess at McDonald's.

I thought I might reconsider my talk, now, by inquiring into just these items, including a couple of sub-items: item number two included attending training at a place called Hamburger University and also included my first blowjob. Stephen says, however, I was right not to include that "blue material." It wouldn't have played well in the Buddha hall.

•   •   •

What can be learned through the select lens of these two biographical points, or in the parlance common to Zen Center, these "conditions of my karmic life"? Let me consider first having an older brother who is a magician. What this does is offer some lessons in form. It provides an opportunity to see someone sewing a cape out of black-and-white checked gingham and adopting a persona based on the motif of checkers, an identity that then embraces anything articulated in a checkered pattern—jaunty checkered caps, checkered socks, a checkered umbrella.

When my brother was fifteen, Mr. Checkers was born and it is an identity he still inhabits today. What I want to believe is that the gingham cloth was on hand already, maybe left over from a church altar banner my mother was making. I prefer this because resourcefulness—responding to the environment—is a cornerstone in my aesthetic. I don't want to think that he just came up with the name Mr. Checkers and then went out and bought the fabric. If you can't make magic from the material in your immediate surroundings, it's no magic I'm interested in.

Having a brother with an alter ego makes gift buying easy. Unlike the full-fledged, complex individual ego who may or may not still respond positively to the licorice all-sorts so eagerly received last year, an alter ego is usually based on just a few prominent features with a high predictive value. You find a stuffed plush dog sporting a checkered vest and you need look no further for your brother's Christmas gift. Watching him receive these gifts was a lesson in the constriction of identity. He had to like these iterations of his chosen self. If he didn't like them, he himself had to change. Perhaps it was precisely this fixity that offered him a relatively stable place to park an identity dissolving in the tumult of adolescence.

I watched him tape Baggies into newspapers, which then became makeshift ovens in which he'd bake a cookie by passing a hand over the sports section. I watched him tuck folded playing cards into oranges, prepping them for when he'd discover them at the birthday party. He e-mailed me recently to tell me he learned the cookie trick in the parking lot of the Highland Palms Convalescent Home after his first magic show, when a resident, a fellow magician, paid him the highest compliment one magician can offer another: he showed him a trick—two, actually. "Right there in the parking lot he showed me a cigarette vanish and the cookie trick."

Fine, he can tell me this now, but then, when I petitioned him to teach me how something was done, he offered only flat refusal, leaving me to study the mirrors, the cut-away doors, the knives with rubber blades on my own when I could get my hands on them. Acting as his assistant made this easy and provided another benefit: the checkered miniskirt my sister sewed for me. The white go-go boots? Those I already had.

Magicians' catalogs arrived in the mail. I got home from school before he did, so this gave me a chance to read them first, to see that there were whole stores devoted to wands, capes, and disappearing chambers. These were items I thought you had to receive by some secret transmission in midnight ceremonies, or have them custom fabricated by fairies, or you had to be born into them. Our mail carrier handed them to me at the screen door.

The access granted by my position gave me training as a cynic. As he lied to the audience, I pictured the queen of hearts, creased and soggy, smuggled inside the orange. I wasn't interested in illusion; I wanted to know how the trick worked—the details of the physical world, the way the Baggie hung on the newspaper, how he measured out the flour, cracked the egg.

I felt betrayed that he couldn't recognize that I was a fellow magician and let me in on these secrets and, before long, I felt bored with his act, with the creed he invoked, and, ultimately, with what must be a paltry kind of magic if it could not be shared. Even then I knew that if I shared my potato chips with my dog, the effect was not one of diminishment, rather they somehow seemed to last longer.

It remains true today that a screwdriver containing several different sizes of bits in its handle intrigues me more than any of those magic supplies designed to be good for just one trick. It still shocks me that you can walk into a hardware store and just buy those marsupial implements.

Knowing I can easily procure one of these screwdrivers, just as now, as an adult, I can have a whole avocado to myself, makes me rethink all the things I thought were hidden, like whether _____ really is _____. But nothing is hidden, asserts the thirteenth-century Zen teacher Eihei Dogen. Or, as Shunryu Suzuki Roshi says, "The world is its own magic."

My brother tried to hide his tricks from me, but this strategy only made me less interested. Rather than stoke his mystique, I just got annoyed with his secrecy and announced whatever intelligence I had been able to gather to the group assembled and left the birthday party to go scout for lizards in the ice plants.

WOULD YOU LIKE _____ WITH THAT?

Now to consider item number two. Working at McDonald's offered, in many ways, an explicit initiation to Zen practice: the rigorous timing of activities, the rotation of roles, adherence to a schedule, the repetition, the elaborated rituals, the emphasis on service, the mid-lunch-rush blur of self and other, registers all ringing up multiple sales, each clerk turning in sequence to the trays of burgers and fries, the crisp snap of five white paper bags opening at once.

The whole notion of fast food might sound anathema to even the most mass-market account of Zen, a system that emphasizes, if nothing else, paying attention to what you're doing. What could be less "Zen" than scarfing down a burger at forty-five miles an hour on the on-ramp to the Dulles Access Road?

But to prepare this fast food, to assemble, ring up, and present it in a bag at this speed actually requires close attention; letting your mind drift is a quick way to get a basket-weave burn on your arm from the fry basket or to get clocked by a box of frozen patties.

It is the rare person who, upon hearing me utter the declarative statement, *My first job was as a hostess at McDonald's,* does not volley the predicate back to me as an interrogative: *A hostess, at McDonald's?* If this question has arisen in your mind, I will tell you what you might not have realized: you can take a tour of your local McDonald's, and you can enlist McDonald's to host your next birthday party. Both of these services fall under the purview of the hostess, as does attending to customer problems—cold fries, limp fries, too few fries. Too many fries? Never.

Giving a McDonald's birthday party involves laying out burgers and fries on a tray, their wrappers quietly rustling against each other, and pre-filling courtesy cups with an orange liquid formulated to trigger a memory of juice. Also, the walk-in freezer held a stock of frozen birthday cakes—chocolate with vanilla frosting topped with Ronald McDonald depicted in his familiar cant of solicitous welcome holding out an array of bright gel balloons. We had our own helium tank on the premises to blow up balloons for the parties, but on a slow afternoon it was often pressed into service for the amusement value of speaking like a duck, especially appreciated when someone ventured to operate the drive-thru speaker in that voice.

The kids lined up along the banquettes and each took the three items and arranged them in front of themselves as I passed before them, as if I were serving *oryoki*, the three-bowl mindful meal often eaten in Zen temples. Offering a tray of burgers to a child, you are bowing whether you intend to or not. Isn't oryoki, with everything you need wrapped up in a neat package, a form of a Happy Meal?

Along with these hospitality functions, if someone failed to show for a shift, as a hostess I was also fully trained in running the register and working the grill, recharging the soft-serve dispenser, whatever was needed.

On the register, the range of what you could do if you were actually there, rather than letting your mind wander, quickly impressed me. Yes, our job was to move the line quickly, but actual people constituted that line! And these people were subject to moods and they had wishes and needs and their wishes were articulated along a relatively finite continuum of combinations of burgers, fries, fountain drinks, and simulacra of desserts. Their tenderness was vast, but the forms they sought were finite, and you could meet at least their explicit requests.

In these quick encounters, I could feel the palpable difference between seeing the person before me and just looking through them to the next transaction; I learned the trick that paying attention doesn't take extra time, it actually gives you more time. A current position description on a McDonald's employment website specifies that one of the key functions of a hostess is "making every single soul feel welcome at the door."

My manager sent me to a daylong training seminar on customer service at Hamburger University in Silver Spring, Maryland. It is this turn of autobiography that is so startling to my friend Stephen and brings on in him what I would call "nostalgia by proxy," a longing to look back on someone else's past, imagining how his life could have been different had he attended Hamburger University. To be able to say, *I went to Hamburger University!* You think you have a general handle on the roster of what you could regret, and then someone tells you she attended Hamburger University. How could you know to aspire to something without knowing it existed?

At Hamburger University, whether the carousel-slide-projector talk touted the proprietary excellence of the russet potatoes used for McDonald's fries or gave precise instructions about how to pack an order so as to keep those fries upright, the one basic message was this: customer service, like the bodhisattva vow, is composed of a vast array—menu!—of possible gestures and responses. It is a posture of being. What I carried away from both this training and from the vow is this: there will always be more you can imagine doing, but you do what you can. Granted, with the former, this mostly translated into selling customers things they didn't yet know they wanted, that is, selling up. Fries? A shake? A pie? Already ordered regular fries? Would you like a large fries? Already ordered large fries? Supersize it? But still, even if the motives were perhaps questionable, there was something in the training that inculcated a kind of alert availability.

At its heart, working at McDonald's proffered an early and thoroughgoing acquaintance with the power of repetition and form.

Asking "May I take your order?" over and over was a constant invitation to notice how form invites expansion within that form. The complexion of my mind at that time was astir in registering the sensation of the subtle and tremendous distinctions within uniformity, just as in Catholic school, when I had marveled at how each person wore their plaid uniform differently, noting where on my friends' thighs their skirts came to an end, how the pleats on, say Janet's (or Rona's!) skirt moved in a way that was impossible to turn away from, while others simply hung flat.

"The line," where all the food was prepared, presented many opportunities for the wholehearted attention Dogen speaks of in the *Tenzo Kyokun*, or *Instructions for the Cook*. For example, when wrapping the burgers in their translucent waxy papers, do so less than wholeheartedly, which is to say, half-assedly, and watch the tray of burgers come unwrapped slowly under the heat lamps. The Egg Mc-Muffin rings required practice so that the crack of the egg took on the iconic circular form, each one distinct, each one perfect, an ovular *enso*. A basic tenet of kitchen work practice at Zen Center holds forth a kind of finesse that isn't about decoration or something being extra. It is the simple, full expression of something that works well because you give it your thorough attention.

And within that realm of form and attention, my first job at McDonald's offered another first, a most exquisite opportunity for exploration, right there in the break room. Greg B. I'll leave it at that, though his name is so generic, it is perhaps possible to use it without violating his privacy. For good measure, I'll change his surname slightly, the way names are transparently masked in some fiction: Brennan. Okay. Throw in another *g*: Gregg. Let him be Gregg Brennan. After all, would he want anyone now to read that he leaned back on the basement break-room couch, blue polyester uniform retaining in the web of its molecular structure a faint sheen from the fry vat, his legs parted enough to make space for me where I knelt before his lap, his hips rising as my head lowered onto what was assuming in my mouth a conformation, the proportions and fluctuant densities of which I would later determine, in consultation with my friend

Meredith, to be of a textbook perfection, the textbook being the copy of *Playgirl* she had just given me for my sixteenth birthday?

At Meredith's slumber party that weekend, we passed the magazine around, kneeling over it head to head, turning the pages from above—"Wait, turn back. I like this one!"—comparing what we found in the magazine to what we were seeing "in the field." Gregg's looked like the centerfold's, I decided. The centerfold radiated a golden quality, the source of which was untraceable. "He's so beautiful, you could sleep with him and still be a virgin!" I posited. Something about this formulation pleased my friend Nancy, the only one among us having regular sex, and I felt she looked at me differently from then on.

Could Gregg—can I—withstand being reminded now that we both wore those paper hats? Yes. We did. In the break room, we took the hats off and afterward we put them back on. Just as is fitting for any ceremony.

Gregg was one of the people who actually looked, if I can say this, hot in his uniform, the blue cap, with its striped band and slightly cocked brim, like an admiral's. In Provincetown, there is a theme week dedicated to leather, latex, and uniforms, though I don't remember ever seeing anyone walking around in a fast food uniform; the predilection tilts more toward protective services, but anything can become erotic given the right constraints and freedoms.

What is it to look hot in a blue polyester tunic with a striped yoke and matching pants? It comes down to this: some people wear their uniforms and some are worn by their uniforms. Gregg wore his uniform, which is to say that to behold him was to behold a living, breathing body, uncompromised by the inertia of the fabric. Perhaps how Gregg's long muscled swimmer's torso outshone all that was standard in his uniform is what Shunryu Suzuki Roshi was pointing to when he said, "When you are all in your robes, I can see your individuality."

I wanted to unbutton that uniform shirt; it didn't matter that the buttons had golden arches embossed on them or that the pockets were just squares of fabric sewn shut. Of course, the timed nature of the operation heightened the proceedings. We had twenty minutes for our break. This is something any Zen practitioner knows, the value of a "container" for focusing the mind.

We banked on the stairs creaking to give us ample notice of anyone coming down for a break. But the stairs were silent for as long as we needed them to be, which, given the fact that it had been, by then, almost ten minutes since we had clocked out, and that Gregg was sixteen years old, was, from zipper down to zipper up, say, four minutes—five max. Only four or five minutes. Four or five minutes have probably elapsed in typing the last few lines, but I doubt I will be chronicling them a few decades from now.

Being time. The unalloyed delight of absorption.

Here in the break room unfolded a five-minute teaching in mindfulness, in bowing, in following the breath, my attention drifting once or twice to the sleeves of soda cup lids stored behind the couch, remembering that I had to stock them after break, and then returning to the breath, his breath.

In his breath, I read: *that*, yes.

What happens if I vary the pressure slightly? *Yes.* How about here? The underside. I'd been studying the frenulum, as much for the word as for what it promised. And here it was. Who needs the word when the tip of your tongue is on the delicate referent? Attention to detail. But not too much. And without a "gaining idea."

Come back to the breath. Appropriate response: more of this, less of that. Functional silence: only such speech as is necessary. Slower. Faster.

Faster.

The relief that comes from not talking at all. As Mark Doty asks in his poem "Bootblack," *What can be said of this happiness?*

All this was so much fine-tuned and robust training for the *doan ryo*, playing the various ritual instruments during Zen services, in which slight variations in pressure and timing in striking a bell or drum can mean the difference between a settled assembly and one where each person feels just slightly off and thinks it's because they didn't sleep well, or that the person in front of them is personally dedicated to annoying them, and all that may be so, but more likely it's that the bell was too shrill or the timing uneven.

Gregg and I went back upstairs and still had time for a snack, one of those apple pies rotating along glowing coils, the sleeves slipping as they made each quarter turn. The heat the filling retained always exceeded my patience in letting it cool. We handed the rectangular pie back and forth until Gregg gave me the last corner, then we clocked back in with a few seconds to spare.

Dharma Road

Brian Haycock

Driving a taxi, like taking one, is an intriguing portal into human nature, a series of intimate interludes in which strangers share a small space. It's an ideal opportunity to practice mindfulness, compassion, and curiosity about your fellow human beings. Brian Haycock, who also writes noir fiction with a Buddhist bent, takes us on a taxi ride on the Dharma Road.

I'm driving back from San Marcos with a fifty-dollar bill in my pocket, feeling pretty good. The sun's out, but it's not blasting away. I've got the radio on, an old Johnny Cash road song going. I've been to Buda, Marble Falls, Pflugerville, Cedar Park . . . I'm thinking I'll work some calls from the radio when I get close to Austin, then try to get something going downtown, maybe make a big day out of it. For a cabdriver, this is heaven.

A 'Vette flashes by on my left, doing eighty. It's silver, lean, and hard, and it's just eating up the highway. I can picture the guy inside, in his leather bucket seat, listening to the surround sound, or whatever sound they have in 'Vettes, watching the highway flow on by. I wish I had a 'Vette.

I'm thinking he must have a radar detector. No one does eighty out here without one. I've been thinking about picking one up, but the cab company doesn't really like to see them in the cabs. Besides, it's not in the budget. I pick up the speed a little, watching the back of the 'Vette pull away up the road, watching for his taillights.

I wish I had a radar detector. But I won't be buying one anytime soon. And I definitely won't be buying a 'Vette on what I'm making in the cab. Or on anything I can even imagine myself making doing something else. That fifty-dollar fare to San Marcos doesn't seem like such a big deal now. Most of it'll be gone as soon as I stop at a gas station to top off the tank.

I'm not feeling so good now.

The Buddha taught that we suffer because we crave what we cannot have. Whatever we have, we always want more. We're never satisfied. There's always something else, something that would make our lives just right if we could only have it. It just eats at us until we get it. And then we lose interest in that and go on to wanting something else. It just goes on and on, and it seems like there's no way out. The guy in the 'Vette probably wants a Ferrari. Or an airplane. And he's no happier with his 'Vette than I am with this cab.

I'd like a Rolls Royce with the cab package, a fast meter, and a never-ending gas card, but I probably won't get that. I'd also like to date Jennifer Aniston, climb Mount Everest, and discover a cure for cancer. It's not going to happen. Not for me. Not this time around.

People wonder about Elvis, how it could have gone so wrong. I think I understand. It was harder for him. Most of us think we'd be happy if we only had a little more money, a better car, a prettier girl-friend. And we keep trying. At the end, Elvis knew none of that could save him. With all he had, he was still empty. He was as destitute as a crackhead curled up in an alley with his teeth grinding down. He wanted something he couldn't have, something he couldn't even name. And he knew he'd never have it. It wasn't the pills that killed him. It was the emptiness. The pills only finished him off.

More than anything, we fear losing what we already have. We become attached to the things in our lives that bring us pleasure, but those things are only temporary. Fleeting. So we hold on, tighter and tighter, but that doesn't work. Everything is changing, all the time, and all our attachments will be broken in the end. The rock-and-rollers will lose their edge, their records will stop selling, and they'll be doing nostalgia tours, wondering where it all went. The beauties will lose their looks, the athletes will slow down. Change is the only constant. Nothing lasts forever. You can't go home again, no matter where you're from.

Most of the changes in our lives are slow and subtle. We don't even notice them. But they add up.

Driving around Austin, you get a sense of constant change in the landscape. There are construction cranes and wrecking balls everywhere you look. It seems like they've always been there. Living here for over twenty years, I feel like I've moved to another city, a little at a time.

When I first moved to Austin, there was a place near where I lived called Beer Park. That's right, Beer Park. This is Texas—people think like that here. There were picnic tables set up, a horseshoe pit, a makeshift stage. Sometimes there were people playing guitars, just kicking it around, having fun. I'd go there after work with some of my friends, have a roast beef sandwich, a glass of beer. It lasted six months. The University of Texas bought the land, tore everything down, and built a maintenance facility on it.

Our lives change more quickly and surely than any landscape. Friends drift off, move away. We move, change jobs, join clubs, take up causes, lose interest in them, fall in and out of love. It's not always a bad thing: we all want some variety, some change to make things interesting. Some of the changes are for the better, some for the worse. But very little in life lasts for long. And nothing lasts forever.

According to the Buddha, the events of our lives have no independent existence. They are only temporary. It's all a house of cards. Everything arises and fades away. Ashes to ashes, all fall down. This is a world of shadow and light, nothing more than a show. It's fun to watch, but that's about all.

The suffering we feel isn't caused by the fact of impermanence itself. Impermanence isn't good or bad, it's just the way things are. It's like gravity, or gas prices, or the long cab lines at the airport. The problem is our habit of craving what we cannot have and becoming attached to things that cannot last. Then, when they're gone, we feel the loss.

I've gotten attached to the cab I drive, number 119. It's an ex-police car with a big V-8, heavy-duty brakes and suspension, about as well built as a car can be. I spend more time in the cab than I spend at home. A lot more. I've driven so many miles in it, I feel like it's an extension of myself, a suit of clothes I put on in the morning. Sometimes it goes in for service and I have to spend an afternoon in another car. I feel uncomfortable, awkward. Everything just feels wrong, and I can't wait to get back in my regular cab. But 119 has over 200,000 miles on it and there's a vibration in the transmission that shouldn't be there. It won't last forever.

When the cab goes down, I'll move on to a new one, and I'll get used to that and I'll probably get attached to it. It's all right. I've got some perspective on it. It's only a car, after all. But when we form strong attachments to things in our lives that cannot last, they lead to suffering in the end. Like anyone, I look back at some of the good times I've had, and I wish I could go back, live that way again. But I can't.

In Buddhism, four sources of suffering are unavoidable: birth, sickness, old age, and death. Birth and the process of growing up are painful, both physically and emotionally. Sickness, old age, and death are great sources of suffering for most people, but the real problem is only our reactions to these changes in our lives.

Life begins in suffering. We are pushed from the warmth and safety of the womb to find ourselves in an uncertain and dangerous world, gasping for breath. The first thing we do is cry. It's a good thing we can't remember our birth. We'd be traumatized.

Old age can only be avoided by dying, so old age is really a good thing. The elderly are fortunate to have lived so long. But it's hard to think of it that way. They have aches and pains and can't do the things they used to do. Old age is hard because we're so attached to our youth. We remember the things we could do then, how good it felt to be young and strong, how fresh and new the world seemed. And we miss that.

We're attached to our good health while we have it, so when we're sick, we suffer from more than just our symptoms. Some people have had health problems for years, and they've gotten used to a certain amount of sickness in their lives. It doesn't seem to bother them as much. People who have been fortunate enough to enjoy good health for most of their lives are in for a shock when they get sick. I get a cold every few years, and that's about it. So far. When I get a cold, I'm the most miserable person on earth. I'm pathetic. I just whine and complain until it goes away. My time will come: I'll get really sick, and I won't be able to handle it at all. That's how attachment works.

And then there's death. We all know it's coming, so it should be easy to accept, but it isn't. We're attached to our lives and want them to go on forever. But they don't, and people who have to face death are truly filled with suffering. Even if they don't let it show.

When the Buddha began to teach, he was asked what his teaching consisted of. He said, "I teach suffering and the end of suffering." Now, after twenty-five hundred years, the Buddha is still teaching the end of suffering. He's teaching it to us.

The way to end our suffering is to let go of our cravings, to give up our attachments to the impermanent events of our lives. If we can learn to accept the temporary nature of all things, to see them simply as events to be appreciated for themselves without trying to hold on to them, then we can live without suffering. That is the basis of Buddhist practice, the entry to the Eightfold Path, the blueprint for a life free of suffering.

If you want to develop mindfulness, there are several options. First, you can join a monastery. This is the traditional way. For thousands of years, seekers have left their lives behind to take up a new life of contemplation and meditation. Little by little, they peel away the layers of delusion that have kept them from seeing the world as it truly is. This way has been proven again and again.

Another way is to spend twelve to sixteen hours a day out on the city streets, flowing through the traffic, seeing the way things move. Practicing mindfulness. This way has not been proven by thousands of years of experience. It's just an adventure.

Not all spiritual practice is about peaceful contemplation. The martial arts are based largely on mindfulness practices. The goal is really to keep your head under extreme conditions and react to the action without becoming distracted. That's cab-driving. Staying focused on the city streets and getting from place to place without getting stuck. It's like a Jackie Chan movie set out in the traffic.

The rookies think they're pretty good drivers. Kings of the road. They think they can just mash the gas pedal into the floorboard and keep it there until they either arrive or crash. Then they get bogged down in traffic, beaten by the mazes of one-way streets and four-way intersections, and before long, they realize there's more to it than knowing how to steer and work the gas pedal. The real cabdrivers learn to get it done on real streets, in real traffic. They plan ahead, react to road conditions as they come up, watch out for potential delays.

It's all about focus. Mindfulness. If you're sitting at a green light fiddling with the buttons on the radio, you're spinning your wheels. If you forget to change lanes until you reach the street you want to turn into, you're just a road hazard for everyone else. Next time, take a bus. Or call a cab.

You hear stories about the wild drivers, the ones who push it all the time. I picked one up at the airport. He told me he'd been a cab-driver for eight months and had piled up fourteen traffic tickets. Then they fired him. He told me he'd gotten one of the tickets for driving on the sidewalk. He also told me—just being helpful—that I was driving too slowly, that I'd never make any money that way.

When I first started driving, a driver told me with a wicked grin, "If you go fast enough, they can't get the number off the cab to report you." He was a great guy to hang around with, a lot of fun. He didn't last that long either.

City driving is really a matter of strategy, and the cabdrivers pick up some good ideas about how to move around without risking tickets and accidents.

Planning is one of the keys to city driving. Before you start out, think about the route you plan to take, taking into account the bottlenecks and other delays you're likely to run into. Know the traffic and how it changes with the time of day. At rush hour, some of the main arteries are nothing but parking lots, while there are residential streets a few blocks away with no traffic on them at all. Be flexible. If the route you're taking isn't working out, look for alternatives. If you can see a problem six blocks ahead, don't wait until you get there to look for another route. And remember to use back alleys and parking lots if they'll get you out of a traffic jam. But don't ever use sidewalks.

Watch for buses, UPS trucks, anything likely to block the road. Avoid bicycles. Watch the lights on the cross streets ahead so you'll know when they're about to change. Get off the line quickly when the light changes. When making a right turn at a red light, remember: It's just a stop sign. Don't sit there.

Sounds simple, doesn't it?

Of course it's simple. This is cab-driving, not Chinese quantum mechanics.

I know. You're disappointed. It's all common sense. You thought there was some cabdriver magic that you could use to get across town in minutes at rush hour. You thought there was some big secret the cabdrivers all knew and no one else could figure out. But it's simple: plan your route, and don't get stuck behind UPS trucks. You knew that.

But that's the point. There's no magic, no secret knowledge. What there is, is mindfulness. Of course you know enough not to get stuck behind a UPS truck. But do you notice the truck from three blocks away? Do you think to change lanes then? Or do you wait until you're stuck, and then curse the driver as he gets out with an armful of packages and a big grin? You can't think that far ahead if you're talking on the cell phone or thinking about what you should have said to your boyfriend when he gave you a couple of tickets to a monster truck rally for your birthday. You can't think that far ahead unless you're paying attention.

It's all about focus. Mindfulness. You can think of cab-driving as an epic martial arts adventure. You're up against the evil amateur drivers. They try to slow you down, block you in, force you from your route. But you don't let them. You see their moves coming from three blocks away, and you anticipate. You're too fast for them. You flow through the traffic. Unstoppable.

And it's all mindfulness.

You really can't reduce city driving to a simple set of rules to follow out on the road. Nothing in life is that simple. The key to city driving is keeping your mind open and alert, being aware of everything going on around you. For a cabdriver, practicing mindfulness on the streets is simply the best way to do the job. You have to be productive out there or you won't make any money. But it's also a way of using work as an opportunity for personal growth. In time, the focus becomes automatic. You get behind the wheel, pull out onto the streets, and it's there. And when you're not driving, it's still there. Focus.

It's not really a choice between monastic life and cab-driving. Any activity will do. Whatever you do, you can find ways to use it to develop a stronger focus, a habit of mindfulness. Your work will benefit—and in the end, so will you.

Driving a cab, you meet a lot of people. In a typical twelve-hour shift, a driver will load twenty fares, about thirty or forty people in all, and spend about fifteen minutes with them. You talk about the weather, sports, good places to eat, what's going on this weekend. You don't talk about politics. Or religion. You don't get to know any of these people. It's all pretty impersonal. You just pick them up and drop them off, and you never see them again.

This gives us a great opportunity to have a positive—or negative— effect on the lives of people without being drawn into the ongoing psychodramas that can turn day-to-day life into such an emotional minefield. For drivers on the Eightfold Freeway, this is where right action comes into play. This is where the Golden Rule rules.

The Buddha taught compassion for all beings. In Buddhism, compassion is generally thought of as an active feeling of empathy, a willingness to share in the suffering of others. It grows from the realization that we are not really separate from each other. We are all parts of a much greater pattern. In other words, we're all in this together. To hurt others is to hurt ourselves. And in daily life, that's not just a saying. It's reality.

Compassion and empathy are central to all religions. In Christianity, there is a great emphasis on the practice of forgiveness. When Pope John Paul II forgave the man who shot and nearly killed him, it was a great spiritual lesson for the world. And the selflessness of such leaders as Mother Teresa and the Dalai Lama is an inspiration for people of all faiths.

Right action means to have compassion for all beings, not just the ones who deserve it. The bad drivers, the self-absorbed creeps, the road ragers, the crackheads—they'll all pay a heavy price for their actions. The toxic passengers will run into real trouble down the line. They're looking for it, and they'll find it. There's suffering in their lives as well. We don't need to add to it. And we don't have to add to anyone else's burdens either.

It's hard making a living behind the wheel of a cab. The drivers have to hustle long hours and handle a heavy load of stress to make it all pay. That can seem like a good excuse to act out. It's not. We're always better off when we're helping others.

I'm at the airport, second up at the cabstand in front of the terminal. I've been waiting in line for almost two hours, and I just want to get going. In front of me is a driver named Ray who always works the airport. He's standing at the back of his cab with the trunk open, a vacant smile on his face. He looks at me, shrugs, looks back at the terminal, fidgets a little. He's watching the stragglers from the previous flights, people who've been using the restrooms, waiting for luggage. They're coming out a few at a time, mostly heading for the parking lots.

I know what he's thinking. He's watching the people as they come out, trying to guess which ones want a cab, how far they'll be going. Some of the drivers have the variables all worked out: the number of people in a group, the way they're dressed, the amount and type of luggage, a long list of factors. Sometimes they'll stand there in the cab line, debating the possibilities, arguing about the people coming out. Sometimes they even bet on it. Ray's thinking about it now, deciding which ones he wants, which he doesn't. He's been in line for a long time, and he's been thinking about the big fare he's going to get, getting attached to the idea of it. He thinks he deserves a good one just for waiting. Not that it matters. Whoever comes out next and wants a cab, that's who he's getting.

It takes a few minutes. Then a woman comes up, in her fifties, well-dressed, trailing an overnight bag on wheels. I'm thinking she's going to a hotel, probably downtown, not a long trip. He's thinking the same but he keeps the smile on, says hello. He picks up the bag, puts it in the trunk, and I can read his lips as he says, "Where would you like to go?"

Apparently, he doesn't like the answer. The smile drops away. He reaches up, slams the trunk. Walks around the car with his lips moving, a nasty look on his face. Pounds a fist into the roof as he opens the door and gets in. The poor woman is still standing there, at the back of the cab, looking shocked. She's wondering what she did wrong. She's probably wondering if she should get in the cab with this guy. He might be dangerous. Or crazy. Finally, she goes around, opens the door, and gets in.

Welcome to Austin, ma'am. Enjoy your stay.

Familiar, isn't it? We get so wrapped up in ourselves that we lose all connection with the people around us. It happens all the time. I know Ray a little, and he's got some issues. He's actually a pretty nice guy, but he keeps to himself most of the time. He's a little on edge. And, like most of us, he didn't see himself sitting in the cab line at the airport when he graduated from high school.

Part of living the dharma is connecting with other people. Seeing the connections that unite us. It's hard to do sometimes. Out on the streets, it's a hard life, and that makes for a great excuse. It's easy to just look out for number one.

This teaching of compassion is one of the cornerstones of all Buddhist practices. In Mahayana Buddhism, compassion is expressed as part of the bodhisattva ideal of living for the benefit of all beings. The practice of *tonglen* involves taking on the suffering of others in a very real way. For some schools, compassion is the main focus of the practice. One school, called Vipassana, or Insight Meditation, emphasizes the development of compassion through rigorous introspection. This practice is called *metta*, or loving-kindness. Loving-kindness—all one word, said with a soft, hopeful smile.

The practice of loving-kindness includes meditations aimed at the development of personal qualities such as serenity and a sense of personal safety that lead in turn to a great compassion for others. For example, we might chant, "May I be safe from physical harm," over and over, like a mantra. With sufficient practice, we attain a feeling of safety and personal security. Once that is achieved, it's easier to be open to the needs of others.

It seems like a lot of work. After all, the point is simply to be a decent human being. That doesn't seem so hard. But these are difficult times, and it's easy to find excuses to let this aspect of our practice slide. We have to take care of ourselves, and we may not have much left over for others.

Loving-kindness doesn't come easy to me, which probably means I should take it up and work extra hard on it. There's a book on the Buddhist shelf at the library, *Gentling the Heart*. When I see the title, I know it's not for me. People who would want to read a book like that probably don't need to be that much more loving toward others. And the people who need it the most—like me, or Ray, out at the airport—won't read it.

You don't see much loving-kindness out on the streets these days. Everyone's battling the traffic, trying to get ahead of everyone else. We could use a few real bodhisattvas out here. People who can help calm things down and show the rest of us how it could be. I'd like to do that myself, but I've got a ways to go. I'm working on it. And I'm learning.

I pull up at the Greyhound station on a Tuesday afternoon, second in the cab line. Business is bad, even for a Tuesday. Midsummer in Austin. It's been slow for weeks. People with money are all vacationing somewhere that's cooler than the surface of the sun. The rest of us are stuck here chasing dollars. There's nothing coming out on the cab radio. I'd go out to the airport and sit in line there, but that hasn't been turning over, either. Besides, this is closer. I keep the air conditioner running, engine on, burning gas.

Nothing happens at the bus station until a bus comes in, and there aren't that many buses. Drivers who work it regularly know the schedule. I don't. I figure I'll just sit there until something happens. I might get a long fare, something to make my afternoon. Some good fares come out of the bus station. Or I might wait two hours for a five-dollar ride. It seems like the best of a long list of bad bets.

I've got those midsummer cabdriver blues. I've got 'em bad.

After a while, I shut off the engine and get out. I'd sit in the shade, but there isn't any. I walk over to the back of the station, where the buses load. There are a few people on the benches there, waiting for the next bus. They all look like they're going to nod off or dissolve in the sun. I'd go inside and check the schedule, which would be the smart thing to do, but I don't want to know.

There's a woman at the back of the station with a little girl. They look lost. She loads some suitcases and a taped cardboard box onto a small cart and sits the girl on top, pushes the cart out to the sidewalk. The girl enjoys the ride, but it's a short one. The woman stands there looking around.

They don't look like they can afford a cab.

Finally she takes the girl by the hand and walks over. "Excuse me, do you know where the Salvation Army is located?"

It's downtown, four or five miles from the bus station. I tell her that.

She looks troubled. The little girl is looking at her reflection in the door of the cab. She can't see much, but she seems entranced. In this heat, she'll be wailing soon enough. The woman thinks it over and asks, "Where can I catch a bus?"

If I were king of the world, or just the head of Capitol Metro, I would put a bus stop right next to the Greyhound station. After all, it is a bus station. But there isn't a stop anywhere near here. I start describing the route she'll have to take to the closest bus stop, which is at Highland Mall. I glance over at the suitcases, the cardboard box sealed with duct tape. I look at the woman. She looks like she has a black eye. Not a bad one, but it's there. I can't do this.

"Come on, I'll give you a ride over there."

"Are you sure? I can't afford to pay you. I know you have to make a living out here."

"It's all right. I'm not exactly getting rich sitting here." I walk over and collect the cart with the suitcases and the box, wheel it over to the cab. I load the trunk. The little girl stands on her toes on the curb, studying the inside of the trunk.

I'm thinking I'm going to give her a ride to the bus stop, then get back in line at the station, but I'm picturing her trying to get the suitcases on a city bus. I make a turn and head for the interstate, downtown. I feel better already. I crank up the air conditioner.

On the way in, we talk. It's what I thought. She was in an abusive relationship, and she's getting out. She's here to start over. She asks if all the people in Austin are as nice as I am, and I tell her, yes, most of them are, but I'm not usually this nice. I'm working on it.

When we get to the Salvation Army, I help her with her bags. The people there are expecting her. She won't be staying at the shelter. They're going to help her get a new start. As I turn to leave, the little girl looks up at me, gives me a beautiful smile, and says thank you. It's the first thing she's said since she left the back of the bus station. It's like the sun coming out on a dark afternoon.

From there, I head over to the Omni and load a fifty-dollar fare to Georgetown, and while I'm there, a call comes out on the radio and I load another coming all the way back downtown and then . . .

No. Of course not. Life isn't like that. It's still a Tuesday afternoon in July. I pull up third in line at the Omni and wait there an hour to load a five-dollar fare going over to the capitol. But I feel good about it. That's what counts.

And a week from now, when I look back at what I've been doing, I'll realize that that was the best afternoon of my week. That was the one time I felt like I belonged in this world, like I had something real and important to do in this life.

Rebel Buddha

Dzogchen Ponlop Rinpoche

*Who is more radical than the Buddha, who overthrows all the conventional
ways we see ourselves and our world? We have a rebel buddha inside us too,
says Dzogchen Ponlop Rinpoche. It's the innate wakefulness that subverts
our illusions and fights for our liberation.*

According to the Buddha, our freedom is never in question. We're
born free. The true nature of the mind is enlightened wisdom and
compassion. Our mind is always brilliantly awake and aware. Nevertheless, we're often plagued by painful thoughts and the emotional
unrest that goes with them. We live in states of confusion and fear
from which we see no escape. Our problem is that we don't see who
we truly are at the deepest level. We don't recognize the power of
our enlightened nature. We trust the reality we see before our eyes
and accept its validity until something comes along—an illness, accident, or disappointment—to disillusion us. Then we might be
ready to question our beliefs and start searching for a more mean-
ingful and lasting truth. Once we take that step, we're starting off on
the road to freedom.

On this road, what we free ourselves from is illusion, and what
frees us from illusion is the discovery of truth. To make that discovery, we need to enlist the powerful intelligence of our own awake
mind and turn it toward our goal of exposing, opposing, and over-

coming deception. That is the essence and mission of "rebel buddha": to free us from the illusions we create by ourselves, about ourselves, and from those that masquerade as reality in our cultural and religious institutions.

The word *buddha* simply means "awake" or "awakened." It does not refer to a particular historical person or to a philosophy or religion. It refers to your own mind. You know you have a mind, but what's it like? It's awake. I don't just mean "not asleep." I mean your mind is *really* awake, beyond your imagination. Your mind is brilliantly clear, open, spacious, and full of excellent qualities: unconditional love, compassion, and wisdom that sees things as they truly are. In other words, your awakened mind is always a good mind; it's never dull or confused. It's never distressed by the doubts, fears, and emotions that so often torture us. Instead, your true mind is a mind of joy, free from all suffering. That is who you really are. That is the true nature of your mind and the mind of everyone. But your mind doesn't just sit there being perfect, doing nothing. It's at play all the time, creating your world.

If this is true, then why isn't your life, and the whole world, perfect? Why aren't you happy all the time? How could you be laughing one minute and in despair the next? And why would "awakened" people argue, fight, lie, cheat, steal, and go to war? The reason is that, even though the awakened state is the true nature of the mind, most of us don't see it. Why? Something is in the way. Something is blocking our view of it. Sure, we see bits of it here and there. But the moment we see it, something else pops into our mind—"What time is it? Is it time for lunch? Oh, look, a butterfly!"—and our insight is gone.

Ironically, what blocks your view of your mind's true nature—your buddha mind—is also your own mind, the part of your mind that is always busy, constantly involved in a steady stream of thoughts, emotions, and concepts. This busy mind is who you think you are. It is easier to see, like the face of the person standing right in front of you. For example, the thought you're thinking right now is more obvious to you than your awareness of that thought. When you get angry, you pay more attention to what you're angry about than to the actual source of your anger, where your anger is coming from. In other words, you notice what your mind is doing, but you don't see the mind itself. You identify yourself with the contents of this busy mind—your thoughts, emotions, ideas—and end up thinking that all of this stuff is "me" and "how I am."

When you do that, it's like being asleep and dreaming, and believing that your dream images are true. If, for example, you dream that you're being chased by a menacing stranger, it's very scary and real. However, as soon as you wake up, both the stranger and your feelings of terror are simply gone, and you feel great relief. Furthermore, if you had known you were dreaming in the first place, then you wouldn't have experienced any fear.

In a similar way, in our ordinary life, we're like dreamers believing that the dream we're having is real. We think we're awake, but we're not. We think that this busy mind of thoughts and emotions is who we truly are. But when we actually wake up, our misunderstanding about who we are—and the suffering that confusion brings—is gone.

A Rebel Within

If we could, we would probably all sink completely into this dream that passes for our waking life, but something keeps rousing us from our sleep. No matter how dazed and confused it gets, our drowsy self is always linked to complete wakefulness. That wakefulness has a sharp and penetrating quality. It's our own intelligence and clear awareness that have the ability to see through whatever blocks our view of our true self—the true nature of our mind. On the one hand, we're used to our sleep and content with its dreams; on the other hand, our wakeful self is always shaking us up and turning on the lights, so to speak. This wakeful self, the true mind that is awake, wants out of the confines of sleep, out of illusion-like reality. While we're locked away in our dream, it sees the potential for freedom. So it provokes, arouses, prods, and instigates until we're inspired to take action. You could say we are living with a rebel within.

This rebel is the voice of your own awakened mind. It is the sharp, clear intelligence that resists the status quo of your confusion and suffering. What is this rebel buddha like? A troublemaker of heroic proportions. Rebel buddha is the renegade that gets you to switch your allegiance from sleep to the awakened state. This means you have the power to wake up your dreaming self, the impostor that is pretending to be the real you. You have the means to break loose from whatever binds you to suffering and locks you in confusion. You are the champion of your own freedom. Ultimately, the mission of rebel buddha is to instigate a revolution of mind.

GETTING TO KNOW YOUR MIND

All the teachings of the Buddha have one clear message, which is that there is nothing more important than getting to know your own mind. The reason is simple—the source of our every suffering is discovered within this mind. If we're feeling anxious, that stress and worry are produced by this mind. If we're overwrought by despair, that misery originates within our mind. On the other hand, if we're madly in love and walking on air, that joy also arises from our mind. Pleasure and pain, simple and extreme, are experiences of mind. Mind is the experiencer of each moment of our life and all that we perceive, think, and feel. Therefore, the better we know our mind and how it works, the greater the possibility that we can free ourselves from the mental states that weigh us down, invisibly wound us, and destroy our ability to be happy. Knowing our mind not only leads to a happy life; it transforms every trace of confusion and wakes us up completely.

To experience that awakened state is to know freedom in its purest sense. This state of freedom is not dependent on external circumstances. It does not change with the ups and downs of life. It's the same whether we experience gain or loss, praise or blame, pleasant or unpleasant conditions. In the beginning, we only glimpse this state, but those glimpses become increasingly more familiar and stable. In the end, the state of freedom becomes our home ground.

Two Aspects of the Mind

Buddhism talks about mind in different ways. There is the mind that is confused or asleep, and the mind that is enlightened or awake. Another way to describe the mind is to talk about its relative and ultimate aspects. The relative aspect refers to confused mind; the ultimate aspect is its enlightened nature. Relative mind is our ordinary consciousness, our commonplace dualistic perception of the world. "I" am separate from "you," and "this" is separate from "that." There appears to be a fundamental division within all of our experiences. We take for granted that good exists apart from bad, right apart from wrong, and so forth. This way of seeing tends to breed misunderstanding and conflict more often than harmony. The ultimate aspect of mind is simply the true nature of our mind, which is beyond any polarities. It is our fundamental being, our basic, open, and spacious awareness. Imagine a clear blue sky filled with light.

Stuck in the Conceptual World

When we don't pay attention, the conceptual world takes over our whole being. That's a pretty sad thing. We can't even enjoy a beautiful sunny day, watching leaves blowing in the wind. We have to label it all so that we live in a concept of sun, a concept of wind, and a concept of moving leaves. If we could leave it there, it wouldn't be too bad, but that never happens. Then it's "Oh yeah, it's good to be here. It's beautiful, but it would be better if the sun were shining from another angle." When we're walking, we're not really walking; a concept is walking. When we're eating, we're not really eating; a concept is eating. When we're drinking, we're not really drinking; a concept is drinking. At some point, our whole world dissolves into concepts.

As the external world is reduced to a conceptual world, we not only lose a wholesome part of our being, we lose all the beautiful things in the natural world: forests, flowers, birds, lakes. Nothing can bring us any genuine experience. Then our emotions come into play, supercharging our thoughts with their energy; we find there are "good" things that bring "good" emotions, and there are "bad" things that bring "bad" emotions. When we live our life like this every day, it becomes very tiresome; we begin to feel a sense of exhaustion and heaviness. We may think that our exhaustion comes from our job or our family, but in many cases, it's not the job or family itself—it's our mind. What's exhausting us is how we relate to our life conceptually and emotionally. We risk becoming so stuck in the realm of concepts that nothing we do feels fresh, inspired, or natural.

Perceptual mind, conceptual mind, and emotional mind are three aspects of relative mind, our mundane consciousness, which we usually experience as a continuous stream. But in reality, perceptions, thoughts, and emotions last only for an instant. They're impermanent. They come and go so quickly that we're unaware of the discontinuity within this stream, of the space between each mental event. It's like watching a thirty-five-millimeter film. We know it's made up of many single frames, but due to the speed at which it moves, we never notice the end of one frame and the beginning of the next. We never see the imageless space between the frames, just as we never see the space of awareness between one thought and another.

We end up living in a fabricated world made up of these three aspects of relative mind. Layer by layer, we have constructed a solid reality that has become a burden, locked us into a small space, a corner of our being, and locked out much of who we really are. Usually, we think of a prison as something made of walls and prisoners as people locked inside, removed from the world for their crimes. Such inmates have basic routines that get them through the day, but the possibilities for a full experience and enjoyment of life are severely limited.

We are confined in a similar way, locked inside the prison walls of our conceptual world. The Buddha taught that what lies at the bottom of all this is ignorance: the state of not knowing who we truly are, of not recognizing our natural state of freedom and our potential for happiness, fulfillment, and enjoyment of life.

OUR NATURAL STATE OF FREEDOM

This ignorance is a kind of blindness that leads us to believe that the movie we're watching is real. As I mentioned earlier, when we believe that this busy mind—this stream of emotions and concepts—is who we truly are, it's like being asleep and dreaming without knowing we're dreaming. When we don't know we're asleep and in a dream state, we have no control over our dream life. The Buddha taught that the key to waking up and unlocking the door of our prison is self-knowledge, which extinguishes ignorance like a light being turned on in a room that has been dark for a very long time. The light immediately illuminates the whole room, regardless of how long it has been dark, and we can see what we haven't seen before—our true nature, our natural state of freedom.

Freedom can happen swiftly. One moment, we're bound by something, the sum total of our life—our concepts about who we are, our position in the world, the force and weight of our relationships to people and places; we're caught in the fabric of all that. Then, at another moment, it's gone. There is nothing obstructing us. We're free to walk out the door. In fact, our prison dissolves around us, and there's nothing to escape from. What has changed is our mind. The self that was caught, trapped, is freed the minute that the mind changes and perceives space instead of a prison. If there is no prison, then there can be no prisoner. In fact, there never was a prison except in our mind, in the concepts that became the brick and mortar of our confinement.

This is not to say that there are no real prisons—no jails or jailers, no forces in the world that can confine, inhibit, or restrict us. I'm not saying that it's all just a thought that can be swept away. We should not ignore any aspect of our reality. But even those prisons and negative forces arose from the thoughts of others; they're all products of someone's mind, someone's confusion. Even though we can't do much about that right away, we do have the power to work with our own mind now, and eventually we'll develop the wisdom to work with the minds of others.

UNCHANGING MIND

When the Buddha taught about this impermanent and composite (or "put together") nature of the relative mind, he did so in order to introduce his disciples to the ultimate nature of mind: pure, unfabricated, unchanging awareness. Here Buddhism departs radically from theological concepts like original sin that view humankind as spiritually tainted by some hereditary violation of divine law. The Buddhist view asserts that the nature of all beings is primordially pure and replete with positive qualities. Once we wake up enough to see through our confusion, we see that even our problematic thoughts and emotions are, at heart, part of this pure awareness.

Seeing this naturally brings us a sense of relaxation, joy, and humor. We don't need to take anything too seriously, because everything we experience on the relative level is illusory. From the point of view of the ultimate, it's like a lucid dream, the vivid play of mind itself. When we're awake in a dream, we don't take anything that happens in the dream too seriously. It's like going on the big rides at Disney World. One ride will take us up in the night sky with stars all around and the lights of a city below. It's so beautiful and we enjoy it, but we don't take it to be real. And when we ride through the haunted house, the ghosts, skeletons, and monsters might surprise us for an instant or two, but they're also funny, because we know they aren't real.

In the same way, when we discover the true nature of our mind, we're relieved from a fundamental anxiety, a basic sense of fear and worry about the appearances and experiences of life. The true nature of mind says, "Why stress out? Just relax and enjoy yourself." That's our choice, unless we have an exceptionally strong tendency to fight all the time; then even Disney World becomes a horrible place. That's also our choice. Our modern world is full of options these days, so wherever we are, we can do it either way.

Many people have asked what this kind of awareness is like. Is the experience of this "true nature" like becoming a vegetable, being in a coma, or having Alzheimer's? No. In fact, it's nothing like that. Our relative mind becomes better functioning. When we take a break from our habitual labeling, our world becomes clear. We're free to see clearly; think clearly; and feel the living, wakeful quality of our emotions. The openness, spaciousness, and freshness of the experience make it a beautiful place to be. Imagine standing on a scenic mountain peak and looking at the world in all directions without any obstructions. That is what's called the experience of the nature of mind.

Freeing Ourselves from Ignorance

If knowledge is the key to our freedom, then how do we move from a state of unknowing to knowing? The logic of the Buddhist path is very simple. We begin from a state that is confused and dominated by ignorance; by cultivating knowledge and insight through study, contemplation, and meditation, we free ourselves from ignorance and arrive at a state of wisdom. Therefore, the essence of this path is the cultivation of our intelligence and the development of our insight. As we work with our intelligence, it becomes sharper and more penetrating; finally, it becomes so sharp that it cuts through the very concepts and ignorance that keep us bound to suffering. What we're doing is training our mind to free itself; we're exercising, working out, pumping up our rebel buddha.

Intelligence is not simply quantitative, a matter of how much we know. It is active; it functions. It's the arms and legs of the wisdom to which it's attached. It's what gets us moving and gets us to our goal. When we begin to break through those conceptual barriers, we not only change ourselves, but we begin to change the world around us. It's not always easy. It requires great conviction because we're challenging what is closest to us—our definition of self, both our personal self and the self of others. Whether it's a suffering self or a tyrannical self, it's what we know and have always cherished. But when you see the reality of your true self, you see it nakedly—stripped of all concepts. It's one thing to say, "The emperor has no clothes"; it's another thing to declare that and be the emperor yourself.

THE MYTH OF THE SELF

Imagine that you look down at your hand one day and see that it's clenched in a fist. You sense that you're holding on to something so vital that you can't let it go. Your fist is clenched so tightly that your hand hurts. The ache in your hand travels up your arm, and tension spreads throughout your body. This goes on for years. You take aspirin now and then, have a drink, watch TV, or take up skydiving. Life goes on, and then one day you forget about it, and your hand opens: there is nothing inside. Imagine your surprise.

The Buddha taught that the root cause of our suffering—ignorance—is what gives rise to this tendency to "cling." The question you should ask yourself is, "What am I clinging to?" We should look deeply at this process to see if anything is there. According to the Buddha, what we're clinging to is a myth. It's just a thought that says "I," repeated so often that it creates an illusory self, like a hologram that we take to be solid and real. With every thought, every emotion, this "self" appears as thinker and experiencer, yet it's really just a fabrication of mind. It's an ancient habit, so ingrained in us that this very clinging becomes part of our identity as well. If we weren't clinging to this thought of "me," we might feel that something familiar was missing—like a close friend or a chronic pain that suddenly disappears.

Just like gripping an imaginary object, our self-clinging doesn't accomplish much for us. It only gives us a headache and ulcers, and we quickly develop many other kinds of suffering on top of that. This "I" becomes very proactive in protecting its own interests, because it immediately perceives "other." The instant we have the thought of "I" and "other," the whole drama of "us" and "them" develops. It all happens in the blink of an eye: we cling to the "I" side and decide whether the "other" is for us, against us, or merely inconsequential. Finally, we set our agenda: toward one object, we feel desire and want to attract it; toward another, we feel fear and hostility and want to repel it; and toward another, we feel indifference and simply ignore it. Thus, the birth of our neurotic emotions and judgments is the result of our clinging to "I," "me," and "mine." Nor are we exempt from our own judgments. We admire some of our qualities and build ourselves up, disdain others and tear ourselves down, and ignore much of the pain we're really feeling because of this inner struggle to be happy with who we are.

Why do we persist in this when we would feel so much better and more relaxed if we just let go? The true nature of our mind is always present, but because we don't see it, we grasp what we do see and try to make it into something it's not. Such complications seem to be the only way the ego can survive—by creating a maze or a hall of mirrors. Our neurotic mind becomes so full of twists and turns that it's difficult to keep track of what it's doing. We expend all of this effort just to convince ourselves that we have found something solid within the insubstantial nature of our mind: a single, permanent identity—something we can call "me." Yet in doing so, we're working against the way things truly are. We're trying to freeze our experience, to create something solid, tangible, and stable out of something that doesn't have that character. It's like asking space to be earth or water to be fire. We think that to give up this thought of "I" would be crazy; we think our life depends on it. But actually, our freedom depends on letting it go.

Enlightenments))

Jack Kornfield

It's such an intimidating word—enlightenment—and raises so many questions. Is it real or some impossible ideal? Can I meet an enlightened person, and if I do how will I know it? Is it something an ordinary person like me can even aspire to? One way or another, we all ask ourselves these questions, however we define the ultimate goal of human life. The answer, says Jack Kornfield, is yes, enlightenment is real and reachable, and it expresses itself in many different ways.

On a meditation retreat several years ago, late one evening after the dharma talk, a woman raised her hand and asked one last question: "Is enlightenment just a myth?" When we teachers went back to our evening meeting, we asked each other this question. We exchanged stories about the creative freedom of Ajahn Chah, the enormous field of *metta* around Dipa Ma, the joyous laughter of Poonja, and of our own awakenings. Of course there is enlightenment.

But the word *enlightenment* is used in different ways, and that can be confusing. Is Zen, Tibetan, Hindu, or Theravada enlightenment the same? What is the difference between an enlightenment experience and full enlightenment? What do enlightened people look like?

Approaches to Enlightenment

Early on in my practice in Asia, I was forced to deal with these questions quite directly. My teachers, Ajahn Chah in Thailand and Mahasi Sayadaw in Burma, were both considered among the most enlightened masters of Theravada Buddhism. While they both described the goal of practice as freedom from greed, hatred, and delusion, they didn't agree about how to attain enlightenment, nor about how it is experienced. I started my monastic training practicing in community with Ajahn Chah. Then I went to study in a monastery of Mahasi Sayadaw, where the path of liberation focuses entirely on long silent meditation retreats.

In the Mahasi system, you sit and walk for weeks in the retreat context and continuously note the arising of breath, thought, feelings, and sensations over and over until the mindfulness is so refined there is nothing but instantaneous arising and passing. You pass through stages of luminosity, joy, fear, and the dissolution of all you took to be solid. The mind becomes unmoving, resting in a place of stillness and equanimity, transparent to all experience, thoughts and fears, longings and love. Out of this there comes a dropping away of identity with anything in this world, an opening to the unconditioned beyond mind and body; you enter into the stream of liberation. As taught by Mahasi Sayadaw, this first taste of stream-entry to enlightenment requires purification and strong concentration leading to an experience of cessation that begins to uproot greed, hatred, and delusion.

When I returned to practice in Ajahn Chah's community following more than a year of silent Mahasi retreat, I recounted all of these experiences—dissolving my body into light, profound insights into emptiness, hours of vast stillness and freedom. He understood and appreciated them from his own deep wisdom. Then he smiled and said, "Well, something else to let go of." Ajahn Chah's approach to enlightenment was not based on having any particular meditation experience, no matter how profound. As Ajahn Chah described them, meditative states are not important in themselves. Meditation is a way to quiet the mind so you can practice all day long wherever you are; see when there is grasping or aversion, clinging or suffering; and then let it go. What's left is enlightenment, always found here and now, a release of identification with the changing conditions of the world, a resting in awareness. This involves a simple yet profound shift of identity from the myriad, ever-changing conditioned states to the unconditioned consciousness—the awareness that knows them all. In Ajahn Chah's approach, release from entanglement in greed, hatred, and delusion does not happen through retreat, concentration, and cessation but from this profound shift in identity.

How can we understand these seemingly different approaches to enlightenment? The Buddhist texts contain some of the same contrasting descriptions. In many texts, nirvana is described in the language of negation, and as in the approach taught by Mahasi Sayadaw; enlightenment is presented as the end of suffering through putting out of the fires of craving, the uprooting of all forms of clinging. The elimination of suffering is practiced by purification and concentration, confronting the forces of greed and hate and overcoming them. When the Buddha was asked, "Do you teach annihilation? Is nirvana the end of the things as we know them?" he responded, "I teach only one form of annihilation: the extinction of greed, the extinction of hatred, the extinction of delusion. This I call *nirvana.*"

There is in the texts, as well, a more positive way of understanding enlightenment. Here nirvana is described as the highest happiness; as peace, freedom, purity, stillness; and as the unconditioned, the timeless, the undying. In this understanding, as in Ajahn Chah's approach, liberation comes through a shift of identity—a release from attachment to the changing conditions of the world, a resting in consciousness itself, the deathless.

In this understanding, liberation is a shift of identity from taking anything as "self." Asked, "How is it that one is not to be seen by the king of death?" the Buddha responded, "For one who takes nothing whatsoever as I or me or mine, such a one is freed from the snares of the king of death." In just this way, Ajahn Chah instructed us to rest in awareness and not identify with any experience as I or mine.

I found a similar practice in Bombay with Sri Nisargadatta, a master of Advaita. His teachings about enlightenment demanded a shift from identifying with any experience to resting in consciousness wherever you are. His focus was not about annihilation of greed and hate. In fact, when asked if he ever got impatient, Nisargadatta joyfully explained, "I see, hear, and taste as you do, feel hunger and thirst; if lunch is not served on time, even impatience will arise. All this I perceive quite clearly, but somehow I am not in it. There is awareness of it all and a sense of immense distance. Impatience arises; hunger arises. Even when illness and death of this body arise, they have nothing to do with who I am." This is enlightenment as a shift in identity.

So here we have different visions of enlightenment. On the one hand, we have the liberation from greed, hatred, and delusion attained through powerful concentration and purification, emphasized by many masters from Mahasi and Sunlun Sayadaw to Rinzai. On the other hand, we have the shift of identity reflected in the teachings of Ajahn Chah, Buddhadasa, Soto Zen, and Dzogchen. And there are many other approaches; if you practice Pure Land Buddhism, which was the most widespread tradition in China, the approach to enlightenment involves devotion and surrender, being carried by the Buddha's "grace."

To understand these differences, it is wisest to speak of enlightenment with the plural s—as enlightenments. It's the same way with God. There are so many forms: Jehovah, Allah, Brahma, Jesus, Kali, and so forth. As soon as followers say they know the one true God, conflict arises. Similarly, if you speak of enlightenment as one thing, conflict arises and you miss the truth.

We know that the Buddha taught many different approaches to enlightenment, all as skillful means to release grasping of the limited sense of self and return to the inherent purity of consciousness. Similarly, we will discover that the teachings on enlightened consciousness include many dimensions. When you actually experience consciousness free of identification with changing conditions, liberated from greed and hate, you find it multifaceted, like a mandala or a jewel, a crystal with many sides. Through one facet, the enlightened heart shines as luminous clarity, through another as perfect peace, through another as boundless compassion. Consciousness is timeless, ever present, completely empty and full of all things. But when a teacher or tradition emphasizes only one of these qualities over the others, it is easy to be confused, as if true enlightenment can be tasted in only one way. Like the particle and wave nature of light, enlightenment consciousness is experienced in a myriad of beautiful ways.

GATEWAYS TO ENLIGHTENMENT

So what practices lead to these enlightenments? Most centrally, Buddhism uses the liberating practices of mindfulness and lovingkindness. These are supported by the practice of virtue, which frees us from being caught in reactive energies that would cause harm to ourself or others. Added to this are practices of composure, or concentration, where we learn to quiet the mind; and practices of wisdom, which can see clearly how all things arise and pass, how they cannot be possessed. Through these practices come purification and healing and the arising of profound compassion. Gradually, there is a shift of identity from being the person who is caught in suffering, to liberation. Releasing the sense of self and all the changing conditions of the world brings "stream-entry," the first stage of enlightenment.

The most common gates to stream-entry in the Theravada tradition are the gateway of impermanence, the gateway of suffering, and the gateway of selflessness. When we open through the gateway of impermanence, we see more and more deeply how every experience is born and dies, how every moment is new. In one monastery where I practiced, we were trained to experience how all of life is vibration. Through long hours of refined concentration, we came to sense all the sounds and sights, the breath, the procession of thoughts— everything we took to be ourself—as a field of changing energy.

Experience shimmered, dissolving moment by moment. Then we shifted our attention from the vibrations to rest in the spacious heart of awareness. I and other, inside and outside—everything dropped away and we came to know the vast stillness beyond all change. This is enlightenment through the gate of impermanence.

Sometimes we enter enlightenment through the gate of suffering. We sit in the fire of human experience, and instead of running from it, we awaken through it. In the *Fire Sermon*, the Buddha declares, "All is burning. The eye, the nose, the tongue, the body, the mind, the world is burning. With what is it burning? It is burning with the fires of greed, of hatred, and of delusion." Through the gate of suffering we face the fires of desire, hate, war, racism, and fear. We open to dissatisfaction, grief, and loss. We accept the inherent suffering in life and we are released. We discover that suffering is not "our" pain, it is "the" pain—the pain of the world. A profound dispassion arises, compassion fills the heart, and we find liberation.

My friend Salam, a Palestinian journalist and activist, passed through the gate of suffering when brutally beaten in Israeli prisons. This kind of suffering happens on every side in war. When I first met Salam in San Francisco, he was being honored for his hospice service. I asked him what brought him to this work. "One time I died," Salam told me. Kicked by a guard, he lay on the floor of the jail with blood coming out of his mouth, and his consciousness floated out of his body. Suddenly, he felt so peaceful—a kind of bliss—as he saw he wasn't that body. "I was so much more: I was the boot and the guard, the goat calling outside the walls of the police station. I was all of it," Salam told me. "When I got out of jail, I couldn't take sides anymore. I married a Jewish woman and had Jewish-Palestinian children. That is my answer." Salam explains, "Now I sit with people who are dying because they are afraid and I can hold their hands and reassure them that it's perfectly safe." He awakened through the gate of suffering.

Sometimes we awaken through the gate of selflessness. The experience of selflessness can happen in the simplest ways. In walking meditation, we notice with every step the unbidden arising of thoughts, feelings, sensations, only to observe them disappear. To whom do they belong? Where do they go? Back into the void, which is where yesterday went, as well as our childhood, Socrates, Genghis Khan, and the builders of the pyramids.

As we let go of clinging, we feel the tentative selflessness of things. Sometimes boundaries dissolve, and we can't separate ourself from the plum tree, the birdsong, or the morning traffic. The whole sense of self becomes empty experience arising in consciousness. More and more deeply, we realize the joy of "no self, no problem." We taste enlightenment through the gate of selflessness and emptiness.

There are many other gates: the gates of compassion, of purity, of surrender, of love. There is also what is called the "gateless gate." One teacher describes it this way: "I would go for months of retreat training, and nothing spectacular would happen, no great experiences. Yet somehow everything changed. What most transformed me were the endless hours of mindfulness and compassion, giving a caring attention to what I was doing. I discovered how I automatically tighten and grasp, and with that realization I started to let go, to open to an appreciation of whatever was present. I found an ease. I gave up striving. I became less serious, less concerned with myself. My kindness deepened. I experienced a profound freedom, simply the fruit of being present over and over." This was her gateless gate.

EXPRESSIONS OF ENLIGHTENMENT

Whatever our gate to enlightenment, the first real taste, stream-entry, is followed by many more tastes as we learn to stabilize, deepen, and embody this wisdom in our own unique life. What does it look like? The facets of enlightenment express themselves marvelously in our teachers. Each manifests enlightenment with his or her own flavors.

Dipa Ma, a wonderful grandmother in Calcutta, was one of the great masters of our tradition. A tiny person with a powerfully trained mind, Dipa Ma expressed enlightenment as love. She devotedly instructed her students in mindfulness and loving-kindness and then she hugged them—putting her hands on their head, face, and shoulders, whispering *metta* phrases. They got drunk on love. Like Dipa Ma, Ammachi, a Hindu teacher from South India, manifests enlightenment as the "hugging guru." She goes into a trance, and all night long she holds people; she might take as many as two thousand people onto her lap and hug them. This is enlightenment as love.

For Zen Master Suzuki Roshi enlightenment was expressed by being just where you are. A woman told Suzuki Roshi she found it difficult to mix Zen practice with the demands of being a householder: "I feel I am trying to climb a ladder, but for every step upward I slip backward two steps." "Forget the ladder," Suzuki Roshi told her. "When you awaken, everything is right here on the ground." He explained how the desire to gain anything means you miss the reality of the present. "When you realize the truth that everything changes and find your composure in it, there you find yourself in nirvana." Asked further about enlightenment, Suzuki Roshi said, "Strictly speaking there are no enlightened beings; there is only enlightened activity." If you think you are enlightened, that is not it. The goal is to let go of being anyone special and meet each moment with beginner's mind.

Mahasi Sayadaw, the Burmese master, expressed enlightenment as emptiness. Watching him on his visits to America, we saw that he rarely laughed or judged. Instead, he exuded a quiet equanimity. Events and conversations would happen around him while he remained still. He was like space—transparent, nobody there. This is enlightenment as emptiness.

For Ajahn Jumnien, a Thai forest master, awakening is not only empty; it's full. His robe is covered in hundreds of sacred medallions, and he employs dozens of skillful means to teach—guided meditations, sacred chants, mantras, chakra and energy practices, forest medicines, animal stories, and shamanic rituals. His dharma is all-hours, nonstop, full of life and joy. There's a sense of abundance in him, and happiness just pours out like a fountain. He expresses enlightenment as fullness.

Thich Nhat Hanh expresses enlightenment as mindfulness. When he has come to teach at Spirit Rock, two or three thousand people sit meditatively on the hillside and eat their apples mindfully in preparation for his arrival. A bell is rung, and he walks slowly and deliberately up the road—*so* mindfully that everyone sighs, "Ahhh." The consciousness of three thousand people is transformed just seeing this man walk, each step the whole universe. As we watch, we drop into the reality of the eternal present. This is where we awaken. Enlightenment as mindfulness.

The Dalai Lama expresses enlightenment as compassionate blessing. For instance, once at the end of his stay at a San Francisco hotel, he asked the management to bring out all the employees. This meant the people who chop vegetables in the kitchen, who clean the carpets late at night, who make the beds. The big circular driveway filled with all those who made this hotel work but who were usually unrecognized. One by one, he looked at each one with full presence, took each person's hand, and said, "Thank you," moving unhurriedly just to make sure that he connected with each one fully. The Dalai Lama personifies enlightenment as compassionate blessing.

Ajahn Chah's manifestation was the laughter of wisdom. Whether with generals or ministers, farmers or cooks, he would say, "When I see how much people are struggling, I look at them with great sympathy and ask, 'Are you suffering? Ahhh, you must be very attached. Why not let go?'" His teachings were deep and straight to the point. He'd say, "If you let go a little, you'll be a little happy. If you let go a lot, you'll be a lot happy. If you let go completely, you'll be completely happy." He saw suffering, its cause, and that freedom is possible in any moment. He expressed enlightenment as wisdom.

When people read these stories, they might ask, "How do they relate to me? I want these enlightenments. How do I get them? What should I do?" The jewel of enlightenment invites us to awaken through many skillful means. Mahasi Sayadaw would say, "To find emptiness, note every single moment until what you think to be the world dissolves, and you will come to know freedom." Ajahn Chah would say, "Just let go, and become the awareness, be the one who knows." Dipa Ma would say, "Love no matter what." Thich Nhat Hanh would say, "Rest in mindfulness, this moment, the eternal present." Ajahn Jumnien would say, "Be happy for no cause." Suzuki Roshi would say, "Just be exactly where you are. Instead of waiting for the bus, realize you are on the bus."

So, is enlightenment a myth? No. It is not far away. It is freedom here and now, to be tasted whenever you open to it. In my role as a teacher, I have the privilege of seeing the blessing of enlightenments awaken in so many meditators who come to dharma practice and become transformed though its many expressions. From their initial tension and struggle with life, their doubt and distress, I watch their bodies ease, their faces soften, their dharma vision open, their hearts blossom. Some touch what Buddhadasa called "everyday nirvana." Others come to know a deep purity of mind and experience a taste of liberation directly.

The Buddha declares, "If it were not possible to free the heart from entanglement, I would not teach you to do so. Just because it is possible to free the heart, there arise the teachings of the dharma of liberation, offered openhandedly for the welfare of all beings."

Aim for nothing less.

The Sword Disappears in the Water

Bonnie Myotai Treace

How do great teachers transmit the truth that is beyond concept to those of us still stuck in the mind of words and ideas? The famed koans of the Zen tradition are stories of how the old Buddhist masters of China used irony, paradox, example, and shock—whatever it took—to wake their students up to a deeper way of being. Since then, masters from China, Japan, and now the West have added their own commentary to this dialogue of enlightenment, including the American Zen teacher Bonnie Myotai Treace, Sensei. The old masters are still trying with all their might to communicate their profound experience to us. The question is, with what mind can we hear it?

THE IRON FLUTE, CASE 90

Main Case

There once was a little hut called Fei'tien, meaning "rich field," where a monk lived for thirty years.

(Fugai: Maybe he did not know how to move.)

He had only one tray made of clay.

(Fugai: Expensive things are not always precious.)
One day a monk, who studied under him, broke that tray accidentally.
(Fugai: The real treasure appears from the breaking.)
Each day the teacher asked the student to replace it.
(Fugai: Why do you want another?)
Each time the disciple would bring a new one, and the teacher threw it out saying, "This is not it. Give me back my old one!"
(Fugai: I would open my hands and laugh.)
(Genro: If I were the disciple, I would say, "Wait until the sun rises in the West.")
(Fugai: I will search for it before I am born.)

Genro's Poem

It is broken;
(Fugai: The whole tray remains.)
Run fast after it.
(Fugai: The sword disappears in the water.)
(Genro: The disciple cannot understand it.)
(Fugai: It has returned to him already. Call an iron kettle a bell; call the earth heaven . . . what's wrong?)

This koan is from one of my favorite collections, "The Iron Flute." It was brought together by Master Genro in the late 1700s. He gathered koans from Tang- and Sung-dynasty teachings and commented on them. His successor, Fugai, then added a commentary and poem to illuminate the koan's point. It's a wonderful collection in that you get a line of the koan, and then it's as if there is someone standing offstage whispering conspiratorially to you, "Here's the point of what was just said." Unfortunately, these helpful additions are often as challenging as the original koan. But there is a nice sense—if we sit with these whisperings—of having many people working on our behalf, for our awakening.

"The Iron Flute" collection is so called because it takes up koans that deal with doing the impossible. How do you play an iron flute? The holes are closed. How do we do that which can't, but somehow must, be done? How do we reveal what has never been concealed? "The Iron Flute" koans have an undercurrent of refreshing vitality that often strikes me like cool water does; they are meant to help cut through stagnancy, designed not to let any kind of staleness define our journey. Before we get into this koan, it seems important to reflect briefly on how koan study works.

Because "The Iron Flute" koans are more modern in their presentation than some of the other collections we use, their language is a little easier to grapple with. Rather than asking for an intellectual understanding, koans demand that we experience, realize, and ultimately reveal their spirit. In working with a koan, the student who says, "Well, what this means is that all things are one," is rung out by the teacher's bell. That doesn't reach it; that's an explanation. What is "all things are one," realized? If it's not realized, it's not going to transform your life, it's not going to heal your suffering, or enable you to live at ease, at peace in the midst of life and death.

Some of the koan work of Zen is designed to keep spiritual practice from becoming just another variety of self-deceit. It doesn't take much to talk convincingly about Zen, given the proper research materials or time to think. But koan study is designed to ask, "How does the koan live?" If it doesn't live here and it doesn't live now, the koan is not living.

In order to engage koans as our life rather than as just another system of thought, Zen requires that we work with a teacher. In order to work with a teacher, there needs to be a student. We often skip over this: It's easy to waste time going through the motions of entering the room for a face-to-face teaching, but to not really be a student—to just be someone who wants to debate, or to prove something. Often, a real spiritual meeting is not available even though the bows have been made. Yet once a student develops, it is inevitable that a teacher will appear in their life. They create each other.

•   •   •

To meet the teacher in this koan, the student has to enter the hut where the teacher is teaching. To identify with the student is to be in this hut—we don't know where: a small place called "the rich field." In this confined space—the space that seems to have nothing to offer, the place that traps us—there is richness. To enter the koan is to identify with this environment, not to separate from it. We're asked to consider: Is there more to what confines us than we might immediately assume?

Then we meet a nameless teacher. I particularly like this koan because the teacher is nameless. The monk, too, is not given a name—a dubious honor traditionally reserved for the nuns and traveling laywomen who appear nameless throughout the koan collections. Here the nameless monk has broken the only tray in the hut and is being compelled to realize "What is it that's irreplaceable, unbreakable, and that serves continually?"

The teacher demands, "Bring it to me!" "Show me the tray!" The one who experienced the breaking—in this case the monk—needs to deal with the brokenness. It's your job, the teacher implies; it's nobody else's responsibility. But how can the student produce what doesn't exist?

There once was a little hut called Fei'tien, meaning "rich field," where a monk lived for thirty years. Fugai whispers from the sidelines, *Maybe he did not know how to move.* Is he stuck? Or is he at the center of the universe? It is not clear at this point in the koan, but we need to allow either possibility. Again these comments are delicious, because Fugai is saying, "Don't assume the obvious. Check it out. Maybe the teacher here has nothing to teach." Not knowing how to move could indicate confinement, or it could be the freedom of not knowing, not needing, no other place, no other time: this place and time filling the universe.

He had only one tray made of clay. Fugai says, *Expensive things are not always precious.* Fugai is helping here to point out that the situation of this destitute teacher in his simple hut with its meager supply of serving implements is sufficient; there's more going on than a complaint about the student's clumsiness. The student's situation is in some way the human situation. Whether it is a tray, or a human body, what we have to serve from can seem fragile, and there is only one. What is it that's precious? What is the treasure of the hut?

One day a monk broke that tray accidentally. Fugai says, *The real treasure appears from the breaking.* The body breaks, things change, life ends. Only when impermanence is fully apprehended do we really have the chance to serve, to give without bargaining. So far, the monk had only been able to serve tea in small measured cups; his teacher wants him to realize and overflow with intimacy. But first, the cup and tray—the idea and the body—have to be released.

Each day the teacher asked the student to replace it. Fugai asks, *Why do you want another?* Don't think it is somewhere else, some earlier time. Fugai whispered as loudly as he could, but the monk had that same storm in his brain that we all use to drown out the clear song of the iron flute. Don't look elsewhere for it, we're told; don't hesitate or try to remember. Don't call it by your name, or any other name. Just serve.

Each time the disciple brought a new one, the teacher threw it out, saying, "This is not it. Give me back my old one!" Fugai makes two comments here. First he says, *I would open my hands and laugh.* Then he says, *I will search for it before I am born.* His teacher, Genro, comments, *If I were the disciple, I would say, "Wait until the sun rises in the West."* Remaining after all the commentary is still the matter of this life. The teacher is asking each of us to bring out the tray, to serve not our limitations but what's whole and unbreakable, our true self. It's easy to identify with all the places we've been hurt and abandoned, but can we identify with the timeless wholeness that weathers every abuse, every condition? If we can't, we may spend this life protecting ourselves and never risk really living. That's why this is such an important koan to realize, over and over.

Another koan, "Keichu Makes Carts," can help clarify how this one works. This is a koan from the "Gateless Gate," the first koan collection students encounter in training. The koan says: Master

Gettan asked a monk, "Keichu made a hundred carts. If he took off both wheels and removed the axle, what would be vividly apparent?" Keichu was regarded in ancient Chinese mythology as the inventor, the "Adam," of carts. When Keichu is mentioned, we know we're in the realm of primal being, of the original vehicle, the original construction. Keichu's presence is a cue to pay attention not just to the story, but the state of consciousness involved. This original cart; he made a hundred of them. Take away the pieces, take away the parts, and what is it that's vividly apparent?

The axle and the wheels are meant to represent all the stuff, all the bits. If we say that what's apparent when the parts are removed is nothing, that doesn't really reach it. Nothing is an idea. Show me nothing. The moment you show it, say it, make it, you have turned it into something.

"A pile of mechanical bits: wheels, spokes, axles"—we might say that is what is made apparent. Still, where do you find yourself in the koan? This koan could be rephrased as "God made the original person, made a hundred of them, made ten million of them; take away the eyes, the ears, the noses, the shoulders, the fingers, the feet, the guts, the skin—now what is clearly revealed? What is vividly apparent?" Who are you?

We grow old, go blind, lose our hearing, can no longer have sex. You've been beautiful, and suddenly you get a skin disease. You've been married, now you're a widow. Some way of defining yourself changes radically. Who are you? All the parts and pieces are taken away—all the roles and identities. What's revealed? Aitken Roshi comments on this using the example of the bicycle. He says,

> Zazen is like learning how to ride a bicycle. You have to steer, pump, keep your balance, watch out for pedestrians and other vehicles—all at once. You are riding a pile of parts with your pile of parts. After you learn to ride, however, what then? You are free of those parts, surely. You are one with the bicycle, and the bicycle keeps its own balance. It steers and pumps itself, and you can enjoy your ride and

go anywhere—to the store, to school, to the office, the beach. You have forgotten sprockets and handle bars. You have forgotten that you have forgotten. Likewise, when Keichu made those carts he was lost in cutting and fitting.

Being one, not separating—the bike rides itself, the dance dances itself. But if we abandon cause and effect in this "forgetting," the koan is not complete. When we carry the tray across the room and carelessly drop it, it breaks. If we drive carelessly, we could hurt someone. When one person has ecstatic sex, their partner may still end up bruised and frightened. The limitless body doesn't mean not taking absolute care of this one, and absolute care of that one. So how to proceed?

Aitken Roshi says,

Take it all off! Take off all those parts. Take off all that meat, take away the gristle, the fat, the marrow, the protein, the vitamins, the calcium, the phosphorus, the atoms, the electrons, the neutrons, the protons—what is crystal clear?

We don't want to do that. We don't want to let go of our preoccupation with our body, and we don't want to let go of the comfort of familiar patterns of thought. To get over the seduction of our own thought is not easy. We're either seduced by self-hatred or self-love. "Everything I think and do is inadequate, I'm stupid, I'm too tall, my neck's too long, my eyes are wrong, my hair's too curly or too straight, I don't work as well as I should, I'm not as smart as I should be, I ought to be doing more, I ought to take better care of myself. Let me define for you why I should not have breathing room on this earth." Or we fall into the other pit: "Let me show you this beautiful thought I've had, let me explain to you why you should respect me, why you should hear me, why your life won't be complete unless you know all about me and my stuff and what I've done and accomplished." Most of us are too busy talking to ourselves to even contemplate what might be vivid and apparent should we ever learn to shut up.

The attachment to the body, pro or con, is similar in that most people tend to swing wildly back and forth between body hate and body love. In explaining our misconception of the body as reality, Daido Roshi has often described a cartoon he'd like to produce in which there's this huge cornucopia of abundant food and other "stuff" we like—apples, bananas, cows, cabbages, music, literature. Everything that we're going to take in is contained in this cornucopia. A sperm and egg come together and form a little being. From the moment of inception, the cornucopia begins to spill into the mouth and eyes and sense organs of the being. It grows and begins to walk and then to stride, and the cornucopia keeps flowing. Very shortly after the flowing in begins, the flowing out begins—the creative outflow of the body—all the piss, poop, songs, poems, and so on. The being grows older, becomes bent, gets smaller and smaller. Then, finally, poof—and the being is gone. The question implicit in the animation is, "Who are you?" Are you the cornucopia of goodies? Are you the pile of stuff behind? Where are you? Where do you find yourself?

The koan can be so viscerally discomforting that we'll do whatever we can to avoid confronting it directly. We feed ourselves with guilt, or we look back at our trail and admire it: "Look what I've made!" We look back at our constructions and are either disgusted or delighted.

But when it's all taken apart, who are we?

The tray that is broken comes alive through the continual questioning of the teacher, "Bring me the tray! Reveal it!" The student doesn't just leave the hut and evade the issue, go down-valley and have a drink. He keeps coming back. "Well, how about this wooden tray?" Or "I've glued together some of the clay pieces and constructed this other thing." He keeps addressing the issue, though he's looking in the wrong place. The tray is needed, the wholeness of our life is demanded. What excuse is acceptable? "I'm sorry—my mother dropped me, I chipped. I'm sorry, I can't because I'm too sleepy. I'm sorry, but I'm not smart enough. I don't even understand the question, so please excuse me." The demand is always there; life can't happen without you. Please, present the tray, present your life. The time has come.

There are those who will persist and find the treasure in the hut. In one fascicle of Master Dogen's *Shobogenzo*, called "The Sounds of the Valley Stream," he writes,

> It is pitiful that we are living in a treasure mountain and can't see it. If we develop an enlightenment-seeking mind, everything becomes the practice of enlightenment, even if we are in the midst of various worlds of samsara [cyclic existence], even if we have already wasted much time—it doesn't matter. It is still possible to develop an enlightenment-seeking mind in this lifetime.

This is like that beautiful story of the pirate who came to the Buddha. The pirate in his youth was convinced by a shaman that the way to become powerful was to create a necklace of the knuckles of the people he killed. So the pirate spent his life murdering and assembling this gruesome necklace of body parts in order to be powerful and invulnerable. Then he met the Buddha and, stripped raw of all his delusions, encountered the horror of what he had created, the brokenness of his tray. He said to the Buddha, "It's too late, I have done what you cannot even imagine." The Buddha said, "I see what you've done—the world of suffering is immeasurable, the ocean of suffering is vast, but the moment one turns toward the shore of enlightenment, it is revealed."

No matter how far out on the sea of suffering we've sailed, all that is required is to turn toward awakening. It's never too late, but it takes that turning, and no one can do that for us.

Dogen says, "It is very difficult to find people who wish to study the true Buddhist teaching." Throughout our history, saints and sages are quite rare. If we try to explain the Buddha-seeking mind, people shut their eyes and ears and run away from the truth; they don't have any introspection, they only have resentment.

It's so perpetually tempting to present our objection, our resentment. It takes most of us a very long time to look within, genuinely, vigorously. I remember I went through a period at the monastery when it seemed that all I could feel was resentment. I wasn't at peace. I was calmer in many ways, but I didn't feel at peace. Every dharma talk would get me angry. I could barely stay on my little black mat, and everything seemed pretentious and ridiculous—"Maybe we should all just go have brunch and not pretend that this practice does something." My attitude was black, and I was ready to take apart the training, the teacher, the koans, the patriarchal horror of all major world religions, the fool's game of all spiritual practices. One morning it dawned on me that I was in an intolerable crisis, and that I had better engage it in crisis mode. I had to quit silently complaining and do something to take care of it, or else this was how I was going to live and die. All I could muster was zazen (sitting meditation), and I began to sit like I never had before. Because there was nothing else, because there was an intractability to the loneliness that no one else could touch, because I knew there was really nowhere else to go that would be "better"—zazen, Saturday night until midnight, or all night if that's what it took. It began to turn around, and the practice became my own.

It is difficult to develop a Buddha-seeking mind, but when you do, you should never abandon your initial resolve. "From the first, never seek the Buddhist way to receive others' praise." Approval, affirmation, someone saying you're right, you're on the right track, you're doing the right thing is how we usually learn. The hard point is that none of us will ever really be satisfied with somebody else's standard of practice. We don't have their imperative, their death, their life, but we do have our own. When we trust that, we can't go wrong. Dogen reminds us not to be swayed by criticism either: We know that there are dogs that bark at good people. Don't worry about those barking dogs, and don't resent them either. It is better to say to them, "You beasts, awaken your Buddha-seeking mind!"

In the poem, Genro writes, "It is broken; / Run fast after it." Fugai comments: *The whole tray remains.* To realize this directly is to have eyes like shooting stars, with every action snatching a bolt of lightning. Run fast after it, Genro says. Don't be stopped, resolve it, take care of it. Do whatever it takes to serve, to realize, to be yourself. Fugai says, *The sword disappears in the water:* There is no longer any sense of you and it, you and the koan, you and your practice. Completely immersed in the way; the way becomes you. The resistance gone, the sharp edges move through the body of water as needed. Genro says, *The disciple cannot understand it.* Fugai says, *It has returned to him already.* Still, he goes looking for it, outside himself. Call an iron kettle a bell—there is no substitute. If it doesn't ring through you from the top of your head to the tips of your toes, it's not the bell. Fugai says, *[C]all the earth heaven . . . what's wrong?*

It's possible to conclude with something more positive than "I'm a wounded healer, I'll serve from my brokenness." That's still an idea. We can bury ourselves in shit and call it heaven, but ultimately the situation stinks. It doesn't serve. More than just selling ourselves another story, we can realize, and bring the truth of this koan to life. That unnamed teacher who calls every day, "Bring me the tray!" is still calling. The koan is never over; it is only now, and that makes for an incredibly rich field. Everything we need is in the "small hut" of this moment; and everything depends on whether we come forward with the original tray.

Adoption

Leza Lowitz

Yuto is a healer of hearts; he's Japanese, Jewish, universal. His adoptive mother, the poet Leza Lowitz, tells a beautiful story of how love, if only we let it, bridges all divides.

I am standing on a cliff fifty feet above the Japan Sea, balanced on a precipice between two oceans. I don't know how life has brought me to this place, this beautiful rock on the Izu Peninsula on the island of Honshu. But I'm here, with my husband and dog. We've hiked up twenty miles to stand on this small point of rock on the Dogashima coast, watching the waves crest below and the falcons crest above.

It's my birthday; the dawn of a new year. I sit down on this line of solid land that cuts into the cliff and give thanks to all who held my hand to pull me up the mountain of life. I feel safe, yet I am literally perched on a narrow, dangerous place on a cliff that drops straight down to the ocean. But it's not the literal I am interested in. Deep in my heart, I feel a sense of security and peace that I've never felt before. So I shift my weight to one foot. I lift the other foot up, place it onto my thigh. I look straight ahead and hold my focus. If I look down I will be overcome with fear. I hold my tree pose, breathing deeply. Strength and courage flood my cells. I repeat my mantra: "I am calm, I am poised . . . at the center of life's storms, I stand serene."

It's taken me forty-four years to get here.
I've searched half the world for this feeling.
And I know, of course, that it is fleeting.

I don't have a Zen master, a guru, or even, really, a religion. But neither did Tu Fu, Basho, Miyamoto Musashi, and countless other poets and wanderers who made their way through hills and valleys, over mountains and rivers, to seek solace. They didn't have to sit in a meditation hall and stare at a wall to look inside. They just looked around and paid attention to what was near them. Their teachers *were* the mountains, rivers, rocks, and trees. Their parents were Mother Earth, Father Sky. Then they woke up. Or should I say, were *awakened.* I'm waiting for my epiphany. I've found ten thousand other ways to be a mother, but I'm still waiting for a child.

ELEGY

I have a friend who took his three-year-old boy up to the mountains in the Japanese countryside. The boy ran ahead excitedly, as little boys will do. There was a wooden footbridge. It hung over a steep ravine, a hundred feet deep. The boy ran ahead onto the footbridge. The footbridge was made of planks of old wood. Not many people walked in the mountains anymore. There were gaps in the planks. Big gaps.

The father watched.

Every year on the date the boy died, my friend posts a memorial picture of his son on his blog. The boy playing a drum set. Standing in front of a samurai helmet. Smiling for the camera. Making the peace sign with both hands. No words, no commentary. Only his son's picture and the word "elegy."

To remember. To honor.

Life is not safe. I know that. Nothing is certain. Things we hope for, dream about, come or don't come, and then are gone.

I meet with my friend often. In our own ways we both mourn the children we do not have. Somehow we have been drawn together in this strange world to mirror each other's pain. To give each other comfort and hope. We *will* move on, our mutual presence seems to say. We give each other that.

HEARTLINES

My husband is *chonan*. In Japan, this is a serious business. *Chonan* means the oldest son and heir to the family name and whatever fortune the family has acquired. While we'd been "away" in the paradise of Northern California for ten years, his younger sister had been doing the dad's cooking and laundry. But his sister, now in her thirties, wanted to start her own life—open her own business, move on. We couldn't ask her to take care of the dad forever. It was Shogo's turn—our turn.

I hadn't wanted to go back to Tokyo, the busy life, the pollution, the stress. But I loved my husband, and wanted to be with him. And I knew that a good marriage was based on compromise, even sacrifice. After all, the root of the word sacrifice is *sacred*. In the highest sense, to sacrifice is to do something completely for someone else, with no personal gain. As an independent American woman, that took some getting used to.

And it was time to start a family.

I'd gone about trying to have a child the way I'd gone about everything else in my life: one part perseverance, one part "trusting the process." And I thought, as many do, that "if it's meant to be, it will be." I had a full, fantastic life and no regrets. But after eight years, I did something I'd never done before in quite the same way. I got down on my knees and prayed.

And then my beloved aunt got cancer. Her one regret was that she did not have children. She worked all her life in child protective services, and had wanted to adopt. She urges me forward with a force and conviction that only impending death can render.

I learn of an Australian psychologist who adopted an infant in Japan. She gives me the name of the government agency—Jido Sodan Jo. The application asks questions like: Why do you want a child? What kind of upbringing and education would you give it?

What are the most important values you would share with a child? What about religion? Filling out the application is challenging, but it is an opportunity for Shogo and me to become very clear on what our values are. So we send in our application and wait.

BLOODLINES

Everyone says Japan is a difficult country to adopt from. Not only are there few children up for adoption, but it's the only country in the world where you need to get the extended family's approval for the process.

Bloodlines are seen as all-important; one's ancestors are one's link to the past. The family registry, or *koseki*, goes back generations and lists each birth and marriage, tying family to family. When we got married, I did not take my husband's name, and this caused a commotion at the ward office when the clerk said there was no "official space" to put my own name on the form.

My husband stood his ground. "Well, *make* a space," he said, knowing that was impossible. One thing about bureaucracy is that it most definitely *cannot* make a space. It would have been much easier for him to request or insist that I change my name, but he didn't. He just waited for the bureaucrat to find a way to remedy the situation. I kept my own name and was added to the *koseki*.

Then doubts start to flood my mind. If we succeed in adoption, I'll be bucking the system again.

I know how difficult it is to raise a child, let alone one who is adopted in a country that is not particularly open to adoption. In Japan, most adoptions are kept secret. Some children don't even find out until their parents die.

So we brace ourselves and ask my husband's father for permission. I find out, to my surprise, that his own father was adopted. Samurai on one side, gangster on the other. My husband has them all in his ancestry—geisha, gangster, samurai, rickshaw driver. This assortment of characters pleases me, makes me feel less strange for my difference, more welcome. My father-in-law says yes.

We ask his sister, since she lives with us. She says yes. We breathe a big sigh of relief. But still I worry. All the possible scenarios tumble through my mind: I am a Westerner and the child will not look like me, so everyone will know he or she is adopted. I know of foreign women who don't take their half-Japanese children to school because their children are ashamed and don't want their peers to know they are *hafu*. And because the child is "different," I don't want him or her to be the victim of *ijime*, school bullying. That could lead to *hikikomori*, someone who is afraid to leave the house and spends their childhood at home. Even worse it could lead to *jisatsu*—suicide. I know I am being neurotic, already thinking about the difficulties the child will face in grade school, middle school, junior high, high school, and beyond. I know I am already being a mother.

I share my fears with my husband. We were both beaten up in school.

"We turned out okay," he says. It was why I studied karate and meditation, which ultimately led me to Japan.

"Yeah, but we got our asses kicked a lot!"

"Maybe *we* went through it so our child wouldn't have to," he says.

"That's a nice thought," I shake my head. If only that were how it worked.

We decide that we are already a rainbow family, he with his long hair and stay-at-home job, me with my red streaks and funky yoga studio, not to mention his family's eccentric lineage and our strange pit-bull mutt. In a conservative neighborhood in a conservative country, we already stand out as freaks. Why not embrace it completely?

PERPETUAL YES

The agency calls about a little girl. We say yes. Nothing happens. Months later they call about a boy. We wait. They offer the child to another family. Many young couples are waiting to adopt, and we are low on the list due to our ages.

I have to do something proactive. I am fiercely committed to living my dreams. If I'm not, who else will be? I contact a dozen adoption agencies. Most of them don't write back. The few who respond say they don't work with families who live abroad. We apply in Vietnam. We wait some more.

Finally, I make Shogo call the orphanage. I insist that he tell them to stop calling us every month to ask if we are interested in a different child.

"Tell them to put a perpetual 'yes' on our file, okay? Tell them that whatever child they have available, we are interested."

"Whatever child?"

"Yes. Whatever child."

I want to say all those things like "It isn't fair" and "Why us?" but I already know the answers to those questions, that there are no answers. This is our fate, our journey, our path.

And somehow, miraculously, it works. The little boy they called us about a few months ago is available again. "Yes!" we say, eager to meet the child who is destined to be ours. But when they come to our house to tell us about him, the information is sketchy at best.

"Do you have a picture?" I ask.

No picture.

This astounds me. Japan is the land of the camera—how could they not have a picture?

"Are you interested or not?" they ask. They're not messing around with this child. He's suffered enough.

"We're interested," we say together.

And for the second time in my life, I get down on my knees and pray.

MOTHERING ZEN

We visit Yuto in the orphanage for hours, days, weeks, months. Finally we can bring him home for an overnight. Then, finally, we can bring him home forever, just after his second birthday.

We go to a playground where he can see the bullet trains passing overhead. At the playground, he comes up to the other kids and wants to play with their toys, or play ball, or play with them in general. He likes to hold hands. He wants contact, touch, closeness. Because he grew up in an orphanage where everything was communal, he misses it. He has no concept of personal ownership.

The first time we give him Ai-Ai, the stuffed monkey we'd brought to take with him in the car—he tries to leave it at the orphanage. We have to convince him that he can keep it. He's never had a single thing of his own.

He is the opposite of other kids, who have to learn how to share. He brings his own toys to share, but the other kids don't take much interest in them. I don't want to try to make sense of things like this, or explain everything to him. He'll learn. I want to cut a path in this crazy forest of life with him. Sitting Zen. Walking Zen. Playing Zen. Mothering Zen. It's all practice, and we have a lifetime.

But my aunt doesn't. I want him to meet her before she dies.

So we bring him to San Francisco. He loves his seven-year-old cousin Shaviv, but he cannot pronounce *Sh*, so he calls him Habib. My sister tells me Habib means "friend" in Hebrew.

We see a homeless man with a cat on the street in front of Macy's on Union Square. The cat has been hit by a car and the man needs money for its hospital bills. Everyone rushes by the man and the cat, but Yuto pulls my arm, insists on petting the cat. Then he sits down on the pavement and tries to pick up the cat to hug it. I tell him the cat is hurt and he shouldn't touch it. So he pets it instead. Now people stop to look at the little boy sitting on the sidewalk, blocking their path. Some mothers pull their children away. A photographer stops to take a picture. Others put money in the basket. More children come to sit by his side.

Somehow, he brings together the splintered worlds of strangers. He is a healer of cats and hearts, a small wonder in this world of so many wonders. If I ever felt any doubts, I do not now.

All That Divided Us Will Merge

Though there are many customs for birth in Japan—the mother returning to her parents' house, a celebration of the child's first solid foods—we've missed them all. In California we hold a Jewish baby-naming ceremony for Yuto. Many people from my mother's community gather to welcome him, though we are strangers. Yuto is given the name Benjamin after his maternal grandfather, who came from Lodz, Poland, and Walter Benjamin, the Jewish writer-philosopher and member of the resistance in World War II. There is a ceremony where we throw all our sins into the Napa River. Any time between Rosh Hashanah and Yom Kippur, in the Jewish tradition, it is customary to throw breadcrumbs into a body of water as a symbolic act of repentance. The ritual is called Tashlich, a sending out. We gather at a waterfront to "cast away" the sins of the past and resolve to have a better year in the one to come.

My mother and stepfather, father and stepmother, my sisters and their sons are there. The whole family has gathered to heal and rejoice. It seems to be a holy time all over the world. In India it is the Hindu Ganesh festival, celebrating beginnings and removing obstacles. In the Muslim world, it is Ramadan.

My mother's friends, most of whom I don't know, come up to congratulate us. Some tell me their stories, of how they too were adopted, or how they adopted children, and what a wonderful *mitzvah* it is.

Tossing bread into the water, everything is still. It is a beautiful moment.

The congregation has prepared a blessing for the occasion. It says: *May the one who blessed your ancestors bless you. We hope that you will be a blessing to everyone you know. Humanity is blessed to have you.*

Yuto sits atop his father's shoulders wearing his beaded *yarmulke*, smiling and dancing. Yuto is Jewish and Japanese; he is universal.

I look at Shogo and see he too is crying.

Humanity is blessed to have you.

The adults gather and say the Shabbat prayer:

And then all that has divided us will merge
Then compassion will be wedded to power
And then softness will come to a world that is harsh and unkind
And then both women and men will be gentle
And then both men and women will be strong
And then no person will be subject to another's will
And then all will be rich and free and varied
And then the greed of some will give way to the needs of many
Then all will share equally in the Earth's abundance
And then all will care for the sick and the weak and the old
And then all will nourish the young
And then all will cherish life's creatures
And then all will live in harmony with each other and the
    environment
And then everywhere will be called Eden once again.

My mother ordered a cake for Yuto decorated with Pokemon, though Yuto seems to be the only one there who does not know who Pokemon is. He devours the cake, which says: "Mazel Tov, Yuto. Welcome to the Tribe."

My aunt passes away. I am stricken with grief. She is my beloved, my friend, my mentor, my guide. But I cannot cry forever. Yuto has been given a pogo stick and wants to bounce on the sidewalk. It is dangerous, but he can't be stopped. He seems impervious to pain, though I know he is not. It's just that he learned not to cry at the orphanage, where help might not have come as quickly and plentifully as it would in different circumstances.

Suddenly, he points to the pavement.

"Cho cho! Cho cho!"

A butterfly lay on the ground. A beautiful orange and black monarch.

"*Nette imasu*"—it's sleeping. I use the Japanese euphemism for death.

He leans over its lifeless body. "*Shinda?*" he asks. Is it dead?

I wonder how, and where, he has learned that word.

"Yes," I say, scooping up the butterfly in my hands and bringing it over to the garbage.

But this will not do.

"*Hana! Hana!*" he stomps his feet and motions to a potted daisy bush in front of the house. Understanding, I carry the butterfly over and put it to rest on the bed of flowers. He covers it with a leaf. Then he points up. *Sora*, he says. Sky.

Satisfied, he takes my hand and leads me back to the pogo stick, where he bounces and bounces until dinnertime.

Dead Like Me

Ira Sukrungruang

How is it that the most significant and inescapable fact of life is the one we work hardest to deny? A question worth contemplating. Meditating on death, said the Buddha, is the most helpful thing we can do. To our surprise, it brings love, joy, and virtue into our lives. Maybe, as these thirteen contemplations on death by Ira Sukrungruang show us, the trick is not to take it too seriously. How transformative would that be?

ONE

My dog lies in the shape of a crescent moon, her front and back paws curling toward each other. She dreams, I am sure, of her greatest moment—the day she brought back a decomposing deer leg. She was not over two then, just a pup, and the leg was twice—maybe three times—the length of her spaniel body. What must she have thought when she came upon such a discovery? What joy did it bring her? She emerged from the expanse of Illinois grass that towered over her a champion, hefting the weight of that deer leg in her small mouth, dragging it to us, breathing in short audible bursts through her nose.

I don't remember who took it from her, who was brave enough

to touch the dried and crusted flank. But I do remember how my dog offered the leg as a gift. How she expended so much energy to bring it to us—this dead and rotting leg. How she did not stay in that field, hidden by prairie grass, and feast.

This is what I think about as I watch her sleep, eight years later. There is more white under her chin and her eyes have become cloudier. And in those years she has given us more presents: a dead and frozen downy woodpecker, mice, a vole, a rabbit, unfortunate squirrels.

Her paws twitch.

Her mouth twitches.

She makes tiny squeaks.

In her dreams, she is off—the ageless dog—scampering across endless flat fields after prey that can never escape her boundless energy.

Two

We joke, my wife Katie and I, about my upcoming death.

"Don't you dare die," she says. "We don't have life insurance on you yet."

"I've been feeling pain in my left arm." I grab my chest dramatically. "And my heart hurts."

"If you die, I swear I'll kick your ass."

"I'll try to hold off a little longer, but no guarantees."

"I'm just saying I need that insurance money."

This type of joking is almost a daily routine, and because it is routine, it is, in fact, a real issue, with real fears. Because underneath our banter is the recognition that I will die. Perhaps sooner than most. Because I am over three hundred pounds and in love with starches and deep-fried food. Because I am a diabetic. Because, though I exercise, I eat more than my body can contain. Because my body is finally feeling youth slip away and suddenly my knees/back/ankles/hips hurt. Because now, I pay for my late nights.

Sometimes joking about what we fear most is the only way to confront it.

When we finally get life insurance, Katie says, "Okay, you can die now."

"I'll pencil it in."

"Maybe next year," she says. "I get more money the longer you last."

Three

Lord Buddha: How many times do you think about death?

Monk Number 1: I think about death every day.

Lord Buddha: Too little. How about you?

Monk Number 2: I think about death with every bite of food.

Lord Buddha: Not enough. And you?

Monk Number 3: I think about death with every breath in and every breath out.

Lord Buddha: Perfect.

Four

When it got to be a certain hour of night, my friend and I spoke only of dying. We spoke about loss. We spoke in hushed tones, afraid that if we got louder someone would hear us, two tough boys being open, being vulnerable. Worse yet, we didn't want our talk to be omens.

My friend was layered in muscle. He worked at the lumberyard at night, and spent his afternoons in the gym pumping iron. He took supplements, drank protein shakes, and was a carb-eating machine.

He leaned against my minivan in the garage, and the summer night brought the song of crickets. He said, "Crickets live less than a year."

"Ooh," I said, "Mr. Science."

"Longer if they stay warm."

"Look at you—the Polish fact machine."

He chuckled and stretched his right bicep, as big as my head. "What would you do if you had a year to live?"

I shrugged. "Lots, I guess." The truth: probably the same thing I do now. Sit outside listening to crickets with him. When you're nineteen, what else is better?

"I'd stop working out," he said. "I'd stop doing any sort of exercise."

I made a sound that said, Whatever. My friend was obsessive about the gym. If he wasn't there, he was at work. If he wasn't at work, he was in my garage talking about dying. I couldn't imagine him without dumbbells in his hands. I mean, this was the guy who'd bought an electric contraption to shock his muscles into shape.

"For real," said my friend. He flexed his left arm. "You know how much time I put in to make these?" He flexed his right. He lifted his shirt to show me his abdominals.

"A lot of time," I said. I had the opposite body. Fat and flabby. I slouched on an aluminum chair.

"I work out more than I sleep." My friend yawned. "If I had a year to live, I'd stop doing anything healthy."

"You can stop now," I told him. "Take a few days off."

He smirked, thinking that what I'd said was absurd.

"I can't stop."

"Why?"

"I'm afraid."

"The irony." My friend admitted his time at the gym was to stave off death. He kept his body in prime condition so it could fight off sickness and age. What he didn't know was that longevity and living are two different things. What he didn't know was that dying happens to the healthy too. Dying happens to everyone.

My friend said, "A cricket is loudest right before it dies."

"Did you make that up?"

He smiled. "Trust a Polack."

FIVE

They were uneven, those stitches, like railroad tracks drawn in a clumsy hand, arcing across the curve of her stomach. It doesn't hurt, she said. I don't know they're there at all. I wanted to ride across her wound with my fingers, to understand why she had been gone for so long while I'd waited and watched, closing and opening my eyes, thinking she might appear in her usual spots: sewing by the window, reading a Thai magazine upstairs, sipping coffee under Buddha. I did not know what a hysterectomy was, did not know that it meant losing the parts that give life. I called for her, louder and louder each time, and the neighborhood echoed with my voice. I feared losing her then, and knew I would keep losing her—each minute, each second. I knew this even when she did finally come back and I hid my face in her hair, ashamed of the wet coming from my eyes. I wondered what other things we were going to lose, what other things had already been lost. What will you do? she said, her hand hovering over the stitches. What will you do when I am gone?

Six

I concentrate on breathing. I count my breaths. I prevent anything from entering my mind. Sometimes it works. Sometimes it fails. When it fails, I toss and turn. I sigh loudly. My wife lying beside me tells me to "Settle!" in the same stern voice she uses with our dogs when they howl at a cat. "Sorry," I tell her, and lay board still, my body tight, like one united muscle. I concentrate on her breathing. I count her breaths. But my mind, my damn mind, has gone to the places I do not want it to tread. Fear clenches my body. I shut my eyes. I shake my head. I try to disrupt my thoughts with movement. But my mind imagines a life without. Without my wife. Without my mother. Without all of those I love. I panic. My hands ball up. My toes curl tight. I take shallow breaths. And my heart. It thuds in my chest so loud and fast I think this could be it, the heart attack I have been waiting for.

This. Is. It.

I'm dying.

I'm not.

I play games to chase the fear away. Imagine myself eating my favorite food. Imagine the taste of that food. Imagine the joy of eating that food. Or, picture myself snorkeling some unknown sea. Picture myself among so many colorful fish. Picture myself as one of the colorful fish. Sometimes it works. Sometimes it fails. When it fails, I am frozen and sweating and clutching the covers tight in both hands. Waiting.

SEVEN

I should be ready for this. I'm counting down.

EIGHT

My wife had an addiction to this TV series that appeared on cable, *Dead Like Me*. The show was about reapers, who'd once been part of the living but who now worked in the business of death. Each day, reapers met in a greasy spoon, and the head reaper—played by the charismatic Mandy Patinkin—gave out Post-it Notes with a first initial and last name and also the time and place the reaper had to be in order to claim the soul. *Dead Like Me* took the scythe and black hood away from death, and gave the job to a mix of crazy characters. The series showcased inventive and outrageous ways people die. Example: the main character, George, was killed by a space-station toilet seat plummeting to the Earth. Those were my favorite parts, those eccentric deaths.

Most of the time, however, the series centered on George. She hated her job of taking souls—understandably. And George clung hard to her former life. She followed her younger sister around in her new, unrecognizable body. She kept breaking into her old house and leaving clues to her existence. She couldn't let go. Even in death, she was suffering from her former life, which as a Buddhist scared the hell out of me.

Buddhists believe in leaving no footprint, but a great majority of us do just that. We want to be remembered. We want to remember. I'm always struck by the question, "How do you want people to remember you?" Often this is asked of celebrities, politicians, the rich and famous. And often, the answer is stock: "As a good father." Or, "As a person who gave." Or, "As a person who tried hard." Not once have I heard, "I don't."

But on a minor scale, we ask ourselves this very question every day—not straightforwardly, not directly—but it is implicit in our daily routines, the decisions we make, the people we keep company with. It is in many ways why some of us collect things, why some of us can't throw things away. Who will remember us if we don't leave these clues? Who will speak of us when we are gone? I wonder whether being alive is about being remembered.

George the reaper says: "We lead our lives, and when they end, sometimes we leave a little of ourselves behind. Sometimes we leave money, a painting, sometimes we leave a kind word. And sometimes, we leave an empty space."

Nine

My mother tells me we live this life for our next lives, and I wonder if that's living. Ever since I can remember, she has said over and over again that it is happening. She talks about her death in the present tense. Present tense—at this moment, right now. I remember her saying this when I was seven. She continues to say this. It is happening.

She's right, of course. The moment we are born, we are dying. Our cells are moving and changing by the nanosecond. Young, we don't care. We don't feel it. We don't register time because there are so many things to do, so many things left to accomplish. Too much fun to be had. But at a certain age, time registers. Suddenly the phrases, "Time flew by, didn't it?" or, "I can't believe the year is over" creep into our language. Suddenly we recognize—though many of us don't want to—that we have expiration dates.

My mother knows this. She has known this for a good many years, even though many in her family lived well into their nineties. She wants me to know it, too. She wants me to be aware of it myself.

It is happening.

Ten

"Vampires have it bad," a girl I used to date once told me. "All they do is suffer. They can never experience the ecstasy of mortality. They're denied death."

"Unless you have a wooden stake," I said. "Or some holy water and a good dose of sunshine."

I met her in debate class in my freshman year of college, and we dated for a week because we didn't know what to do with ourselves. Meeting in debate meant we were always on opposite sides of an issue. Abortion: she found it unholy; I was for a woman's right to choose. Capital punishment: she was for death to criminals; I was for life sentences with possibility of parole. In that week of our intimacy, the topic we often circled around was death. She was obsessed by it, knew bizarre death facts.

"A cockroach can live without a head. True story. Then it starves."

"There was a news reporter who killed herself on the air. True story. Boom, gun shot in the head."

"Tennessee Williams died—true story—because he choked on a bottle cap."

After a few days, I couldn't take any more true stories. She wasn't a goth girl. There were plenty of them on campus, wandering like zombies in tight groups, usually English majors. She didn't listen to death metal. She didn't stare off into space or mumble incantations. She appeared to be typical. A blue jeans and sweatshirt kind of girl. Someone you wouldn't mind bringing home to meet Mom and Dad.

Except the death thing.

Her fascination scared me, made me look for death at every turn. When I crossed the street, I made sure no car came because, according to her, four thousand pedestrians a year died in auto-related accidents. When I ate, I chewed carefully, with the knowledge that two thousand people died last year alone because of choking. I smoked less because she liked to describe the lungs of a dead smoker.

It didn't occur to me that her infatuation with death might have been a telltale sign of depression. I was barely eighteen, self-centered, and my first year of college was proving to be rough, and here was this girl in debate who intrigued me with her arguments in class, even though I disagreed with everything she said.

Finally, during lunch at the cafeteria, I said, "Can't we talk about butterflies and bunnies?'

"They die, too, you know?" she said, chewing a chicken tender.

"Please don't talk about this anymore."

"Okay," she said.

"Let's try something else."

But there was nothing else to talk about, and without her talk of death, there was nothing between us at all. We sat in silence, eating our lunches.

When she was done, she rose with her tray and said, "You should try being a vampire."

Eleven

Lord Buddha says, "Do not mourn me." He lies supine under a bodhi tree that is shaped like an umbrella. Monks have gathered around their teacher. The young ones pat away moisture from their eyes. The older ones are resolute. They wait for one last lesson.

Lord Buddha says, "This is a joyous moment." His body begins to glow. There was one other time his body lit up like this: the moment of enlightenment.

Lord Buddha says, "I will be free of this body that housed suffering." He closes his eyes. Ready.

Twelve

Lately, I've had this urge to document everything. Wherever I go, I take a picture. Usually, it is of something that moves me. The light between trees. Pelicans and cormorants on a dock. Sunlight off a pond. Sometimes, I set the timer on my camera and pose dramatically. I think about my poses. I think about my facial expression. My poses are usually silly. I stick my tongue out. I play a role, like a quick-shot cowboy or gangsta. These pictures aren't for me. They're never for me. They're for my wife. My family. My friends. I want them to remember me and the things I love in case I'm not there anymore to tell them why I love these things. When I get home, I rush to the computer. I make sure to organize my photos into folders labeled by the date. This is important. Again, it's not for me.

You can know my days by what pictures I take. You can know my life by what face I make. If something happens, there is evidence that I exist. If something happens . . .

THIRTEEN

In W. S. Merwin's poem "For the Anniversary of My Death," he writes: "Every year without knowing it I have passed the day . . ." I always pause at that line. Its profundity takes my breath away. We wake up each day and fill it with activity. At the end of the day, some of us will sleep and wake again, and some of us will continue sleeping. The poet César Vallejo wrote in his poem "Black Stone Lying on a White Stone" that his death would come on a Thursday: "I will die in Paris—and I don't step aside—perhaps on a Thursday, as today is Thursday, in autumn." Vallejo died, for the record, on a Friday in spring.

These poets and many more who have broached the topic of death have gotten me thinking about the cliché "death follows you." I'm not sure death follows anyone. I think, in fact, we follow death.

Recently, I listened to my sister-in-law, who is in seminary school, speak at her father's memorial service. In the soft cadence of her voice, in her pointed prose, I was struck by the details of his life, his joys, his happiness. He was a man who lived, who loved, and was loved. My sister-in-law's speech on that gusty Illinois afternoon spoke of living regardless of religious affiliation or lack thereof.

Buddha said: "If we keep death in front of us, if we are aware of it, we will live better lives."

Before Buddha closed his eyes, before he gave in to his death, what was it, I wonder, he saw? Was it a bird trilling in the tree? Was it his disciples' orange robes fluttering in wind? Was it the sunlight peeking through branches? I would like to think that before his last breath he saw the shape of contentment, and that contentment guided him into whatever his next life was.

For the time being, for me, not knowing must suffice.

Age-Old Affinity

Misha Becker

*"There is a mysterious kinship between the very young and very old,"
writes Misha Becker, "a kind of recognition: we are standing on the
edge of the world." Here's her touching story of the connection between
someone at the end of life and someone just at the beginning.*

Exiting the elevator, Olivia and I turn right and make our way
down the long, carpeted corridor to Mrs. Everley's room. Air fresh-
ener poorly masks the smell of urine. I wonder if my baby, who rides
peacefully in her stroller, is bothered by the odor. It is a peculiar
smell, one I have come to associate specifically with the dying.

The residents we encounter in this assisted living facility fawn
over Olivia when we pass by. They ask the usual questions: A girl or
a boy? How old? Is she your first? But they ask with a stronger curiosity than younger people do. In the Nigerian language Bole, the
same word is used for both grandmother and granddaughter (*dìya*),
and grandfather and grandson (*dìka*). And in many African cultures
grandparents jokingly refer to their grandchild as their "husband"
or "wife." There is a mysterious kinship between the very young
and very old, a kind of recognition: *we are standing on the edge of
the world.*

We have been visiting Mrs. Everley, who is ninety-four, every
week since Olivia was seven weeks old. Before my daughter was born

I assumed that I'd take a hiatus from my hospice volunteering, just as I'd be taking a leave from work. But then it occurred to me that my maternity leave would be the perfect time to sit with hospice patients, as long as I could bring my baby along. With a whole semester away from my students, my schedule would be free of lecturing, grading, and other work obligations. My baby would be too young to have her own agenda, outside of nursing and napping.

Mrs. Everley has always loved children, but is not interested in having an adult volunteer sit with her. She barely tolerates the nursing assistants and other paid caregivers. She isn't cold or unfriendly, just particular. She complains about the aides who dress and bathe her, help her in and out of her recliner, and bring her meals. But she needs help with more and more tasks, and anxiety creeps in when she is alone. Before Olivia and I started visiting, the only person who seemed to soothe her was her granddaughter, Janice. But with her own family and busy life, Janice needed relief. Janice wondered whether a baby might offer some comfort, or at least a diversion, for her grandmother.

Janice's intuition was spot on. Each week, we are greeted with plumes of adoration, all in Mrs. Everley's pillowy, lilting Virginian accent: "My precious angel! My darlin'! She is the most beautiful baby I've ever seen! Bless his heart." She always says, "Bless his heart," even though she knows Olivia is a girl.

Unlike the other patient we visit, Mrs. Everley knows exactly who we are, even though she's not quite clear on why we show up every week. Mrs. Everley has told everyone about Olivia: her whole family, other residents of the facility. She even confided to the hospice chaplain, "Don't tell anyone, but a woman comes to see me and brings her baby!" She missed us the week we were out of town. Olivia has, in fact, been lifted to something like celebrity status.

When I first met Mrs. Everley she was lucid and chatty. Between gilded praises for Olivia she would stroll through her orchard of memories and pick stories to tell. Happy ones: when she had her six-year-old daughter's hair curled into shiny ringlets for her first professional photograph. Sad ones: when she learned she couldn't have more children, or when her daughter passed away. Stories about the future: she would point to paintings in her apartment, such as the Chinese-style one across the room, and tell me which great-grand-child wanted to have it after she was gone. When she couldn't find a word or lost part of her story she would gently laugh at herself, like my grandmother did before her dementia became severe.

Mrs. Everley reminds me a little of my grandmother, a Southern Christian version of my Californian Jewish grandmother. Three years before Olivia was born I sat beside her as she was dying. Her irregular breathing had slowed, her already unsteady mind tilted further from its erstwhile balance. Over the course of three days I learned to read her unspoken signals. When she pointed to her lips, I kissed them. When she reached for my hand, I let her hold it. When she touched my face, I leaned forward and let her stroke my hair. I watched in wonder as she touched her own face, feeling the ridge of her nose, the curve of her brow, her long-turned-silver hair, her parched lips. The body saying good-bye to itself.

After this experience I sought out a hospice organization I could get involved with as a volunteer. Partly I was inspired to help others traverse this awesome and terrifying path, as I had my grandmother. Partly, though, my motivation was selfish. I wanted to be in the presence of this profound change, a body stepping into the border-lands. Sitting with the dying reminds me to ask unsettling questions: Will I be comfortable in my body when I can't walk or use the bath-room without help? How will I feel when my mind no longer re-members itself? Will I hold on with a vise grip or surrender to the tide of the universe as it pulls me away from this Earth? Sitting with the dying also reminds me, importantly, of the essential sameness between us humans. Someday I too will be like this. Incredibly, so will Olivia.

Details of daily living don't stop mattering to the dying. Mrs. Everley fretted over a stain on her blouse, losing one earring, a hoarseness in her voice. She didn't want us to come on Tuesdays because that was when she had her hair done. Southern hospitality had saturated her bones over the years. One week she insisted on sharing with me some chocolates brought to her by friends from her church; another week she offered me the last of her favorite cookies.

Once when we arrived for our visit, Mrs. Everley was being helped by an aide with her toileting. When I knocked on the apartment door the aide came out and asked who I was. I told her I was a volunteer. I could hear Mrs. Everley asking in the bathroom, "Is it the woman with the baby? Please ask them to wait!" It distressed her that she might miss us. Afterwards she apologized profusely for having kept us waiting.

Early on in our visits Mrs. Everley cradled Olivia in the crook of her arm. "Yes, darlin', there's your momma right there," she reassured her, even though Olivia never cried. "She won't ever leave you. That's right. She won't ever leave you, precious angel." Later, when Mrs. Everley didn't want to hold Olivia, she would just gaze at her sitting on my lap.

During last week's visit Mrs. Everley told me how her husband, who had been a Methodist, converted so that they could worship as a family at the same Baptist church. She asked me if I belonged to a church. I was a bit reluctant to tell her I was a Buddhist, thinking she might not approve or understand what it was. But when I told her that I attended a local Zen Buddhist center, she seemed satisfied. She even commented, "You know, I can tell you are a Buddhist. You look like you would be a Buddhist." I don't know what she meant by that, but it seemed to be a remark of approval. She wanted to make sure Olivia would grow up in a spiritual community.

Since we started visiting Mrs. Everley four months ago, Olivia has been growing in all the myriad ways babies do: smiling, cooing, holding her head up, rolling over, babbling, and now sitting up and grabbing things. And Mrs. Everley has been un-growing in the ways of the dying. In the past few weeks her mind and body have edged further toward frailty. She has more and more trouble coaxing words from the corners of her mind, more confusion about where she is. She no longer understands how to use the phone to call her granddaughter, Janice.

I wonder if today's visit will be our last. Mrs. Everley has left her recliner for a hospital bed, where she lies curled on her side. She moans a little but is otherwise unresponsive when Janice tries to wake her.

Like the labor of childbirth, which can telescope into a days-long affair, the process of dying can stretch on for days or even weeks. Mrs. Everley is "transitioning," as they say in hospice lingo, but we don't know yet if she is actively dying. My own grandmother lived for two more weeks after my visit, without eating or drinking—she did suck on water-dipped sponges. Her spirit took its time unwinding, her body undoing, her mind unknowing. But death can also, unpredictably, happen quickly.

I wait a long while before approaching.

"Mrs. Everley? I brought Olivia to see you."

As if Olivia's name were a magic word, Mrs. Everley's eyes spring open and she lifts her head. "Oh, you came to see me! My darlin', precious angel . . ." she trails off. Olivia is particularly lively, excitedly proclaiming "Da da da da da!" in her cute, singsong voice. She jumps on the bed while I hold her body, my small bundle of energy. Every time Olivia jumps or babbles Mrs. Everley smiles and laughs a little. She drifts in and out of consciousness, in and out of intelligibility. For a while Olivia leans against her fragile hip, grabbing her bony fingers or the loose, mottled skin of her arm. Mrs. Everley doesn't seem to mind at all.

We stay for half an hour like this, me holding Olivia as she jumps on the bed, Mrs. Everley sometimes sleeping, sometimes waking. Finally I sense that Mrs. Everley needs to rest.

"Mrs. Everley, we're going to go now. We really enjoyed our visit."

She quickens. "Oh, please come back again."

"We will. We'll come back and see you again. Good-bye now."

"Good-bye."

I don't question the genuineness of Mrs. Everley's enthusiasm over Olivia, but I confess it surprises me. Her response is so visceral, it's as if Olivia channels a line of adrenaline straight to Mrs. Everley's tired-out heart. Maybe Olivia does have magical powers. Maybe all children do. They who have so recently entered through the doorway of life have the power to forge a profound connection to those about to make their exit. New skin touching old skin, two beings passing one another on the great highway of life. I can conjure a soft-focus image of their private conversation: The elder asks the younger, "What is it like on the other side?" The younger smiles and coos.

Or maybe Mrs. Everley is simply charmed by youth's vivacity and fascinated with its unspent possibilities. For Olivia's part, I doubt she is actually aware of what she sees before her: a long ribbon of life now fraying. She encounters this dying woman with the same emphatic curiosity she does everything else in her rapidly expanding world. In some sense, their affinity is to be expected. They have much in common: few teeth, little hair, incontinence. A close proximity to laughter and to tears. An uncertain degree of awareness of exactly where they are and why they are there. Neither of them will remember these visits. How wonderful that they should know one another.

Why Meditate?

Matthieu Ricard

*It's the first question everyone asks—why meditate?—and rightly so.
It's not naïve to ask why we'd do something so strange, and the deep
philosophy and psychology behind it is not immediately obvious,
particularly when the goal is not something simple like relaxation
or calm, but profound transformation, even enlightenment. Matthieu
Ricard, a French-born Buddhist monk, former scientist, and close
student of some of the great Tibetan teachers of our time, is perfectly
equipped to answer this deceptively simple question.*

Take an honest look at yourself. Where are you in your life? What
have your priorities been up till now and what do you intend to do
with the time you have left?

We are a mixture of light and shadow, of good qualities and defects. Are we really the best we can be? Must we remain as we are
now? If not, what can we do to improve ourselves? These are questions worth asking, particularly if we have come to the conclusion
that change is both desirable and possible.

In our modern world, we are consumed from morning till night
with endless activity. We do not have much time or energy left over
to consider the basic causes of our happiness or suffering. We imagine, more or less consciously, that if we undertake more activities
we will have more intense experiences and therefore our sense of

dissatisfaction will fade away. But the truth is that many of us continue to feel let down and frustrated by our contemporary lifestyle.

The aim of meditation is to transform the mind. It does not have to be associated with any particular religion. Every one of us has a mind and every one of us can work on it.

Is Change Possible?

The real question is not whether change is desirable; it is whether it is possible to change. Some people might think they can't change because their afflictive emotions are so intimately associated with their minds that it is impossible to get rid of them without destroying a part of themselves.

It is true that in general a person's character doesn't change very much over the course of their life. If we could study the same group of people every few years, we would rarely find that the angry people had become patient, that the disturbed people had found inner peace, or that the pretentious people had learned humility.

But as rare as such changes might be, some people do change, which shows that change is possible. The point is that our negative character traits tend to persist if we do nothing at all to change the status quo. No change occurs if we just let our habitual tendencies and automatic patterns of thought perpetuate and even reinforce themselves, thought after thought, day after day, year after year. But those tendencies and patterns can be challenged.

Aggression, greed, jealousy, and the other mental poisons are unquestionably part of us, but are they an intrinsic, inalienable part? Not necessarily. For example, a glass of water might contain cyanide that could kill us on the spot. But the same water could instead be mixed with healing medicine. In either case, H_2O, the chemical formula of the water itself, remains unchanged; in itself, it was never either poisonous or medicinal. The different states of the water are temporary and dependent on changing circumstances. In a similar way, our emotions, moods, and bad character traits are just temporary and circumstantial elements of our nature.

A Fundamental Aspect of Consciousness

This temporary and circumstantial quality becomes clear to us when we realize that the primary quality of consciousness is simply knowing. Like the water in the above example, knowing or awareness is neither good nor bad in itself. If we look behind the turbulent stream of transient thoughts and emotions that pass through our minds day and night, this fundamental aspect of consciousness is always there. Awareness makes it possible for us to perceive phenomena of every kind. Buddhism describes this basic cognitive quality of the mind as luminous because it illuminates both the external world through perceptions and the inner world of sensation, emotion, reasoning, memory, hope, and fear.

Although this cognitive faculty underlies every mental event, it is not itself affected by any of these events. A ray of light may shine on a face disfigured by hatred or on a smiling face; it may shine on a jewel or on a garbage heap; but the light itself is neither mean nor loving, neither dirty nor clean. Understanding that the essential nature of consciousness is neutral shows us that it is possible to change our mental universe. We can transform the content of our thoughts and experiences. The neutral and luminous background of our consciousness provides us with the space we need to observe mental events rather than being at their mercy. We then also have the space we need to create the conditions necessary to transform these mental events.

Wishing Is Not Enough

We have no choice about what we already are, but we can wish to change ourselves. Such an aspiration gives the mind a sense of direction. But just wishing is not enough. We have to find a way of putting that wish into action.

We don't find anything strange about spending years learning to walk, read and write, or acquire professional skills. We spend hours doing physical exercises to get our bodies into shape. Sometimes we expend tremendous physical energy pedaling a stationary bike. To sustain such tasks requires a minimum of interest or enthusiasm. This interest comes from believing that these efforts are going to benefit us in the long run.

Working with the mind follows the same logic. How could it be subject to change without the least effort, just from wishing alone? That makes no more sense than expecting to learn to play a Mozart sonata by just occasionally doodling around on the piano.

We expend a lot of effort to improve the external conditions of our lives, but in the end it is always the mind that creates our experience of the world and translates this experience into either well-being or suffering.

If we transform our way of perceiving things, we transform the quality of our lives. It is this kind of transformation that is brought about by the form of mind training known as meditation.

WHAT IS MEDITATION?

Meditation is a practice that makes it possible to cultivate and develop certain basic positive human qualities in the same way as other forms of training make it possible to play a musical instrument or acquire any other skill.

Among several Asian words that translate as "meditation" in English are *bhavana* from Sanskrit, which means "to cultivate," and its Tibetan equivalent, *gom*, meaning "to become familiar with." Meditation helps us to familiarize ourselves with a clear and accurate way of seeing things and to cultivate wholesome qualities that remain dormant within us unless we make an effort to draw them out.

So let us begin by asking ourselves, "What do I really want out of life? Am I content to just keep improvising from day to day? Am I going to ignore the vague sense of discontent that I always feel deep down when, at the same time, I am longing for well-being and fulfillment?" We have become accustomed to thinking that our shortcomings are inevitable and that we have to put up with the setbacks they have brought us throughout our lives. We take the dysfunctional aspects of ourselves for granted, not realizing that it is possible to break out of the vicious cycle of exhausting behavior patterns.

From a Buddhist point of view, the traditional texts say every being has the potential for enlightenment just as surely as every sesame seed contains oil. Despite this, to use another traditional comparison, we wander about in confusion like a beggar who is simultaneously rich and poor because he does not know he has a treasure buried under the floor of his hut. The goal of the Buddhist path is to come into possession of this overlooked wealth of ours, which can imbue our lives with the most profound meaning.

TRAINING THE MIND

The object of meditation is the mind. For the moment, it is simultaneously confused, agitated, rebellious, and subject to innumerable conditioned and automatic patterns. The goal of meditation is not to shut down the mind or anesthetize it, but to make it free, lucid, and balanced.

According to Buddhism, the mind is not an entity but a dynamic stream of experiences, a succession of moments of consciousness. These experiences are often marked by confusion and suffering, but we can also live them in a spacious state of clarity and inner freedom.

We all well know, as the contemporary Tibetan master Jigme Khyentse Rinpoche reminds us, that "we don't need to train our minds to improve our ability to get upset or jealous. We don't need an anger accelerator or a pride amplifier." By contrast, training the mind is crucial if we want to refine and sharpen our attention; develop emotional balance, inner peace, and wisdom; and cultivate dedication to the welfare of others. We have within ourselves the potential to develop these qualities, but they will not develop by themselves or just because we want them to. They require training. And all training requires perseverance and enthusiasm, as I have already said. We won't learn to ski by practicing one or two minutes a month.

Refining Attention and Mindfulness

Galileo discovered the rings of Saturn after devising a telescope that was sufficiently bright and powerful and setting it up on a stable support. His discovery would not have been possible if his instrument had been inadequate or if he had held it in a trembling hand. Similarly, if we want to observe the subtlest mechanisms of our mental functioning and have an effect on them, we absolutely must refine our powers of looking inward. In order to do that, our attention has to be highly sharpened so that it becomes stable and clear. We will then be able to observe how the mind functions and perceives the world, and we will be able to understand the way thoughts multiply by association. Finally, we will be able to continue to refine the mind's perception until we reach the point where we are able to see the most fundamental state of our consciousness, a perfectly lucid and awakened state that is always present, even in the absence of the ordinary chain of thoughts.

What Meditation Is Not

Sometimes practitioners of meditation are accused of being too focused on themselves, of wallowing in egocentric introspection and failing to be concerned with others. But we cannot regard as selfish a process whose goal is to root out the obsession with self and to cultivate altruism. This would be like blaming an aspiring doctor for spending years studying medicine before beginning to practice.

There are a fair number of clichés in circulation about meditation. Let me point out right away that meditation is not an attempt to create a blank mind by blocking out thoughts—which is impossible anyway. Nor is it engaging the mind in endless cogitation in an attempt to analyze the past or anticipate the future. Neither is it a simple process of relaxation in which inner conflicts are temporarily suspended in a vague, amorphous state of consciousness. There is not much point in resting in a state of inner bewilderment.

There is indeed an element of relaxation in meditation, but it is connected with the relief that comes from letting go of hopes and fears, of attachments and the whims of the ego that never stop feeding our inner conflicts.

MASTERY THAT SETS US FREE

The way we deal with thoughts in meditation is not to block them or feed them indefinitely, but to let them arise and dissolve by themselves in the field of mindfulness. In this way, they do not take over our minds. Beyond that, meditation consists of cultivating a way of being that is not subject to the patterns of habitual thinking. It often begins with analysis and then continues with contemplation and inner transformation. To be free is to be the master of ourselves. It is not a matter of doing whatever comes into our heads but of freeing ourselves from the constraints and afflictions that dominate and obscure our minds. It is a matter of taking our life into our own hands rather than abandoning it to the tendencies created by habit and mental confusion. Instead of letting go of the helm and just allowing the boat to drift wherever the wind blows, freedom means setting a course toward a chosen destination—the destination that we know to be the most desirable for ourselves and others.

THE HEART OF REALITY

Meditation is not, as some people think, a means of escaping reality. On the contrary, its object is to make us see reality as it is, right in the midst of our experience, to unmask the deep causes of our suffering, and to dispel mental confusion. We develop a kind of understanding that comes from a clearer view of reality. To reach this understanding, we meditate, for example, on the interdependence of all phenomena, on their transitory character, and on the nonexistence of the ego perceived as a solid and independent entity.

Meditations on these themes are based on the experience of

generations of meditators who have devoted their lives to observing the automatic, mechanical patterns of thought and the nature of consciousness. They then taught empirical methods for developing mental clarity, alertness, inner freedom, altruistic love, and compassion. However, we cannot merely rely on their words to free ourselves from suffering. We must discover for ourselves the value of the methods these wise people taught and confirm for ourselves the conclusions they reached. This is not purely an intellectual process. Long study of our own experience is needed to rediscover their answers and integrate them into ourselves on a deep level. This process requires determination, enthusiasm, and perseverance. It requires what Shantideva calls "joy in virtuous ways."

Thus we begin by observing and understanding how thoughts multiply by association with each other and create a whole world of emotions, of joy and suffering. Then we penetrate the screen of thoughts and glimpse the fundamental component of consciousness: the primal cognitive faculty from which all thoughts arise.

LIBERATING MONKEY MIND

To accomplish this task, we must begin by calming our turbulent mind. Our mind behaves like a captive monkey who, in his agitation, becomes more and more entangled in his bonds.

Out of the vortex of our thoughts, first emotions arise, and then moods and behaviors, and finally habits and traits of character. What arises spontaneously does not necessarily produce good results, any more than throwing seeds into the wind produces good harvests. So we have to behave like good farmers who prepare their fields before sowing their seeds. For us, this means the most important task is to attain freedom through mastering our mind.

If we consider that the potential benefit of meditation is to give us a new experience of the world each moment of our lives, then it doesn't seem excessive to spend at least twenty minutes a day getting to know our mind better and training it toward this kind of openness. The fruition of meditation could be described as an optimal way of being, or as genuine happiness. This true and lasting happiness is a profound sense of having realized to the utmost the potential we have within us for wisdom and accomplishment. Working toward this kind of fulfillment is an adventure worth embarking on.

The Power of an Open Question

Elizabeth Mattis-Namgyel

The Buddha's great insight—the epiphany he had under the Bodhi Tree—was that things are fine as they are. In fact, they're more than just fine—the true nature of the universe, our own true nature as sentient beings, is joyful, pure, and awakened. It is also completely open, beyond reference points, and full of energy, and because that threatens our narrow sense of self, we struggle to solidify our experience using a variety of strategies that only drain the joy and spontaneity from our lives. Elizabeth Mattis-Namgyel, a Western-born teacher in the Tibetan Vajrayana tradition, offers this insightful catalog of our self-defeating strategies and calls on us to find the courage to live in reality as it is.

Hundreds of years after the Buddha's enlightenment, a great scholar and illustrious follower of the Buddha, Nagarjuna, discovered the Middle Way teachings. And out of his love for them he exclaimed: "I pay homage to he who has abandoned all views."

Nagarjuna was speaking about the Buddha, of course. And the views he refers to cut far deeper than philosophy. For these are the subtle assumptions and beliefs we have about the world: namely, that happiness can be found within the world of things, or conversely, that we must reject the world to find happiness. These assumptions affect the very way we respond to things viscerally, energetically, emotionally, and conceptually.

The Buddha didn't just intellectually question these assumptions; he tried them on for size to see if they would fit. And when he found that they only led to wanting and rejection, excitement and anxiety, he gave up on them and sat in meditation beneath the Bodhi Tree. This is exactly what we have to do.

Meditation practice provides the perfect context for observing our beliefs and recognizing the tug-of-war we have with our own experience. Just sit quietly for five minutes and watch what happens. Unless we have some accomplishment in meditation, we won't know what to do with all the activity. We become overwhelmed by the energetic play of the mind, pummeled by our own thoughts and emotions, bewildered by our inability to sit in peace. We will want to do something. And we really only have two means of escape from all this mayhem: we can either spin out into thought, which is an exaggeration of experience, or we can suppress or deny it.

Exaggeration and denial describe the dilemma we have with mind, and not just in meditation. Exaggeration and denial operate in conjunction with all our fantasies, hopes, and fears. When we exaggerate experience, we see what isn't there. And when we deny it, we don't see what is. Both exaggeration and denial are extraneous to the true nature of things, the nature we experience when we just stay present.

EXAGGERATION

When we sit down to practice, it takes but a moment to spin out into thought—to get lost in fantasy. Suddenly we can't remember the date of our last tetanus shot. We start to go over our schedule. When can we see the nurse? But in the meantime, what if we step on a nail? What if we get lockjaw?

We take these thoughts so seriously. We get all worked up, feeling that it's all so important, and then, suddenly, someone coughs and the sound penetrates our fantasy bubble and it pops . . . Where are we?

Oh, right. We're on a group retreat in a room full of people. Our eyes were open but we didn't see a thing. Our ears were open but we didn't hear or feel the world around us because we basically had checked out. The practice instructions didn't enter our minds, because all the while we were tending to important imaginary matters, driven on by the momentum of our thoughts.

Exaggerations embed themselves in our individual thoughts and emotions as well as our national ones. We have seen how the stability or instability of our national economy, for instance, depends largely upon our individual and collective hopes and fears. Hopes and fears morph into speculations, fantasies, dreams, and nightmares—all of which show up on the path to the "American dream." While they may shape our economy, they certainly don't lead us into a direct relationship with reality.

Exaggeration disengages us from the present to one degree or another, which means we lose our connection to the world around us. In the case of the economy, when the prosperity bubble pops, it forces us back to life's basics: food and rent. We start to ask some basic questions: "How can I simplify my life? How can I adapt to the changes I see around me? Maybe I should start a garden, maybe get some chickens to farm some eggs."

In the case of meditation practice, when our fantasy bubble pops, we return to the basics of our breath, our bodies, our connection to other beings and the world around us, the wisdom of our tradition. All these things bring us back to the present moment. When we start to practice meditation, we may be astounded by how often our mind is off musing and how rarely we are awake to the basic realities of life. But soon the practice quiets our mind, and we begin to understand the difference between staying present and spinning out into fantasy. Meditation practice provides us with a context to question whether or not we even have a choice between relaxing with the rich energy of our experience or distracting ourselves with busyness.

DENIAL

After exaggeration, there is really only one other means of escape from the raw energy of experience: denial. And when we sit down to practice, there is always plenty of denial, suppression, and blocking.

Thoughts come with energy, sensation, and emotion, and that's no problem. But what do we do when the energy, sensations, thoughts, and emotions get uncomfortable? What do we do with all the unwanted experiences we have in meditation? The tension in our neck: what will we do with that? What about all those wild uncontrollable thoughts? What about dullness, negative emotions, fatigue, speed, nuttiness, boredom, and basic unpleasantness?

"Unwanted" refers to the disappointments we experience when our hopes and expectations of how we want things to be don't work out. We have preferences as to how our experience should be: a respite from ordinary life; some time out to be "spiritual"; a pleasant state of mind. But when we sit down to meditate, our mind just seems to rough us up. We don't know how to relate to the dynamic energy of mind, because it seems to come at us like an enemy. But the fact that we reject so much of our experience should indicate to us that we're on the wrong track.

Denial turns our awareness away from our discomfort in search of liberation despite our experience. Does this sound familiar? The Buddha left his forest hermitage because he realized that spiritual development was not possible through denial of the physical world, thoughts, emotions, and perceptions. In other words, he understood that attaining enlightenment was not possible through rejecting or denying the occurrences that make up our life.

The unique beauty and kindness of the Buddha's approach is that it never suggests we need to experience anything other than what we experience. The Buddha never said that some thoughts are bad or wrong and we should reject them. Thoughts and emotions— all manner of occurrences—arise in our lives, and we can't control them. Buddha's first teaching begins with a deep exploration of suffering and its causes. Buddhist contemplation provides us with an opportunity to develop a new relationship to suffering as opposed to our usual approach of denying unwanted experience. In this way, challenging circumstances become gateways for liberation. In this spirit, the Buddhist teachings emphasize the practice of including and deeply penetrating to the nature of all things rather than rejecting experiences.

Once, during a difficult retreat where a lot of turbulent thoughts and emotions kept arising in my practice, my teacher, Dzigar Kongtrül Rinpoche, explained to me that the disturbances I encountered came from a subtle resistance I had toward my experience. Rinpoche reminded me that the attitude of practice was to extend respect and gratitude toward mind and experience. When we respond to anything that arises with judgment or aggression, we experience the pain of it. The next time I sat down to practice I stopped pushing at my experience. It amazed me to see what a difference it made. It was such a small adjustment, yet I felt as if a heavy weight had been lifted. And most importantly, these instructions initiated me into enjoying my mind in practice.

Creative Energy

Exaggeration and denial are the strategies reactive mind uses to avoid the natural creative energy that presents itself to us in each moment of experience. We can learn a lot by observing, in our own bodies, how we work with this energy. For example, say we have a strong rush of aggression, desire, or fear. A mix of thoughts, emotions, and physical sensations surges throughout our body. What do we do with that energy? People often say, "Go ahead, release it. Let it out. If you hold it in, it will just get worse." In one way this is true. This can happen. Yet when we continue to vent our anger, get excited and lose ourselves in the heat of the moment, or start to panic when we're afraid, we deplete our energy, lose our vibrancy, our composure and confidence. We often do things we wish we hadn't. We may suspect that perhaps we could have done things differently: rerouted our energy in a more positive direction . . . although we're not sure how. On the other hand, if we suppress this energy, it gets blocked and we get a tight neck, clenched jaw, stiff back, and shallow breath. We can watch our bodies harden and bend with age. Our way of working with energy shapes our physique, our posture, and the way we carry ourselves as we move through the world. It all has to do with how we respond to this incredible wealth of energy that can potentially flow through us in a natural and ordinary way.

KNOWING THINGS

When we speak about reactive tendencies of exaggeration and denial, we may wonder exactly what it is that we are reacting to. Think about this. How do you perceive things, and why do you respond to them in the way that you do?

We have different ways of knowing things. Most commonly we know "things" through our habitual objectification of them. For example, we often speak about the objectification of women. When we objectify something, we draw a boundary around it and therefore can only know it in a limited way. Who, for instance, is that sultry woman on the billboard—the one in that cool black dress holding a martini? Who is she aside from the one-dimensional image we have of her, an image based upon our fantasies, our desires or insecurities? Undoubtedly, she has a longing for happiness, like all of us. She also feels the pain that comes with that longing, which is touching and beautiful in its way.

Human beings are complex: we have fresh moments and rotten moments. We have creative and destructive moments, too. We are crazy and predictable, glorious and miserable. Sometimes human beings seem like the lowest form of life on earth . . . then suddenly we find someone doing something brilliant, touching, and humane. There is a depth and richness in a human being that we can never capture or pin down. In truth, everything is like this—like shifting sands. Try to find "things" if you can. Try to find them before you objectify them, hem them in with concepts, tamper with them, or embellish them by exaggerating or denying their existence. Do you see what I'm getting at here? No matter how hard we search, in the realms of science, psychology, or otherwise, we will never reach an absolute conclusion in the world of "things." The world that we objectify will never offer us a full experience. A full experience only comes from our ability to know the truth of thinglessness. When we speak about the boundarylessness of things, we are pointing to knowing their truth, or essence. As we saw before: we cannot find a true boundary or edge to any thing, because all things exist in dependence upon other things. When we experience the interdependent and boundaryless nature of things, we don't feel the heaviness of the world against us—the world as opposed to me. Instead we feel the fullness of the world, and we are part of that fullness. When we stop objectifying things, in effect, we have nothing other to react to.

Tolerating Things

In Tibetan, the word *zopa* often translates as "patience," "endurance," or "tolerance." I don't think we have an English equivalent that describes the depth and meaning of this word—at least I haven't found one yet. While *zopa* has many usages, the most provocative I've found is described by the nineteenth-century wandering yogi Patrul Rinpoche, in his text *The Words of My Perfect Teacher*. He describes *zopa* as "the ability to bear the truth of thinglessness or boundarylessness." What does it mean to tolerate thinglessness? Good question.

Normally, "tolerating" something means "putting up with" it. We tolerate things on principle. We tolerate things we cannot change and things we'd rather not confront for fear of the consequences. We tolerate the coffee at the office, our neighbor's dog, that nasty recurring rash on our cheek, and our own and others' idiosyncrasies.

Tolerating the boundarylessness of things—*zopa*—is different. It means that we change our attitude toward the thing itself, whatever that thing may be: a challenging state of mind, the redness of the sunset reflecting on a beautiful mountain, pleasant and unpleasant meditation experiences, our boss. We experience a shift of habit when we stop objectifying, embellishing, or turning away from the fullness of expression. We start to know things in a different way. To bear or tolerate thinglessness means not running away from a bigger experience.

The way we know things depends upon the mind, nothing more. Most of us have moments of deep contentment when we don't feel a need to alter, express, run from, or invest some special meaning in our experience in any way. Deep contentment shows us that, at least momentarily, our habit of cherishing and protecting ourselves from what we call "other" has subsided. In moments like these, we have stopped objectifying things. We can let things be. And when the mind rests at ease in this way, it accommodates everything, like space.

Space, by nature, allows objects to come into being, to function, to expand, to contract, to move around, and to disappear without interference. Space doesn't do—it allows. It never creates objects, and it never destroys them, which is just another way of saying that space doesn't elaborate upon or reject what moves through it. Space relies upon nothing, yet everything relies upon the yielding nature of space. For this reason, the most prolific writer and meditation master of the Nyingma lineage, Kunchyen Longchenpa, talked about space as the universal metaphor for the mind that finds the Middle Way of being.

THE TRUTH OF THINGS

Initially, as we search for the Middle Way, we will need a little boost—a bit of strength and verve to be exact—in order to be able to abide in thinglessness. What will happen? We don't know. And we haven't yet habituated ourselves to the spacious quality of mind. Our long-standing impulse to objectify and run with our experiences is virtually automatic. So we should know, "going in," that a little discomfort may arise. That's what happens when we break any habit, isn't it?

Although tolerating thinglessness seems foreign to us, we actually do it all the time. Think of what happens when we ask a question: curiosity and wonder keep our mind in suspense, and we engage our experience without objectifying it. Our mind stays wide open, alert, and ready for possibility. We may even say we have reached the height of our intelligence when we ask a question.

Koans take the art of questioning into the realm of practice. Koans are questions that emerge from dualistic, conceptual mind. Yet we cannot answer them in the same way in which we asked them. In search of an answer they take us beyond the mind of objectification. We usually associate koans with Zen practice. Perhaps Zen practitioners got the idea of koan practice from the Buddha himself.

My friend Larry studied koans with his Zen teacher, the late Kyudo Nakagawa Roshi, for many years. He once told me that Roshi would often give different students the same koan to study. Sometimes the students would come to Roshi with similar answers. Roshi might dismiss the answer from one student and accept the same answer from another student. The reason for this, as Larry explained it to me, had to do with whether or not the student presented the answer with the confidence of a direct experience. In other words, the purpose of a koan is to transcend the dualism of the question in order to arrive at the Middle Way of being. When the student had arrived in this way, Roshi was satisfied. Otherwise, no matter how clever or correct the answer was, to Roshi it was just another answer.

We may recall that the Buddha grappled with a koan: "How can beings find happiness in the face of old age, sickness, and death?" The Buddha's question assumed an objectified self that yearned for freedom from an objectified notion of suffering. By definition his question was dualistic. Yet his answer, as you may remember, emerged from the realization of boundarylessness. It took him beyond the realm of objectified things and objectified self. It revealed to him a whole new way of knowing things—a way of knowing free from the struggle and limits of ordinary dualistic mind.

We can never reach a conclusion about the Middle Way through objectification. Boundarylessness, by definition, is inconclusive. What we can know, however, is the profound fullness and limitless nature of all things. To know things in this way is the experience of liberation.

The Wisdom of a Broken Heart

Susan Piver

Buddhist practice could be taken as a cool, detached process—observing with clarity and objectivity all that arises in the moment, both inside and outside. That's an essential part of Buddhist meditation, but there must also be heart. As Susan Piver teaches us in this story of a difficult time in her own life, it's not just about observing what happens to you and how you react; you have to make friends with yourself and your life. That's the true secret of Buddhist practice, the wisdom of a broken heart.

A few months after my longtime boyfriend and I had broken up, I was charged with conducting a business meeting at a restaurant over lunch. I was pretty sure I was on the road to recovery from the breakup and had been genuinely looking forward to this opportunity to discuss an exciting new project with the other attendees, colleagues I respected and admired. I made a reservation at a favorite restaurant, which we had been to many times before and was always delicious. Yes, I thought, I'm going to be okay. I have a good job. I work with wonderful folks. Our meeting is going to be fun. I am moving on, damn it.

So I drove to the meeting with a lovely feeling of things returning to normal. The seven of us, as I had requested, were seated at the
only round table in the restaurant large enough to accommodate a
group of that size. We were settling ourselves around the table, wav-
ing hello, pulling out papers, and turning off pagers, when everything completely fell apart for me. *The waiter had brought us a basket
of jalapeño cheddar-cheese cornbread.*

Oh no. *He* loved jalapeño cheddar-cheese cornbread. A mere
glimpse of those crumbly, orangey squares flecked with green blot-
ted out all feelings of normality and, once again, my world turned
upside down. Tears stung the back of my eyeballs and I gruffly
pushed back my chair to try to make it to the ladies' room, but not
quite in time—the tears had already begun to fall. There's no hope,
I thought. Just when I thought I was getting my life back, a piece of
bread caused it to disintegrate once again.

I sat down in one of the stalls and tried to cry without making any
noise, which, as anyone who has attempted this knows, only leads to
a bulbous nose and a Mount Rushmore–sized headache. Somehow I
soldiered on and made it through the meeting, and when I got home
at the end of the day I was too tired to cry anymore, so I just lay on the
couch. For about six hours. When I finally dragged myself to bed, I
thought, I'll never get over this. Why? Why do the waves of grief just
keep coming? What is happening here, and will it ever end?

At this point, I realized that there was very little, maybe nothing,
I could do to predict, modulate, and manage these unpredictable
waves of grief. Trying to fight them would be like trying not to have
nightmares by staying awake all night just in case one might arise. It
was just too exhausting. I had to accept that these episodes were
simply a part of my life for the time being and I was going to have to
learn to deal with them instead. But how?

Soon after this, I was attending a talk by a Tibetan Buddhist
monk at a local meditation center. He was young, not yet thirty, but
already highly respected as a scholar and spiritual adept. After talking about overcoming obstacles such as depression and anxiety, he
was asked about how we can manage our emotions in a world of

ever-increasing danger and uncertainty, how to cope with feelings of paralyzing dread about our safety and the future of the planet. The monk said, "When you are filled with fear, anxiety, or other difficult emotions, the first thing you should always do is make friends with them." Rather than fighting off unpleasant feelings, it is always best to soften, open, and invite them. Fighting wastes valuable time. Allowing them acknowledges the reality of that particular moment and makes it easier to address your circumstances intelligently. For example, if you're walking down a dark street trying to pretend you're not afraid, you might miss the valuable signals fear offers you when you tune in and open to it.

And so it is with a broken heart, or any other problem, really. You may have been taught to attack a problem when you encounter it, either by trying to fix it right away or else eradicating it. I'm not suggesting that this is never a good idea, but there is another option which is not often thought of, which is to extend the hand of friendship to your situation. This is an extraordinary thing to do. Making friends with your broken heart, instead of trying to mend it or banish it, begins by simply making room for it to exist. You could even invite it to sit down with you, since you've probably been hating it or trying to ignore it. When grief and disappointment threaten to overwhelm you, instead of bemoaning them, turning away, or shrinking in fear of them, you could feel them. Instead of trying to shout them down, either by talking yourself out of what you're feeling (It's all his fault, anyway), making up a story about what it all means (I always attract the wrong guys), or collapsing on the couch with a bottle of gin (to deaden the pain), invite in your feelings and get to know them.

For example, when you feel grief, where does it manifest in your body? Does it weigh down your chest, close your throat, or make your shoulders ache? How about disappointment or anger or any of the other feelings that have become your companions? If your emotion had a color, what would it be? If your emotion could speak to you (instead of the other way around), what would it say? When you suddenly feel a pang of emotion, whether positive or negative, can you go back and pinpoint the exact moment it arose? These are useful questions. Just like getting to know a new friend, the first step is simply to find out about her.

This process is really, really hard, so you need to appreciate yourself and what you are going through. So many problems result from the inability to simply be kind to yourself. Please develop some sympathy for yourself, which is different from self-pity or self-indulgence. Imagine if you knew that your best friend or your child or your mom was going through what you are experiencing—wouldn't your heart ache for her? Wouldn't you feel that if only there were something you could do to help, you would do it? Wouldn't you think about her night and day with kindness, hoping for her to find peace?

Ask yourself honestly: have you felt these things about yourself?

If you have, that is wonderful; you are a great friend. If you haven't, you could try to offer kindness to yourself. You know that the ultimate kindness, the best thing you can do for a friend, is simply to be there with her and for her when she's falling apart. Offering advice is not helpful unless you've been asked directly to give it. You know that trying to talk her out of what she's feeling or convince her that it's not a big deal is unkind. Telling her to buck up already is certainly not helpful. What helps more than anything? Simple, unquestioning, ultra-patient companionship. Be by her side. Take her to a movie to get her mind off the situation. Check in with her throughout the day just so she'll know someone is thinking of her. Listen to her patiently, no matter how many times you've heard the story; feel sad with her when she cries and relieved when her spirits begin to rise.

What helps more than anything is to be gentle toward yourself. Gentleness doesn't mean being all "poor baby" or coddling yourself in any way. Real gentleness has way more precision and intelligence than that. Gentleness means simply that you acknowledge and embrace your own experience from moment to moment, without judgment. Without trying to fix it. Without feeling ashamed of it— or, if you do feel ashamed of it, do not feel ashamed of your shame! In this way, gentleness is actually an advanced form of bravery. You aren't afraid to take on your own suffering, even though you don't know how or when it will end; still, you agree to feel it. Somehow, this acceptance begins to calm things down. On its own timetable, gentleness begins to pacify even the most raging emotions. Gentleness is the spiritual warrior's most powerful weapon.

The best way to cultivate gentleness toward yourself, thought by thought and moment by moment, is through the sitting practice of meditation. In fact, meditation, which is sitting with your self, your thoughts, emotions, and yearnings and simply allowing them to be as they are, *is* the practice of gentleness itself. There is no better teacher than this.

Most likely, there will be only a few times in your life when you'll reach the limit of what you can bear. It may be from falling ill, the death of a parent, or even the loss of a most precious possession, such as your home, and of course it can also be because of a broken heart. To face these extraordinary times, you need to take extraordinary measures. Most of the tactics touted as "extraordinary measures," however, are really ways of escaping the reality of what we must face, our emotions. Certainly drinking, drugging, random sex, and sleeping all the time are ways to avoid emotional pain, but even healthier means, such as positive thought, physical exercise, therapy, or simply forcing yourself to move on, are also methods of stepping *away* from what ails you, rather than toward it. And stepping toward it and going into it do not just mean lying around crying all the time. It means meeting your emotions and relating to them, not as enemies to be conquered, but as wounded friends from the front, needing your loving attention. As the Zen teacher and poet John Tarrant says, "Attention is the most basic form of love. Through it we bless and are blessed."

The Child Within

Thich Nhat Hanh

The great Thich Nhat Hanh has so many sides: Zen teacher, poet, political thinker, courageous activist. He is also an extraordinary psychologist, with a deep understanding of the Western psyche and its wounds. His unique presentation of Buddhist psychology for the modern world is what we need to heal.

In each of us, there is a young, suffering child. We have all had times of difficulty as children and many of us have experienced trauma. To protect and defend ourselves against future suffering, we often try to forget those painful times. Every time we're in touch with the experience of suffering, we believe we can't bear it, and we stuff our feelings and memories deep down in our unconscious mind. It may be that we haven't dared to face this child for many decades.

But just because we may have ignored the child doesn't mean she or he isn't there. The wounded child is always there, trying to get our attention. The child says, "I'm here. I'm here. You can't avoid me. You can't run away from me." We want to end our suffering by sending the child to a deep place inside, and staying as far away as possible. But running away doesn't end our suffering; it only prolongs it.

The wounded child asks for care and love, but we do the opposite. We run away because we're afraid of suffering. The block of pain and sorrow in us feels overwhelming. Even if we have time, we don't come home to ourselves. We try to keep ourselves constantly entertained—watching television or movies, socializing, or using alcohol or drugs—because we don't want to experience that suffering all over again.

The wounded child is there and we don't even know she is there. The wounded child in us is a reality, but we can't see her. That inability to see is a kind of ignorance. This child has been severely wounded. She or he really needs us to return. Instead we turn away.

Ignorance is in each cell of our body and our consciousness. It's like a drop of ink diffused in a glass of water. That ignorance stops us from seeing reality; it pushes us to do foolish things that make us suffer even more and wound again the already wounded child in us.

The wounded child is also in each cell of our body. There is no cell of our body that does not have that wounded child in it. We don't have to look far into the past for that child. We only have to look deeply and we can be in touch with him. The suffering of that wounded child is lying inside us right now in the present moment.

But just as the suffering is present in every cell of our body, so are the seeds of awakened understanding and happiness handed down to us from our ancestors. We just have to use them. We have a lamp inside us, the lamp of mindfulness, which we can light anytime. The oil of that lamp is our breathing, our steps, and our peaceful smile. We have to light up that lamp of mindfulness so the light will shine out and the darkness will dissipate and cease. Our practice is to light up the lamp.

When we become aware that we've forgotten the wounded child in ourselves, we feel great compassion for that child and we begin to generate the energy of mindfulness. The practices of mindful walking, mindful sitting, and mindful breathing are our foundation. With our mindful breath and mindful steps, we can produce the energy of mindfulness and return to the awakened wisdom lying in each cell of our body. That energy will embrace us and heal us, and will heal the wounded child in us.

LISTENING

When we speak of listening with compassion, we usually think of listening to someone else. But we must also listen to the wounded child inside us. Sometimes the wounded child in us needs all our attention. That little child might emerge from the depths of your consciousness and ask for your attention. If you are mindful, you will hear his or her voice calling for help. At that moment, instead of paying attention to whatever is in front of you, go back and tenderly embrace the wounded child. You can talk directly to the child with the language of love, saying, "In the past, I left you alone. I went away from you. Now, I am very sorry. I am going to embrace you." You can say, "Darling, I am here for you. I will take good care of you. I know you suffer so much. I have been so busy. I have neglected you, and now I have learned a way to come back to you." If necessary, you have to cry together with that child. Whenever you need to, you can sit and breathe with the child. "Breathing in, I go back to my wounded child; breathing out, I take good care of my wounded child."

You have to talk to your child several times a day. Only then can healing take place. Embracing your child tenderly, you reassure him that you will never let him down again or leave him unattended. The little child has been left alone for so long. That is why you need to begin this practice right away. If you don't do it now, when will you do it?

If you know how to go back to her and listen carefully every day for five or ten minutes, healing will take place. When you climb a beautiful mountain, invite your child within to climb with you. When you contemplate the sunset, invite her to enjoy it with you. If you do that for a few weeks or a few months, the wounded child in you will experience healing.

With practice, we can see that our wounded child is not only us. Our wounded child may represent several generations. Our mother may have suffered throughout her life. Our father may have suffered. Perhaps our parents weren't able to look after the wounded child in themselves. So when we're embracing the wounded child in us, we're embracing all the wounded children of our past generations. This practice is not a practice for ourselves alone, but for numberless generations of ancestors and descendants.

Our ancestors may not have known how to care for their wounded child within, so they transmitted their wounded child to us. Our practice is to end this cycle. If we can heal our wounded child, we will not only liberate ourselves, but we will also help liberate whoever has hurt or abused us. The abuser may also have been the victim of abuse. There are people who have practiced with their inner child for a long time who have had a lessening of their suffering and have experienced transformation. Their relationships with their family and friends have become much easier.

We suffer because we have not been touched by compassion and understanding. If we generate the energy of mindfulness, understanding, and compassion for our wounded child, we will suffer much less. When we generate mindfulness, compassion and understanding become possible, and we can allow people to love us. Before, we may have been suspicious of everything and everyone. Compassion helps us relate to others and restore communication.

The people around us, our family and friends, may also have a severely wounded child inside. If we've managed to help ourselves, we can also help them. When we've healed ourselves, our relationships with others become much easier. There's more peace and more love in us.

Go back and take care of yourself. Your body needs you, your feelings need you, your perceptions need you. The wounded child in you needs you. Your suffering needs you to acknowledge it. Go home and be there for all these things. Practice mindful walking and mindful breathing. Do everything in mindfulness so you can really be there, so you can love.

THE ENERGY OF MINDFULNESS

The energy of mindfulness is the salve that will recognize and heal the child within. But how do we cultivate this energy?

Buddhist psychology divides consciousness into two parts. One part is mind consciousness and the other is store consciousness. Mind consciousness is our active awareness. Western psychology calls it "the conscious mind." To cultivate the energy of mindfulness, we try to engage our active awareness in all our activities and be truly present with whatever we are doing. We want to be mindful as we drink our tea or drive through the city. When we walk, we want to be aware that we are walking. When we breathe, we want to be aware that we are breathing.

Store consciousness, also called root consciousness, is the base of our consciousness. In Western psychology it's called "the unconscious mind." It's where all our past experiences are stored. Store consciousness has the capacity to learn and to process information.

Often our mind is not there with our body. Sometimes we go through our daily activities without mind consciousness being involved at all. We can do many things by means of store consciousness alone, and mind consciousness can be thinking of a thousand other things. For example, when we drive our car through the city, mind consciousness may not be thinking about driving at all, but we can still reach our destination without getting lost or having an accident. That is store consciousness operating on its own.

Consciousness is like a house in which the basement is our store consciousness and the living room is our mind consciousness. Mental formations like anger, sorrow, or joy rest in the store consciousness in the form of seeds (*bija*). We have a seed of anger, despair, discrimination, fear, a seed of mindfulness, compassion, a seed of understanding, and so on. Store consciousness is made of the totality of the seeds, and it is also the soil that preserves and maintains all the seeds. The seeds stay there until we hear, see, read, or think of something that touches a seed and makes us feel the anger, joy, or sorrow. This is a seed coming up and manifesting on the level of mind consciousness, in our living room. Now we no longer call it a seed, but a mental formation.

When someone touches the seed of anger by saying something or doing something that upsets us, that seed of anger will come up and manifest in mind consciousness as the mental formation (*cittasamskara*) of anger. The word "formation" is a Buddhist term for something that's created by many conditions coming together. A marker pen is a formation; my hand, a flower, a table, a house, are all formations. A house is a physical formation. My hand is a physiological formation. My anger is a mental formation. In Buddhist psychology we speak about fifty-one varieties of seeds that can manifest as fifty-one mental formations. Anger is just one of them. In store consciousness, anger is called a seed. In mind consciousness, it's called a mental formation.

Whenever a seed, say the seed of anger, comes up into our living room and manifests as a mental formation, the first thing we can do is to touch the seed of mindfulness and invite it to come up, too. Now we have two mental formations in the living room. This is mindfulness of anger. Mindfulness is always mindfulness of something. When we breathe mindfully, that is mindfulness of breathing. When we walk mindfully, that is mindfulness of walking. When we eat mindfully, that's mindfulness of eating. So in this case, mindfulness is mindfulness of anger. Mindfulness recognizes and embraces anger.

Our practice is based on the insight of nonduality—anger is not an enemy. Both mindfulness and anger are ourselves. Mindfulness is there not to suppress or fight against anger, but to recognize and take care of it—like a big brother helping a younger brother. So the energy of anger is recognized and embraced tenderly by the energy of mindfulness.

Every time we need the energy of mindfulness, we just touch that seed with our mindful breathing, mindful walking, smiling, and then we have the energy ready to do the work of recognizing, embracing, and later on looking deeply and transforming. Whatever we're doing, whether it's cooking, sweeping, washing, walking, being aware of our breathing, we can continue to generate the energy of mindfulness, and the seed of mindfulness in us will become strong. Within the seed of mindfulness is the seed of concentration. With these two energies, we can liberate ourselves from afflictions.

The Mind Needs Good Circulation

We know there are toxins in our body. If our blood doesn't circulate well, these toxins accumulate. In order to remain healthy, our body works to expel the toxins. When the blood circulates well, the kidneys and the liver can do their job to dispel toxins. We can use massage to help the blood circulate better.

Our consciousness, too, may be in a state of bad circulation. We may have a block of suffering, pain, sorrow, or despair in us; it's like a toxin in our consciousness. We call this an internal formation or internal knot. Embracing our pain and sorrow with the energy of mindfulness is the practice of massaging our consciousness. When the blood doesn't circulate well, our organs can't function properly, and we get sick. When our psyche doesn't circulate well, our mind will become sick. Mindfulness stimulates and accelerates circulation throughout blocks of pain.

Occupying the Living Room

Our blocks of pain, sorrow, anger, and despair always want to come up into our mind consciousness, into our living room, because they've grown big and need our attention. They want to emerge, but we don't want these uninvited guests to come up, because they're painful to look at. So we try to block their way. We want them to stay asleep down in the basement. We don't want to face them, so our habit is to fill the living room with other guests. Whenever we have ten or fifteen minutes of free time, we do anything we can to keep our living room occupied. We call a friend. We pick up a book. We turn on the television. We go for a drive. We hope that if the living room is occupied, these unpleasant mental formations will not come up.

But all mental formations need to circulate. If we don't let them come up, it creates bad circulation in our psyche, and symptoms of mental illness and depression begin to manifest in our mind and body.

Sometimes when we have a headache, we take aspirin, but our headache doesn't go away. Sometimes this kind of headache can be a symptom of mental illness. Perhaps we have allergies. We think it's a physical problem, but allergies can also be a symptom of mental illness. We are advised by doctors to take drugs, but sometimes these will continue to suppress our internal formations, making our sickness worse.

Dismantling Barriers

If we can learn not to fear our knots of suffering, we slowly begin to let them circulate up into our living room. We begin to learn how to embrace them and transform them with the energy of mindfulness. When we dismantle the barrier between the basement and the living room, blocks of pain will come up and we will have to suffer a bit. Our inner child may have a lot of fear and anger stored up from being down in the basement for so long. There is no way to avoid it.

That is why the practice of mindfulness is so important. If mindfulness is not there, it is very unpleasant to have these seeds come up. But if we know how to generate the energy of mindfulness, it's very healing to invite them up every day and embrace them. Mindfulness is a strong source of energy that can recognize, embrace, and take care of these negative energies. Perhaps these seeds don't want to come up at first, perhaps there's too much fear and distrust, so we may have to coax them a bit. After being embraced for some time, a strong emotion will return to the basement and become a seed again, weaker than before.

Every time you give your internal formations a bath of mindfulness, the blocks of pain in you become lighter. So give your anger, your despair, your fear, a bath of mindfulness every day. After several days or weeks of bringing them up daily and helping them go back down again, you create good circulation in your psyche.

The Function of Mindfulness

The first function of mindfulness is to recognize and not to fight. We can stop at any time and become aware of the child within us.

When we recognize the wounded child for the first time, all we need to do is be aware of him or her and say hello. That's all. Perhaps this child is sad. If we notice this we can just breathe in and say to ourselves, "Breathing in, I know that sorrow has manifested in me. Hello, my sorrow. Breathing out, I will take good care of you."

Once we have recognized our inner child, the second function of mindfulness is to embrace him or her. This is a very pleasant practice. Instead of fighting our emotions, we are taking good care of ourselves. Mindfulness brings with her an ally—concentration. The first few minutes of recognizing and embracing our inner child with tenderness will bring some relief. The difficult emotions will still be there, but we won't suffer as much anymore.

After recognizing and embracing our inner child, the third function of mindfulness is to soothe and relieve our difficult emotions. Just by holding this child gently, we are soothing our difficult emotions and we can begin to feel at ease. When we embrace our strong emotions with mindfulness and concentration, we'll be able to see the roots of these mental formations. We'll know where our suffering has come from. When we see the roots of things, our suffering will lessen. So mindfulness recognizes, embraces, and relieves.

The energy of mindfulness contains the energy of concentration as well as the energy of insight. Concentration helps us focus on just one thing. With concentration, the energy of looking becomes more powerful and insight is possible. Insight always has the power of liberating us. If mindfulness is there, and we know how to keep mindfulness alive, concentration will be there, too. And if we know how to keep concentration alive, insight will also come. The energy of mindfulness enables us to look deeply and gain the insight we need so that transformation is possible.

Body and Mind Dropped Away

Pat Enkyo O'Hara

It's one of the most famous formulations of the enlightenment experience: body and mind dropped away. It's a good guide no matter what our level of practice, but its ultimate meaning is surely elusive, for it was the awakening experience of Eihei Dogen, founder of the Soto school of Zen and one of Buddhism's most subtle and difficult philosophers. Roshi Pat Enkyo O'Hara explains why, paradoxically, dropping away body and mind is the key to a full and unmediated experience of life.

When I first began Zen practice, I read the root manual of Zen meditation by the Japanese master Dogen. The "Fukanzazengi" starts with enticing phrases about the possibility of "emancipation," and finding our "original self " by stepping back and "turning the light inward." I recall vividly my excitement as I read these opening phrases, anticipating the instructions I so desired in order to discover how to use my mind to change my life. And then, in the next section, as the instructions began, I was surprised, and somewhat deflated, to read the detailed guidance about how to hold the body, to sit, to hold one's hands, feet, mouth, ears, and eyes, as well as what kind of cushion to use, clothes to wear, and so on. All of this physical data, and I was looking for the secret of what to do with my mind!

And of course, that was right where I was stuck, thinking that there was a mind practice that did not involve my body, as if my mind were some kind of balloon that floated over me, rather than being integral to every part of my being. Or alternatively, that my body was some kind of chariot that carried my mind around. Either way, I was certainly stuck.

But not uniquely so. At the first retreat center where I practiced, there was little attention paid to posture, as long as one did not move and distract others. Later, when I studied under the Japanese Zen master Maezumi Roshi for over a year, I was constantly corrected for my slumping, imbalanced posture—or was it for my slumping, imbalanced thinking? I had not yet learned that they were two ends of the same stick. During much of this correction, I thought, "Oh, that's just my body—what's the problem?"

Just the Body

There is an old story about Dogen as a young monk visiting China. On a cold and dark morning, he was sitting in deep meditation and was stunned when his teacher, walking behind him, removed a cloth slipper and slapped the dozing monk sitting next to him, saying, "Meditation is not sleeping! Drop away body and mind!" Young Dogen, at that very moment, experienced a great release. Based on his subsequent teaching, we can guess that he discovered that he was pitched into a state of being where all conceptions of body and mind drop away, and what is left is . . . this moment, in all of its ecstatic, crushing, wondrous liveliness, and its inevitable evaporation.

Some scholars say Dogen misunderstood that phrase, "drop away body and mind," that actually his teacher, speaking in Chinese, said something like wipe away the dust of the mind. But what Dogen heard became his core teaching on meditation and on life itself: "Dropping away body and mind, body and mind, dropped away." This phrase in turn became a key way of describing zazen, Zen meditation.

• • •

Seven hundred and fifty years later, a middle-aged woman walks on the snow in upstate New York during a long meditation retreat. As my boot sinks through the crust, through layers of ice and snow to the muddy earth below, my foot, my leg, my whole being lets go, drops, body and mind, earth and sky, being and nonbeing. As the old poet Han Shan said,

> There is a body—there is not a body;
> This is me—then again it is not.

This dropping of all concept of body and mind is like a distorting lens falling away and what is left is a realization that I am the snow, the ice, the earth and sky, while I have not stopped being myself.

Once a student asked me if Dogen's "dropping away body and mind" meant that we should ignore our bodies, not pay any attention to them, numb them? Is dropping away body and mind an instruction to ignore the presence of "body awareness" or "mind awareness," to numb out? Or isn't it rather a teaching to drop all conceptions of body and mind? Isn't to drop to release, to let go of our grasping after abstractions? What would happen if there were no positing of "this is body" and "this is mind"—then what would be left? Without the conception "body" there is just this soft whooshing of sensation, internal and external, of muscle, of skin, of feelings; there is flow. Why would we want to block it out? It is our life!

And when there is pain, there too is the flow of our life. A serious dharma student, suffering from knee pain during a retreat, once told me that she had mastered the art of blocking all feeling in her hips, knees, and feet during zazen! What she had found was a way for her mind to obliterate the bottom half of her body. This is not dropping, this is blocking. She threw out the bottom half of her being, the bottom half of her true nature, of her potential to wake up. When there is pain, physical or emotional, there is an opportunity to investigate thoroughly our own being and the source of our pain and the nature of it. Blocking the pain creates a black box of pain, unknown and unchangeable. Moving toward the feeling, we realize that it is fluid, that it has time and motion and variability. We no longer have stuck our pain in a vault, but we meet it with attention and aliveness. How is it possible to engage in a meditation practice of "waking up" by means of blocking the reality of the moment? To deny our reality blinds us from the world itself, from all beings and experiences everywhere.

When we try to control and separate our experience, we miss so much. Earnest seekers often stumble over the truth they are scrambling for. A Zen master walking with his student on a spring day said, "Do you smell the olive blossoms?" "Yes, Teacher." The master replied, "You see, I am hiding nothing from you." Imagine the student's response: "Is this a mystical teaching? What does he mean 'he is hiding nothing'? What is it about the olive blossoms? What do they signify?" He offered his student everything. The fragrance of olive blossoms in spring doesn't lead to some special state, any more than meditation, zazen, or study leads to something other than what is always here, if we can but drop away our preconceptions.

This is beautifully evoked by a story about two early Chinese Zen masters, Nanyue and Mazu. One day Master Nanyue saw Mazu in the courtyard sitting earnestly in meditation. He asked Mazu what he was doing and Mazu said he was sitting zazen in order to attain buddhahood—awakening. Nanyue then sat down in front of Mazu and began to rub a tile with a rock. Mazu blinked, looked at Nanyue, and asked the obvious, "Why are you rubbing that tile with a rock?" Nanyue kept rubbing and said, "I'm making a mirror." Mazu said, "How can you make a mirror out of tile and rock?" Nanyue replied, "How can you make a Buddha out of sitting in meditation?" Mazu was taken aback, his entire ordering of things fell away, and he whispered, "Master, what then is right?"

That phrase, "What then is right?" is so endearing, in its innocence and direct openness to a new way to realize reality. What then is right? To help Mazu to see for himself, Nanyue resorted to an old saying, "When there is a cart that won't move, do you hit the ox or hit the cart?" As Dogen has pointed out, the implication of this question itself is marvelous: what do we mean by the cart "not moving"? Is it "not moving" and therefore not part of the flow of impermanence that is an aspect of all creation? Or is it not moving in relation to the ox? Or in relation to some third thing? What would that be?

The richness of this Zen parable lies in its subtle waves of meaning. On one level, Nanyue is showing Mazu that it is not the body that needs to be urged but the mind that must turn. On another level, we could consider what it would be to hit the cart, to urge the body to "move," that is, to manifest the becoming of buddhahood. Wouldn't it be to take the posture, to take the traditional cross-legged, upright, living form of meditation, and thus to become a Buddha in that act? That's hitting the cart. Or is it the ox? Are they two?

As for Mazu, he was speechless. Nanyue, taking pity on Mazu, explained, "Are you sitting meditation in order to become a Buddha or to sit meditation? If you are sitting to practice meditation, you know that it has nothing to do with sitting or lying down; if you sit to become a Buddha, the Buddha has no fixed form. In this transient, nonabiding world, do not discriminate. If you are practicing to become a Buddha, you kill the Buddha; if you are attached to meditation, you have not yet entered the principle."

It was as if Mazu had breathed the air of life for the first time. It is said that for him it was like drinking delicious ghee. He was able to drop off his ideas and split off notions of discipline, of doing-in-order-to, of grasping for perfection or Buddha. At once Mazu received this powerful instruction: it is not the body, it is not the mind; it is you.

What is this "you"? Returning to the meditation manual I mentioned at the beginning, the "Fukanzazengi" tells us to learn to step back and turn the light inward, to illuminate the self. Then body and mind drop off naturally, and original self will manifest. What is left when our ideas of body and mind slip away? Right now, what comes to mind is this July moment in the countryside of New York, and so I write,

The air so damp with heat
even the mosquito rests,
silent humming.

One answer to the question of what is left when body and mind
drop away is the wholeness of life right here. Right now, while reading this, take a moment to just stop, look up, and breathe in and
breathe out, and whatever sounds and smells and worlds are right
now swirling around you is what is left when it all drops.

In another chapter of Dogen's writings, "Zenki," Dogen likens
one's life to riding in a boat; you row, you adjust the rudder and
sails, and it is the boat that gives you the ride; without it, you can't
ride. But, he says, "Your riding makes the boat what it is." Again,
dropping the separation between body and mind, between boat
and sailor, we go directly into the life of the boat. It is the living of
your life in your body and mind that makes you who you are. And
actualizing one's life through living it brings us back to a realization
of our whole being. The Christian mystic Thomas Merton described this experience as no longer being involved in the measure-
ment of one's life "but in the living of it." Merton directs us to
a vital aspect of union of body and mind: the living of life as opposed to the theorizing and narrating of it. What makes this living
of it possible? Merton found it in prayer, and Dogen found it in
zazen. Here Dogen expresses this quality of body and mind gathered together:

In the heart of the night,
the moonlight framing
a small boat drifting,
tossed not by the waves
nor swayed by the breeze.

There is no struggle here. The boat drifts, and is not pulled this
way and that by the waves and the wind. It is the natural flow of
meditation; when the struggle is dropped, the mind is not telling the

body to perform in any way, nor is the mind struggling against itself to be any way.

This is what is called *jijuyu samadhi*, the samadhi, or union, of the self receiving and enjoying itself. Imagine the ease of one's whole being giving and receiving to itself, fulfilling itself through its completion. This expression of body and mind meditation renounces all ideas of forcing ourselves to perform a practice and instead offers an image of the ease and natural spontaneity with which a child raises her arm, or a man leans against a tree.

Of course, it doesn't always feel that way, particularly at the outset of meditation practice. But even then, after an hour of what seems like being pushed this way and that by body and mind, there is often an odd and surprisingly pleasant, joyful, and energetic feeling that arises. It is likely that in several tiny time spaces between effort and distraction there were moments of dropping away. The effort and distraction were never necessary, only the willingness to practice as it is. And through time, with practice, these moments grow, and a kind of self-enjoyment of mind and body emerges, and we "drop in" to our natural state. Zazen has been compared to the naturalness of a fish in water. The wavelike motion of a fish as it swims this way and that is like a mind and body that is not controlled, numbed, nor unconscious and automatic. It is playing freely, like a fish or a bird, clouds and water.

Having reached this quality of flow of body and mind, it is easy to become attached to the bliss, and to limit oneself to the pure enjoyment of body and mind at play. This is the "high" quality of samadhi, when our body and mind take on the color of the sky, the green of the trees. Yet there is a far deeper and richer possibility. The realization of body and mind dropped away is only the beginning. When we reach this place that is no-place, again and again, we launch ourselves into life itself. Or, as another Zen saying has it, when we reach the top of a hundred-foot pole, where do we go? We step out, and manifest our body in the ten directions. We let go. Completely, utterly, releasing our grip on even the bliss. And in that release, we find a wilder, open freedom, and responsibility. We meet our relationship with the world. We find we are the world and that there is plenty to do. From the high top of a pole we let go and see where we are, literally, right now.

Sitting on the subway, rickety-rackety sounds, the vibration in my butt, legs, feet. People sleeping, looking up, looking down, looking at me now, and zazen is not sitting or lying down, it is being alive and awake, inside and outside, here and now. Inside: the muscle of compassion, the muscle of steadiness, patience, kindness—it rests, calming fear and anger as they rise and fall. Outside: seeing that no matter what, hidden or revealed, there is kindness and love in each one of these fellow passengers.

When we first sit down to practice with our own body and mind, we might think that they are two. And we practice for a while and we recognize that body is mind and mind is body. And we start by thinking that we and the world are two. And we practice a while longer, and we realize that we and the world are one. And we practice a little longer, and we realize that we must act in the world, and that it is not a matter of one or two. It is just realizing our nature moment to moment, olive blossoms, mosquitoes, standing by a tree, a urine-stained alley. This is jumping off the pole.

Jumping off the pole offers us the possibility to practice for all beings. And while that might sound overly pious, it is in fact true. And somehow I don't think it matters whether we know it or not at the beginning of our spiritual path. Maybe we think we are doing it for our own well-being, our own salvation, our own happiness. How different is that from Mazu's doing it in order to attain buddha-hood? We may be mistaken as we enter the path, but as we move along, like Mazu, we are likely to encounter the real thing.

In an early Mahayana sutra, the *Vimalakirti*, there is a wonderful scene in which the accomplished meditator Shariputra tells of what he learned about meditation from the great and worldly lay teacher Vimalakirti. Shariputra is portrayed as austere and somewhat severe in his expression of meditation. We can imagine him sitting completely sealed in his concentration. One day Shariputra was sitting under a tree and Vimalakirti came by and corrected him, saying true meditation is to appear in the activities of the ordinary people, not abandoning your samadhi and "yet showing yourself in the ceremonies of daily life." What ceremonies of daily life? Those of the marketplace, the commons, the home. In Vimalakirti's case, it was going to bars and brothels and talking with people. For many of us today, it is the ceremony of recycling the earth's resources, talking with an angry neighbor, mindful business practice, or as simple a ceremony as dipping your credit card with the samadhi of dropping away separation.

What is the ultimate most deep and profound realization? It is that we are not separate from markets and bars and subways and pollution and our responsibilities as integral beings in the world. Vimalakirti is urging this holy man to see that we must let go of every shred of self-clinging, to drop off all notions of a separate self, all ideas of reality, of body or mind, let it all drop away. And what is left is the ceremony of daily life.

Consider how we approach these ceremonies of our daily life. The great Duke Ellington gave a wise teaching when he said, "It don't mean a thing if it ain't got that swing." It's true of music, of our meditation practice, of our lives. What is that swing? Isn't it the vitality, the presence, the spontaneity, the free improvisation of play? What meaning, what importance does our life have if it is missing "that swing"? When we encounter reality freshly, with full attention and nonseparation, we will naturally place the beat in the unexpected, yet perfect groove. We ourselves are in that groove and that is how we are able to swing. When we move out of the beat, out of the rhythm, we contract and get stuck again. And that stuck place hinders our ability to serve ourselves and others. Separating our understanding of body and mind, self and other, practice and fruition, we lose the beat and forget that we are all of these dualities. And when we let them drop away we become, as the Zen saying goes, like a dragon in water, a tiger in the mountains.

The Burning Present

Rick Bass

*What are now seen as cutting-edge principles of environmentalism
have been core truths of Buddhism for twenty-five hundred years—
impermanence, the inescapability of cause and effect, the interdependence
of all things, both animate and inanimate. When you add to that Buddhist
compassion for all beings, including those of the future, then it's not
surprising that Buddhists have been committed to and influential in the
environmental movement. Here is Rick Bass, one of America's leading
nature writers and now a columnist for the Buddhist magazine* Tricycle,
on the lessons of the Gulf oil spill.

The Gulf was dying already. For thousands of years, the Mississippi
River, before being dammed and channelized, carried the tops of
old ghost mountains down its winding corridor, emptying the continent's heartland into the delta of south Louisiana. The river built
the incredibly rich land there like a gardener dreaming a new garden, bringing in billions of metric tons of sediment from upstream
and spilling it enthusiastically into the marshes of the vast delta,
which was sinking at a rate miraculously and perfectly in balance
with that replenishment of sediment—as if the marsh itself were a
set of lungs, inhaling but then exhaling: living. The shimmering
grains of clay and organic matter nurtured the shrimp and oysters
just offshore, and made it possible for me as a young person in this

world—this made world, not past or future—to go out onto a pier on the Gulf at night and shine a flashlight into the bay and watch schools of glowing shrimp, like underwater fire, made phosphorescent by my light and by the stir of their own movements, their physical presence in the world, and the excitability of their internal bioluminescence. On a quiet night you could hear them clicking, squealing. *Live in the here and now*, we try to tell ourselves with every breath, but sometimes our love for the world—like our despair—wells up so strong within us that it is like its own burning that makes us feel more present in the world.

So not only is the Gulf despoiled with the poison of our need, being covered with oil, but it is sinking, too. Death is one thing, but extinction is quite another, and worst of all is extinction of habitat, so that not even the dream of resurrection can remain: for without the physical vessel to make visible and better understood the beautiful spirit, isn't it all just smoke, ether, and dreams?

In order to love this world most fully, I need to know the specificities of things. I don't always need to understand them—I like that there remains room in me for mystery and awe—but I do need to see, touch, taste, hear, smell the world's wonders. Maybe it is a kind of spiritual set of training wheels, but if so, I hope I never lose them.

And yet we are losing them.

We wanted oil—oil is attached to every last one of us—and we got it. Such an old, weary lesson, *Be careful what you ask for.*

There is another, hidden story, even larger than the Gulf. We are a visual species; the plumes of crude jetting into the sea weigh heavy on our souls. But just across the U.S. border, up in the tar sands of Alberta, there is another equally horrific image. A gaping pit, an abyss on its way to becoming the size of Florida, exists where Imperial Oil—the largest company in the world—is using the wild Athabasca River to pressure-wash underground sand formations that they gouge up like honeycombs, using huge amounts of energy and clean fresh water to steam the oil from those sands. Native people in the area are dying from drastically abnormal incidences of rare cancers, and Imperial Oil is seeking to transport more giant mining equipment—on trucks over two hundred feet long and three stories high—up the Snake River to Lewiston, Idaho, along the same route where the Nez Perce tribe rescued Lewis and Clark and directed them to the Pacific, shortly before the U.S. betrayed the Nez Perce and chased them toward Canada before killing them.

The Snake River is clotted with aging dams that are leading to the extinction of wild salmon. Imperial's barging of behemoth earth-digging equipment up the Snake will require the expensive reclamation (by taxpayers) of the dams, rather than removing them so the salmon can run wild and free again instead of being caged at sea in bacteria-laden coops, their pulpy flesh rotting from sores.

Once off-loaded from the barges, the giant trucks will creep down the highway at five miles per hour, prowling along Montana's majestic Rocky Mountain Front, where grizzly bears and elk come down out of the mountains and out onto the plains that were once their home.

Sometimes you can see a disaster coming before it happens. The state of Montana envisions this route as becoming a major petro chemical corridor, despite the wishes of the native people on the reservations along this route. As a country we showed we could reverse our support for apartheid in South Africa. But it was easy to give up diamonds; it's not so easy to try to give up subsidized toxic oil. We can labor to save the panda and the rhino but find it harder to commit to salmon and grizzlies. We can protest human rights abuses in China, but the lines get blurrier when the abuses are on our own continent, linked to the flow of our oil.

This business of our physical lives is so complicated. Fight for salmon and grizzlies, but detach from the outcome? Witness the poisoning of the Gulf of Mexico, and of the wetlands, but detach from the extinction of an entire ecosystem?

I'm not there yet. I don't think I can ever get there, and I'm not sure I even want to. What is it in me that holds so tightly to this burning—that refuses to let go of even despair? This puff of life, puff of breath, that we so briefly hold? This dab of soiled clay that is ourselves, made animate for a while.

The Call of the Abyss

Wendy Johnson

*Humility is a watchword of both Buddhism and the environment
movement, for it is the hubris of ego, which declares that we humans
stand alone, serving our own needs without consequence, that causes both
spiritual and ecological suffering. Gardening writer Wendy Johnson gazes
into the geological abyss of the Gulf and asks us to respect nature's depth,
power, and mystery.*

Now in mid-June the 2010 summer harvest begins to ripen in a
flood tide of Dragon Tongue beans, golden beets, and sweet basil,
while three thousand miles to the east on the Gulf of Mexico the
Deepwater Horizon oil spill continues to worsen. Long before
morning meditation I listen to the dawn chorus of summer song-
birds, a brogue tribute to the solstice season. I am thinking of my
sister Sally, who lives on Knight Island, a bridgeless barrier reef in
southwestern Florida. She and a dedicated cadre of women friends
have been walking their beach at daybreak for the past weeks, mark-
ing and protecting scores of loggerhead sea turtle nests as the ancient ones emerge from the Gulf to lay their eggs. A few hundred
miles to the west of Knight Island, in Fort Jackson, Louisiana, vet-
erinarians and volunteers work around the clock cleaning and tending oil-drenched brown pelicans, northern gannets, and laughing
gulls rescued from the epicenter of the oil spill disaster.

I live and garden on the edge of the Pacific Ocean at Muir Beach, where flocks of healthy brown pelicans skim the dark briny water. Watching them, I remember the first Earth Day observance, held on April 22, 1970, almost forty years to the day from the Deepwater Horizon explosion. That Earth Day was a response to the massive oil spill in the Pacific Ocean, just off the coast of Santa Barbara, California, in 1969. Now close to sixty thousand barrels a day are spewing into the deep currents of the semi-enclosed Gulf of Mexico, smothering undersea life with toxic plumes radiating out more than fifty miles from the shattered wellhead.

As a meditator and a gardener, I experience this plume of oil as a visible trace of the compressed plant wealth of the ages. During the Carboniferous period 400 million years ago sunlight fueled the growth of terrestrial and marine vegetation, reducing atmospheric carbon dioxide while retaining carbon stored in dense mats of decomposing plant material hundreds or even thousands of feet deep. Since the discovery in 1859 of this stored ancient sunlight in the form of "black gold," human beings have extracted more than 750 billion barrels of oil from the depths of the earth, fueling an explosion of population and consumption.

"When this is, that is," taught the Buddha, and "from this arising, that arises." These days the Buddha's original teachings of dependent co-arising are particularly potent. I experience my own complicity with and connection to the Gulf oil spill on a daily basis, either as I drive my car twenty-six miles to work or harvest Zen spinach into a carefully reused plastic bag. It is not the arising of conditioned existence that speaks to me now but the wordless call of the *descent* that beckons, down to the depths of the unknown.

The undersea realm of impenetrable darkness, icy temperatures, and the crushing pressure of dense saltwater is called the abyss, from the Greek *abussos*, "without bottom." The site of the Deepwater Horizon rupture is almost a mile down in this oceanic abyss, where the weight of the seawater exerts pressure of more than one ton per square inch. Here, at the exploded wellhead, BP drill lines bore another three and a half miles into the core of the earth.

At this depth unfathomable questions of cause and effect rise unanswered to the surface of the sea.

At a depth of more than twelve thousand feet below the surface the underwater abyss has long been considered lifeless terrain. Yet with the aid of modern science a wealth of alien creatures living in the abyss have been revealed. From the angler fish bearing millions of bioluminescent bacteria to vampire squid dating back 200 million years, whose primitive blood pigment extracts traces of oxygen from thick seawater, to the eerie tubeworms living on the Gulf floor that subsist on food chains sustained by oil and gas seeps, the depths of the abysmal waters hold the largest uncharted reservoir of life on earth. Billions of organisms inhabit this dark and silent world.

Responding to the call of the abyss demands dedication to the descent and to living in the presence of mysteries and problems that can be neither solved nor uncoded. I can sit still at the edge of the Pacific Ocean with an upwelling of sadness and gratitude for my sister on the Gulf of Mexico as long as I remember that there is only one ocean and that all vast bodies of water are connected. In this practice it helps to remember the primal power of the abyss. Twice a day in Nova Scotia, Canada, the Atlantic Ocean pours 14 billion tons of tidal seawater through the Bay of Fundy, a volume of water equivalent to the combined flow of every river on earth. For the last twenty-five years, during the ebb tide of peak oil, a modest provincial power plant on this bay has been generating electricity from the surge of the depths up to the floating surface of the *saha* world. Considering this, I am reminded of an old admonition from the philosopher Nietzsche: "If you gaze long enough into an abyss, the abyss gazes into you."

Having the Lake
to Ourselves

Lin Jensen

In the end, even the biggest and most complex problems still come down to what's in our hearts. Our hard-bitten culture may mock simple virtues like sharing, but they can transform our lives together. Lin Jensen tells a sweet story of sharing a dinner, a lake, a world.

Sympathy is a consequence of inclusion, the affectionate result of an expanded identity that occurs when "self" and "other" are recognized as simply "self." The presence of this newly inclusive sympathetic connection relaxes boundaries and discloses a frame of mind that lets more in. I can best explain this by example.

For several summers, my daughter Krista and I backpacked into the most remote areas of the Sierra Nevada range where we could be alone. We'd leave the trails and, traveling by compass, climb into some high glacial cirque where the topographical map indicated the presence of a lake. And if we found no one else there, we were pleased to have the lake to ourselves. We felt a little proprietary and even exclusive in a way, fishing the lake with no one but the two of us rippling the still waters, hearing only the sounds of our own voices, owning the whole view of the lake without a single intrusion of someone's red, blue, or yellow tent anywhere to be seen with the exception of our own.

We liked the sense we had of entering an unoccupied wilderness and seeing it as if we were the first ever to come that way. Yet we never quite felt relaxed in our solitude until night had fallen because other campers could show up at any time and spoil our good fortune. We'd set conditions that couldn't be enjoyed even when met. A worrisome little distress invariably accompanied having the place to ourselves. And, in addition, it sometimes felt quite selfish to wish for ourselves what we hoped to exclude for others.

This came to a head on a late afternoon at a lake in the Kern River watershed. Krista and I had climbed to 11,000 feet that day and found there a perfect setting. The lake lay still as a mirror reflecting the granite peaks that encircled the basin. The shoreline was dotted with miniature firs and there, in the high altitude spring of late July, the basin grasses were freshly green. The skies were clear with a bright, slanting sun, and night promised a full moon. We were setting up our tent and laying out the supper things, when I saw the two of them with their packs, laboring their way up the outlet stream toward the lake. I felt just that first twinge of mixed disappointment and shame, but this time I was moved to do something I'd never thought to do before. They were a couple, husband and wife I supposed, and having seen our campsite, they veered away from us, straining under the weight of their packs to reach a stretch of shoreline distant from our own. Perhaps they thought to respect our privacy—or theirs. But I intercepted them on their way. "My daughter and I were just getting supper started," I told them. "We've caught fish and have buttered potatoes to go with it. Why don't you join us?"

They did. And when they were included, the distinction between "we" and "they" readily dissolved. These "intruders" on our solitude turned out to be such good companions that I drifted into an easy and natural sympathy with them. We ate together like one family and watched the full moon rise over the basin. Our evening together brought home to me how the pronouns we humans choose to use are indicative of how we identify relationships, and before the four of us crawled into our sleeping bags that night, we'd commented (without apparent perception of irony!) on how fortunate it was that "we" had the lake all to ourselves.

It's imperative that we learn to share the earth. The reluctance to share what we have with "outsiders" is an attitude that worsens the ecological crisis we find ourselves in now. It often manifests as an anxious concern regarding available resources, a worry that breeds competition between us and erodes sympathetic concern for the needs of others. But it also erodes sympathetic concern for earth itself and distracts us from recognizing the cooperative nature of the ecosystem, a cooperation that sustains all earthly life. It's an irony, of the behavior of those who hoard and covet, that it's inherent in the very nature of things that we best help ourselves by helping others.

I don't think most people intend to deprive others of their rightful place and share in the world; it's just that in wanting the lake to ourselves, we forget that there are only so many lakes to go around.

Toward a True Kinship of Faiths

The Dalai Lama

At a time when so much global conflict is driven by religion, it is more important than ever for people of different traditions to learn to coexist harmoniously. A world of many faiths poses challenges for religious practitioners, who must balance acceptance of other faiths with deep commitment to their own. His Holiness the Dalai Lama offers us this manifesto of tolerance, in which religious diversity and personal belief are reconciled.

THE CHALLENGE OF "OTHER" RELIGIONS

For many religious people, accepting the legitimacy of other faith traditions poses a serious challenge. To accept that other religions are legitimate may seem to compromise the integrity of one's own faith, since it entails the admission of different but efficacious spiritual paths. A devout Buddhist might feel that acceptance of other spiritual paths as valid suggests the existence of ways other than those of the Buddha toward the attainment of enlightenment. A Muslim might feel that acceptance of other traditions as legitimate would require relinquishing the belief that God's revelation to the

Prophet, as recorded in the Qur'an, represents the final revelation of the highest truth. In the same vein, a Christian might feel that accepting the legitimacy of other religions would entail compromising the key belief that it is only through Jesus Christ that the way to God is found. So the encounter with an entirely different faith, which one can neither avoid nor explain away, poses a serious challenge to deep assumptions.

This raises these critical questions:

- Can a single-pointed commitment to one's own faith coexist with acceptance of other religions as legitimate?

- Is religious pluralism impossible from the perspective of a devout person who is strongly and deeply committed to his or her own faith tradition?

Yet without the emergence of a genuine spirit of religious pluralism, there is no hope for the development of harmony based on true interreligious understanding.

Historically, religions have gone to great lengths, even waging wars, to impose their version of what they deem to be the one true way. Even within their own fold, religions have harshly penalized those heterodox or heretical voices that the tradition took as undermining the integrity of the inviolable truths that the specific faith represents. The entire ethos of missionary activity—that is, the focus on bringing about active conversion of people from other faiths or no faiths—is grounded in the ideal of bringing the "one true way" to those whose eyes remain unopened. In a sense, one might even say that there is an altruistic motive underlying this drive to convert others to one's own faith.

Given this history and, more important, given the perception of conflict that many religious people feel between maintaining the integrity of their own faith and the acceptance of pluralism, is the emergence of genuine interreligious harmony based on mutual understanding possible at all? Scholars of religion speak of three different ways in which a follower of a particular faith tradition may relate to the existence of other faith traditions. One is a straightforward exclusivism, a position that one's own religion is the only true religion and that rejects, as it were by default, the legitimacy of other faith traditions. This is the standpoint adopted most often by the adherents of the religious traditions. Another position is inclusivism, whereby one accords a kind of partial validity to other faith traditions but maintains that their teachings are somehow contained within one's own faith tradition—a position historically characterized by some Christian responses to Judaism and Islam's relation to both Judaism and Christianity. Though more tolerant than the first position, this second standpoint ultimately suggests the redundancy of other faith traditions. Finally, there is pluralism, which accords validity to all faith traditions.

True Acceptance of the "Other's" Reality

It is understandable, given the seemingly irreconcilable conflict between commitment to one's own faith and a true embracing of religious pluralism, that many people feel that genuine interreligious understanding and harmony require the acceptance of some kind of ultimate unity of all religions. Citing the metaphor of multiple rivers all converging into the great ocean, some suggest that the world's faith traditions, with their distinct doctrinal beliefs and practices, all ultimately lead to the same place. For instance, that place may be union with the Godhead, regardless of however differently this Godhead may be referred to—Jehovah, God, Ishvara, Allah, and so on.

My own view is different. The possibility of genuine interreligious understanding and harmony should not be, and need not be, contingent upon proving the ultimate oneness of all religions. The problem with such an approach is that it demands a precondition that remains impossible for the majority of adherents of the world's great religions. In fact recognition of diversity among the world's faiths is not only essential but also the first step toward creating deeper understanding of each other. True understanding of the "other" must proceed from a genuine recognition of and respect for the other's reality. It must proceed from a state of mind where the urge to reduce the other into one's own framework is no longer the dominant mode of thinking.

To begin, whether we like it or not, the existence of other religions is an undeniable fact. It is also undeniable that the teachings of the great religions provide great benefits to their adherents. Even the Buddha failed to turn the entire population of central India into Buddhists, let alone the entire world. Hinduism, too, failed to convince a significant proportion of the population of the Indian subcontinent of the primacy of the Vedic way to *moksha* (salvation). Similarly for Christians, Jesus did not convert the entire population of the Holy Land into his followers—nor did he try to. From the point of view of Islam, even after the Prophet's appearance in the world, the presence of Jews and Christians remained an inalienable part of the landscape of the Middle East.

It is impossible for the 6 billion human inhabitants of our planet to all follow the same religion. First, the diversity of mental dispositions, spiritual inclinations, and different kinds of conditioning has always been a basic feature of human society, and one set of spiritual teachings would simply not serve everyone. Second, given the long history of the religions—in some cases, stretching over thousands of years—they have evolved in a complex human geography adapted to specific cultural sensibilities and environments, giving rise to different habits of mind. Such things cannot be changed overnight, nor is it desirable that they be. So creating a single religion for the world, whether a new one or one of the old ones, is simply unfeasible.

Especially in today's globalized world, where not only nation to nation but even continent to continent our fates are deeply intertwined, the acceptance of the reality of other faiths is critical for the sake of peace and human happiness. Furthermore, because of modern communication, tourism, and the global economy, the world's religions are in daily contact with one another. The era when a particular faith could exist in the comfort of isolation is gone forever. Given this new reality of our world, the only alternative left to religious pluralism is an increasing sense of division and conflict. So, in brief, the standpoint of religious exclusivism represents a perspective that is not in accord with reality.

From the point of view of a religious person who seeks to live his or her life according to the dictates of a sound ethical way of life, it becomes especially incumbent upon us to accord deep reverence to all faith traditions. In the past these traditions have provided inspiration, meaning, and ethical guidance to millions of people. Today, too, despite tremendous advances in the field of material development and human knowledge, these faith traditions continue to provide solace to millions of our fellow human beings. And in the foreseeable future, these traditions will continue to be a source of deep spiritual inspiration to millions.

Regardless of how one may feel about the specific doctrines of other faith traditions, this fact alone—their service to millions of fellow human beings—makes them worthy of our deep respect. Their profound benefit to others is really the ultimate reason each of us, believers and nonbelievers alike, must accord deep respect to the world's great faith traditions. For a believer, a key element here is to be truly sincere about the values of compassion that are at the heart of one's own faith tradition. For the ultimate reason to accord respect to other religions is to see that they, too, engender the beautiful qualities of the human heart and foster compassion and loving-kindness—exactly the qualities one is striving to attain through one's own faith.

Interestingly, when it comes to actual spiritual practices, which I consider to be the essence of these religious teachings, as opposed to metaphysical or theological formulations, there is profound convergence across all traditions. All carry the message of love, compassion, and universal brotherhood and sisterhood. Based on these virtues, all teach forgiveness, forbearance, contentment, simplicity of life, and self-discipline.

THREE KEY ASPECTS OF A FAITH TRADITION

In addressing the question of the plurality of religion, personally I find it helpful to draw a distinction between what can be seen as three key aspects of a religion: (1) ethical teachings, (2) doctrines or metaphysics, and (3) cultural specifics, such as attitudes to images. The first aspect pertains to the practitioner's daily life, whereby he or she needs to live according to the dictates of an ethics based on compassionate consideration of others' welfare. Essentially, this provides a guideline to the devout on how to live according to the spiritual ideals one espouses within the context of a society. In contrast, the second aspect of religion pertains primarily to its understanding of the ultimate truth, which is inevitably related to what happens to the believer in the afterlife. It is this second aspect that provides the rationale for the teaching on ethics and religious practice that makes up the first aspect. The third aspect, which is often bound up with cultural and historical circumstances, determines how believers may behave at a given place and time.

Once this distinction is drawn, the question of how to deal with the challenge posed for the devout by the plurality of religion assumes a different form. For example, on the level of ethical teachings, there is undeniably a great convergence of the world's great religions. The central message of all these religions is love, compassion, and universal brotherhood and sisterhood. Their presentations may be different—for example, a theistic tradition may admonish its followers to "love thy neighbor" as the wish of God, while a nontheistic tradition may say that, given the law of cause and effect, if one does not wish ill for oneself one should then refrain from doing ill to others. But on this level, the purpose of all religions remains the same: to contribute to the betterment of humanity, to create a more compassionate and responsible human being. Not only are the ethical teachings of the religions essentially the same, the fruits of love and compassion are the same as well. For example, just as Mother Teresa of Calcutta was a product of Christianity's great teachings on compassion, so too a great soul like Mahatma

Gandhi (who demonstrated the power of nonviolence as an effective political means) was primarily a product of India's great religion, Hinduism.

Now, on the metaphysical and cultural levels—our second and third aspects of a religion—clearly there are differences among the religions, some of which are in fact quite fundamental. In the cultural domain, time and historical context may even cause significant differences within a given religion, as in the relatively recent espousal of women priests in the Anglican Church or in the differences between Buddhism in its traditional homelands—for instance, Thailand, Sri Lanka, Japan, and Tibet. But the fundamental arena of difference lies in the second—doctrinal or metaphysical—aspect. For where a religion's doctrines play an active role, the distinctness of the faith traditions becomes most pronounced.

To begin with, even on the basic question of what happens in the afterlife, as well as the origins of the universe, there is much divergence. There is also a difference in the way in which the notion of well-being in this afterlife is defined. Lastly, there are differences in the method—the "path" in the Buddhist language—on how to realize this future well-being. Given these differences, it is no surprise that there are fundamental differences in the conception of what constitutes ultimate truth. Any attempt to find convergence on this doctrinal and metaphysical level is like the well-known Tibetan proverb, "trying to attach a yak's head on a sheep's body." The question, then, becomes what is the purpose of these different doctrinal and philosophical views? Here, I find a historical model from my own Buddhist tradition to be most helpful.

A Buddhist Hermeneutical Principle

Divergence of doctrinal and philosophical standpoints has always been an important part of Buddhism's own self-understanding. Soon after the Buddha's passing away, his followers evolved into distinct schools, each espousing somewhat different doctrinal and philosophical standpoints. Each of these teachings are based on the words of the Buddha, which means that one and the same teacher taught divergent—in some cases, in fact, contradictory—views of reality to his followers. For example, although the standard Buddhist doctrinal standpoint rejects the notion of an independent self, there is also a sutra where the Buddha states that the physical and mental constituents of a person are the burden while the person is the bearer of that burden, thus suggesting the presence of an agent independent of the physical and mental elements that make up a person's existence.

Similarly, there is a statement by the Buddha that karmic actions and their fruits exist, while in general the self that is thought to be the agent of the action and the experiencer of the fruits of the karmic action does not exist. There are also statements in which the Buddha rejects the reality of the external material world but affirms the existence of the world of consciousness. Finally, there are scriptures that reject any notion of the substantial existence of things, both material and mental. Here, then, the Buddha teaches all things to be empty of any substantial reality and that they exist only within the context of interrelated events of cause and effect. In technical Buddhist language, all conditioned things are impermanent and all things and events are dependently originated, thus lacking any objectively identifiable essence that defines their real existence.

Since all of these divergent, even contradictory, teachings were taught by the same teacher, does this mean that the Buddha himself was confused when it came to defining the ultimate nature of reality? Or, does this mean that the Buddha deliberately wished to create confusion in the minds of his followers? Clearly, for a devout Buddhist, both of these alternatives remain unacceptable. Furthermore, the fully awakened Buddha is, for the Buddhists, the embodiment of compassion for all things living—"a great friend even to those who are unacquainted," as a classical text puts it. So, how then are the followers of the Buddha to understand his divergent teachings? This is where the role of hermeneutics comes in.

The principle invoked by Buddhists in attempting to interpret the Buddha's conflicting teachings has to do with the understanding that what the Buddha taught is contingent on the needs of a given context and its potential for efficacy. In a sense, the Buddha, as teacher, did not have free reign on what to teach. His teaching, the dharma, was a cure for the ailments of the spirit, aimed to awaken it to its highest perfection; therefore, it demanded adjustment to the specific context in which it was being taught. In a sense, the dharma is a medicine whose effectiveness can be judged only in relation to the treatment of an illness. Since there are so many diverse mental dispositions, or spiritual and philosophical inclinations, among human beings, there should be equally corresponding numbers of teachings. The idea that there should be only one teaching—a kind of panacea that is valid for all beings—from this point of view is untenable.

For some, the idea that this very life has been created by God is deeply inspiring and also most powerful in providing a spiritual anchor; while for others, the notion of an all-powerful creator is troubling and even untenable. For some, the idea that what we are today is the result of our own past karma and what we will become is determined by how we live today is appealing and beneficial, while others find the idea of future lives and previous births incomprehensible. In fact, if the Buddha were to teach the doctrine of no-self to someone whose mental disposition is such that he or she is likely to understand this in nihilistic terms—as denying the very existence of a person, who is responsible for his or her intentional actions—not only would this be most unskillful on the Buddha's part but, more important, the teaching would be harmful for that person. In fact, to give the teaching of emptiness to someone whose mind is not ready for it is a direct infraction of one of the bodhisattva precepts.

In the case of prescribing medicine, a skilled physician will take into account the specific physical constitution of the patient, his age, fitness, proneness to negative reactions to certain substances, and so on. Depending on this, the physician will prescribe the medicine. Even with respect to one and the same patient, a skilled physician needs to be sensitive to how the patient responds to the dose, as well as different compositions of the medicine, so he can adjust both the dose and the composition as the patient progresses along the path of healing. In the same manner, a skilled spiritual teacher adapts his or her teachings, always maintaining deep sensitivity to the specific needs of a given situation. Therefore, a Buddhist cannot say, when relating to the Buddha's teaching, "this is the best teaching," as if one can make such evaluations independent of the specific contexts.

I often speak of a "supermarket of religions." Just as a supermarket rightly takes pride in its rich and diverse resources of food commodities for sale, in the same manner the world of religions can take pride in its rich diversity of teachings. Now, as for the question of why some people find certain religious teachings more appealing and effective than others, while different individuals have a negative reaction to the same teaching, from the Buddhist and classical Indian religious and philosophical points of view, it has largely to do with the person's own conditioning, including his or her karma. From a theistic perspective, it is a matter of God's mysterious workings. This is, in fact, the key reason I personally advise people to stay within their own traditional faith.

Personally, I find this hermeneutic principle most helpful when relating to the question of other religions, for it explains the value and richness of the great diversity of religions. Each religion, because of a long historical development that involved the experiences of so many generations, has its own beauty, logic, and uniqueness. Most important, this diversity enables the world's religions to serve such a vast number of human beings. In contrast, if there were only one historical religion, not only would the world be impoverished, especially in relation to its spiritual resources and imagination, but also that religion would fail to serve the needs of many people.

Seen from this angle, the diversity of religion becomes not an awkward problem; rather, it becomes an adornment of the human spirit and its long history. It is something to be celebrated rather than bemoaned. Understood thus, the urge to convert others to one's own faith loses its force. In its place arises a genuine acceptance of the reality of other faith traditions. Then, instead of seeing others as an aberration, or at worst as a threat, one can relate to others out of a sense of deep appreciation for their profound contributions to the world.

THE PROBLEM OF FUNDAMENTALISM

Now, one possible response that a faith tradition can make in the face of the plurality of faiths, which is an inescapable fact of the contemporary world, is to embrace fundamentalism. This is, in fact, what many followers of religion have chosen to do. At its heart, fundamentalism is a reaction to a perceived threat to the integrity of one's own religious tradition. Just as we see fundamentalism in the Abrahamic religions, we also see fundamentalism in Asian religions such as Buddhism and Hinduism.

Broadly speaking, the fundamentalists, irrespective of their specific religious affiliation, tend to believe that the contemporary world is rife with immorality and ungodly values, and that the role of the devout is to try to bring human society back to a golden age when the world functioned according to the dictates of a moral God. In their quest for this goal, fundamentalists on the whole believe strongly that their scripture contains the totality of all the truths that are worth knowing, and that it is their responsibility to defend the truths of this scripture against the onslaught of pluralistic or secular ideas that inevitably relativize truth. An important part of the standpoint of fundamentalism is, therefore, to defend the literal truth of scripture and maintain its definitive status. For the fundamentalists, then, the commands of God as they understand them to be revealed in scripture are absolute, atemporal, and nonnegotiable.

Although fundamentalism need not necessarily lead to religious extremism, the line dividing the two remains a fine one. There is, however, one concern that underlies the fundamentalist standpoint, which pluralists need to take seriously. This is the concern that religious pluralism involves relativizing doctrinal truths. Here, if we invoke the distinction I made earlier of the three key aspects of a religion—ethics, doctrine, and culture—we can respond to this concern effectively. While allowing openness to interpretation in matters of practice and culture, which in any case pertain to guidelines for living within a society, even a religious pluralist can accept that the doctrines of his own scripture that primarily pertain to ultimate truth are definitive. In other words, one can be a religious pluralist yet maintain, for oneself, the doctrinal aspects of one's own tradition as representing the definitive truth.

Reconciling "One Truth, One Religion" with "Many Truths, Many Religions"

So, with these considerations as background, how does a follower of a particular religious tradition deal with the question of the legitimacy of other religions? On the doctrinal level, this is a question of how to reconcile two seemingly conflicting perspectives that pertain to the world's religious traditions. I often characterize these two perspectives as "one truth, one religion" versus "many truths, many religions." How does a devout person reconcile the perspective of "one truth, one religion" that one's own teachings appear to proclaim with the perspective of "many truths, many religions" that the reality of the human world undeniably demands?

As many religious believers feel, I would agree that some version of exclusivism—the principle of "one truth, one religion"—lies at the heart of most of the world's great religions. Furthermore, a single-pointed commitment to one's own faith tradition demands the recognition that one's chosen faith represents the highest religious teaching. For example, for me Buddhism is the best, but this does not mean that Buddhism is the best for all. Certainly not. For millions of my fellow human beings, theistic forms of teaching represent the best path. Therefore, in the context of an individual religious practitioner, the concept of "one truth, one religion" remains most relevant. It is this that gives the power and single-pointed focus of one's religious path. At the same time, it is critical that the religious practitioner harbors no egocentric attachment to his faith.

Once at a conference in Argentina, the well-known Chilean scientist Humberto Maturana, who incidentally was a teacher of a close scientist friend of mine, the late Francisco Varela, said that, as a scientist, he should not be attached to his field, for this would obstruct his ability to study it with objectivity. This, I think, is an important insight that we in the religious world should also embrace. It means that I, as a Buddhist, must not feel egocentric attachment to my own faith of Buddhism, for doing so obstructs me from seeing the value of other traditions.

In the context of society, however, the concept of "many truths, many religions" not only becomes relevant but also necessary. In fact, where there is more than one person, already the pluralistic perspective of "many truths, many religions" becomes critical. Thus, if we relate these two seemingly contradictory perspectives to their differing contexts of society and the individual we can see no real conflict between the two.

This still leaves unanswered the question of how we should relate to the divergent and contradictory doctrinal teachings of the religions. From the Buddhist point of view, the belief in a Transcendent God, with its emphasis on the idea of a first cause that in itself is uncaused, amounts to falling into the extreme of absolutism, a view that is understood to obstruct the attainment of enlightenment. In contrast, from the monotheistic religions' point of view, Buddhism's nonacceptance of God and divine creation amounts to falling into the extreme of nihilism, a view that is dangerously close to an amoral and materialistic view of the world.

But, on the other hand, from the theistic religions' point of view, if one believes that the entire cosmos, including the sentient beings within it, is a creation of one all-powerful and compassionate God, the inescapable consequence is that the existence of faith traditions other than one's own are also God's creation. To deny this would imply one of two results: either one rejects God's omnipotence—that is to say, that although these other faiths are false ways, God remains incapable of stopping their emergence—or, if one maintains that although God is perfectly capable of preventing the emergence of these "false" ways, He chooses not to do so, then one rejects God's all-embracing compassion. The latter would imply that, for whatever reasons, God chose to exclude some—in fact, millions—of His own children and left them to follow false ways that would lead to their damnation. So the logic of monotheism, especially the standard version that attributes omnipotence, omniscience, and all-embracing compassion to God, inevitably entails recognition that the world's many religious traditions are in one way or another related to God's divine intentions for the ultimate well-being of His children. This means that, as a devout follower of God, one must accord respect and, if possible, reverence to all religions.

From the Buddhist point of view, given the tremendous diversity among sentient beings, each individual and group with a long history of inclinations and propensities, people find different ways of approach more suited to their own spiritual inclinations and thus more effective for their spiritual development. This alone is adequate ground to develop a sense of appreciation of all faith traditions. From the liberal democratic point of view, too, so long as one subscribes to the ideal that each citizen of a nation must be respected in his or her own right, one is also bound by this principle to respect the faith traditions that these individuals perceive to be the basis of their understanding of who they are as persons.

Given the need for upholding the perspective of "many truths, many religions" in the context of wider society, while the dictates of one's own faith demand embracing the "one truth, one religion" perspective, I believe that a creative approach is called for here—if one wishes to uphold both of these perspectives with integrity.

One might, for instance, make a distinction between faith and respect as two distinct psychological attitudes in relation to the world's religions. Faith is associated with such psychological states as cognitively oriented "belief," as well as more affectively oriented "trust" and "confidence." In contrast, respect is associated with appreciation and reverence, deriving particularly from the recognition of the values and importance of the object for which one has respect.

In the context of religion, then, faith pertains to truth—especially doctrinal truths—as proposed by one's own religion. Therefore, for a devout religious person, it becomes important to reserve faith for his or her own religion, while cultivating respect—in fact, deep reverence—for other religions. In the Sanskrit Buddhist tradition, a distinction is made between three types of faith (*shradda*): faith in the form of admiration, in the form of conviction, and in the form of emulation. Of these, admiration—the first form of faith—is effectively equivalent to respect or reverence, which, as we have noted, can be fully extended to other religions.

There are two broad arguments for this idea of respect for other traditions. The first is the undeniable fact that, as mentioned earlier, these traditions have provided solace and spiritual development, as well as a laudable system of ethics, for millions of people and will continue to do so in the foreseeable future. The second, perhaps stronger, argument is that despite the doctrinal differences between religions (which cannot be bridged), just as the doctrinal teachings of my own faith admirably inform the ethical way of life of my own faith, so the doctrines of other faiths inform no less valid ethical ways of life in the other religions. The doctrines themselves cannot be reconciled, but the way they make it possible to ground strikingly parallel and praiseworthy ethical systems is a wonderful fact. This fostering of deep and active respect for other faith traditions is certainly doable, and it is how I practice myself.

Heart of the Dalai Lama

Pico Iyer

*For thirty-five years, the novelist and essayist Pico Iyer has been a friend,
observer, and student of the Dalai Lama. In this heartfelt personal essay,
he reveals the simple human secret that has made His Holiness the most
beloved spiritual figure in the world.*

When I was your age," the Fourteenth Dalai Lama is telling a
group of six hundred or so young female students at Chikushi Jagakoen school in Fukuoka, Japan, "I was a quite lazy student. I didn't
have much enthusiasm for studying." Though sitting politely, their
hands in their laps, the girls almost visibly come to attention, drawing closer as he says this (they weren't expecting such words from a
celebrated visitor). "So my tutor always kept a whip," he goes on, as
naturally as if he were talking to his oldest friend. "I was studying
with my elder brother, so the tutor kept two whips. One was yellow—a 'Holy Whip'! But I think if you use the 'Holy Whip,' the effect is the same as from the other one, 'Holy Pain.'" Even the girls,
trained to be reserved and demure since birth, cannot contain their
laughter—and delight, perhaps, and relief. Even this man regarded
as an incarnation of a god by his followers is, at some level, just like

them. Even he has been in need of discipline at times, and is in the lifelong business of finding an answer to suffering, or "Holy Pain," as it might be. I scribble down his every word and notice how seamlessly he's transmitting certain fundamental truths of Buddhism. Don't be distracted by externals, or signs of ceremony—a yellow whip hurts just the same as any other whip. Don't think of holiness as something separate from the realm of suffering—if anything, our most sacred duty comes in our response to the realm of suffering, which evolves through a change in perception. Don't think of people as unequal—everyone has to go through the same lessons, and the Buddha himself, master democrat, gave us a sense of power and potential by always reminding us that he was no different from us.

And yet, as ever, the Dalai Lama conveys all this without using the word "don't" at all. "But," he tells the young students, "I believe some years I lost" through not paying attention. "Please pay attention to your studies." It's a tonic and liberating idea: excitement is in the eye of the beholder, a reflection of the choices that we make. He's already told the girls, at the beginning of his lecture, that he's "nothing special," no different from any one of them, in his human challenges (or his human potential). So if they are impressed by the sense of presence, alertness, and kindness they see before them, embodied in one being, they're essentially impressed by an image of what they can be, too, if they so choose. Indeed, by learning from his mistakes, they can go beyond him in certain respects, and pay attention to the possibilities around them from a younger age. At some point, he assures them, he realized that his studies were in fact the most exciting adventure around; it wasn't necessarily that the difficult Buddhist texts changed, but that his way of seeing them did.

He doesn't tell them, I have noticed, that whenever he has a spare moment on the road he turns to a copy of some Buddhist teaching, his greatest joy whenever he isn't inspecting the world around him (to get a deeper, more detailed and empirical sense of what reality looks like). In Yokohama he'll ask an engineer, backstage, before a large lecture, how the soundboard works. When we have lunch with an ambassador from Bahrain, he'll try to learn more about the history of Islam and Arabic culture. When old friends come to meet him in his hotel room, he asks them how things are going in Japan and listens to their answers closely, like a doctor hearing a list of symptoms. One reason he's in this little girls' school in Fukuoka this morning is that so many Japanese mothers, on recent trips, have told him of their urgent concern about alienation among the young in their country, children who shut themselves in their rooms and never have contact with the world, teenage suicides.

The other reason he's here is no less practical: these students, some barely out of kindergarten, are the ones who will make the world we live in thirty years from now, the real power brokers in the larger view of things. On his previous trip to Japan, one year before, the Dalai Lama had spent his one day in Tokyo not visiting politicians or cultivating the media or talking to movers and shakers; he'd spent the entire day visiting two boys' high schools associated with temples, offering them lectures like this one and sitting in meditation with the boys in a school zendo. Children are not only more open to transformation and more in need of positive direction than their elders are; they're also potential more or less incarnate. Two months after this meeting, I'll meet one of Britain's leading young writers, who has worked hard for Tibet, turning a rigorous, scrupulous eye on the events of the day and becoming one of the leading modern historians of India.

"The Dalai Lama came to my school when I was very young," he told me. "I was just in my teens. And it was a school run by Benedictine monks. But somehow it made an incredible impression on me." As soon as he finished his studies, he went to Dharamsala to study in the Library of Tibetan Works and Archives. Later he would spend two months on a punishing trip across Tibet, recording what's really happening there.

It's so easy not to listen to the Dalai Lama, I've found over the decades I've been traveling with him. It's almost impossible not to be inspired by him, to be warmed, to be clarified, to feel that you've come into a presence of rare goodness and uncanny, omnidirectional compassion. I've been lucky enough to know him for thirty-five years now, since I was a teenager, and every November, when he comes to Japan, I travel by his side every day from around 7:30 every morning, when his working day begins, to around 5 p.m., when it concludes. I sit in on his closed-door meetings with parliamentarians, his audiences with old friends, his chats with ceremonial hosts, his discussions with leaders of all Japan's religious groups. It's exhausting even watching him go through his day. He comes down to the hotel lobby for his first event, after four hours of meditation, and finds five Tibetans who have traveled across the island to see him. He stops to receive and bless the ceremonial silk scarves they've brought to him, and as they sob with emotion and gratitude, he gives them heart and tells them not to give up sustaining their culture and their confidence in its survival. And then he goes and does the same thing for the next ten hours, as he's done every day for seventy years.

Yet so often, even as we're being moved by the way he instinctively knows how to see past divisions, laughs to dissolve our tension, or manages somehow to make us feel we're meeting not just a great philosopher and global leader, but also an old friend, we come away—at least I do—with our head in the clouds, unstoppably grinning and with tears in the corners of our eyes. We talk about all that he's given us and all that we've learned from his being—what a great sense of humor!—and we (or at least I) grow wild with our own ideas of him, instead of the ideas he's come to offer to us. Thirteen years ago, I heard from a writer in Hawaii (skeptical, non-Buddhist, famously unimpressionable) that when the Dalai Lama came to his city, he went to the lecture, took down every word he said, and then kept the transcript by his bed, so he could read it again and again.

Now I do the same. It's not hard to transcribe every word, since the Dalai Lama speaks slowly and very deliberately in English and, when he's speaking in Tibetan, his words come to us through a translator. I get a lot of instruction from them as I write. But I get even more when I go back to my desk and read the words over and over, and copy them out again and again, as if they were (and why should they not be?) a text I am studying at college. Even in his second language, the Dalai Lama speaks with meticulous precision, and a quarter of a century of traveling has allowed him to hone his words down so that the simplest-sounding sentence in fact contains volumes of teaching.

"I am a simple Buddhist monk," he says, and once upon a time I'd have been warmed and disarmed by the comment, so modest and transparent. But now, as I listen to him, I hear him say that he's come to this formulation, as to everything he says, through an extended process of research, reflection, and analysis. When he's dreaming, he says, he usually sees himself as a monk, but almost never as the Dalai Lama. When, occasionally, he has faint memories of earlier incarnations, he generally sees himself in a monastic role, but only very rarely as the Dalai Lama. More important, his monastic commitment is one that he has undertaken and that no one can strip from him but himself; the Dalai Lama is a title, a position—a set of rites—that could be taken from him at any moment. When the Thirteenth Dalai Lama was asked who he was, I found out when I researched it, he said, "A simple Buddhist monk."

Listen to the doctor's careful prescription instead of just raving about his bedside manner, I tell myself as he returns to Japan in the bright autumn days for another few days of engagements. It's too easy to fly off into lofty theorizing about the man, into essays on him or abstractions, into comparisons and projections and all the kind of vagueness or myth-making that he would forcefully counsel me against. Maybe on this occasion I can just try to take down what he says—to listen—and to see how every sentence contains a teaching. How even a modest-seeming event at a girls' school can offer as much as some of his most sonorous discourses.

There are rows and rows of six-year-olds, impeccable in their blue skirts and tops and bonnets, lined up in the brilliant sunshine as the Dalai Lama and a small group of secretaries, bodyguards, and attendants arrive (along with my wife and me) at Chikushi Jagakoen.

High schoolers are standing, equally serious and attentive, at their side, and even some college students, in scrupulously quiet styles and pale colors. Fukuoka is a long way from Tokyo and Kyoto, on an island to the south, and not many dignitaries trouble to come here.

But as I walk behind the Tibetan leader on the warm November day, it's clear that we could be walking around any school in Nova Scotia, or Indiana—or the Tibetan Children's Village in Dharamsala. The Dalai Lama bends down to shake each little girl by the hand, sometimes affectionately tweaking a cheek as if this Yuki or Sachi were his great-niece. He engages the high school girls in conversation, looking into their eyes and attending to their answers as if they were his guides to contemporary Japan. "How many of your students speak English?" he asks the teachers on arrival, so he can make best use of the hours. Given that most have at least studied it, he can speak to them directly, and not have to lose time on translations.

One day before, he had been addressing a group of four hundred local Buddhists, from different sects, burying their differences to come together to listen to him direct them toward certain useful texts from Shantideva and Nagarjuna as an answer to loneliness and confusion. In the afternoon, he'd addressed thousands of regular folks in the Kita Kyushu Dome on his usual themes of compassion and responsibility. The previous weekend, in Tokyo, he'd spent a whole day speaking to Chinese individuals living in Japan—looking for common ground, as always—and then had devoted one and a half days to talking to the international media. But now he's giving himself to the schoolgirls as attentively and enthusiastically as if he were visiting the White House or the Vatican.

Japan is the strongest Buddhist nation in the world, of course—until China comes around. More to the point, it's also one of the only ones that opens its doors to the Dalai Lama. Not the least of the ironies of his life is that the most visible and probably most respected Buddhist in the world is not invited to Buddhist Sri Lanka or Burma or Thailand or Vietnam, because they fear the consequences from China. Japan, however, is powerful enough to risk his presence, and the Dalai Lama, in turn, has long turned to Japan for instruction in mixing modern innovation with ancient tradition, and in blending efficiency with humility, hard work with a wish to do better. The previous spring I spent two days with him in Santa Barbara, and did an event with him at New York's Town Hall, but I see him most engaged in the Buddhist part of his public life as he travels around Japan and thinks about how to make strong and deep the future of Mahayana Buddhism.

Now, as the girls sit silently before him in the school auditorium, he offers something of a lesson in "skillful means." With fellow monks and philosophers, I've seen, on this trip as on every other, he will quickly dive into texts and exchange ideas and explanations with the excitement of a lifelong scholar; but with these girls, he'll find the place of common experience between them and him—his life as a student, his life as a brother—and exchange certain basic human principles of attention and self-confidence to kids who may not know or care about the four noble truths. A large part of a doctor's skill comes not in making the diagnosis, but in explaining it in simple, everyday, human terms that any layperson can understand.

The fact that his own English is imperfect is itself a small reassurance—a reminder that he's on the same level as his listeners and is not an all-knowing sage laying down the law from a throne or a mountaintop. His voice goes up and down, never a monotone, and his sentences are as full of emphases and clarity as his famously articulate Tibetan. Yet at the same time, in its calligraphic directness, his solid and succinct English gets the point across with little room for ambiguity, or wild misinterpretations.

As he speaks about our "global family" and the "new reality" of a world without "them and us," the Dalai Lama speaks always with his being, leaning in toward the students, rocking back and forth while sitting cross-legged on his chair, coming to the front of the stage when he arrives so he can make eye contact with as many people as possible. He waves to familiar faces. He looks up at the adornments of the stage. He conveys his humanity through pulling a tissue out of his robes. And when he asks for questions, to my astonishment a hundred hands shoot up, the generally reticent Japanese clearly so engaged by his presentation that their defenses are gone and they're as eager to speak to him as they are to some respected classmate.

One girl after another stands up, and poses a question as direct and to the point as any the Dalai Lama could ask for: "How do I bring peace and love to the world—I'm only small?" "Do you get disappointed trying to protect Tibet and Tibetan Buddhism?" "What do you do if you're losing hope?" Clearly, like most audiences he visits, they've been studying the Tibetan issue in preparation for his trip. But clearly, too, they're posing the questions that are most urgent to them right now—the bullied girl or the scared one, the idealist and the one who is feeling isolated and frustrated. They all get up and find a way to frame question after question that comes from the heart.

The Dalai Lama listens to them as keenly as a physician listens to his patients, and, though he hears variations on the same questions several times a day, he responds to each one with unqualified vigor and intensity. "As soon as you feel some problem, some disappointment," he tells the first questioner, "then you must look at the problem from a wider perspective, through different angles." I realize, with a pang, how close this issue is to his own predicament, with the Chinese government cracking down on Tibetans in Tibet more unsparingly than ever. "Then you can see there's a possibility of a compromise," he goes on. "If you look only in one way, you think, 'I can't accept this.'"

I recall too how on this trip he's been talking over and over about the challenge of forgiveness and how much he admires the way the Japanese, after seeing two of their biggest cities destroyed, did not express hatred toward their American antagonists in war but decided to learn from them. Over and over he's been saying that Japan, particularly as the world's only victim so far of atomic bombings, can both lead the world in the cause of nonviolence and serve as a model for combatants everywhere of how to break the cycle of vengeance. "You suffered," he says, "and yet you turned that experience into a determination to prevent war, not into a hatred of your oppressor." He's speaking to the Japanese girls, clearly, but it's not hard for the rest of us to hear how this might apply to our lives—we all face conflict—and, no less, to the lives of every Tibetan.

Again and again, as the questions continue, I see how compressed and practical his responses are. Asked about getting discouraged in his work for Tibet, he answers, without hesitation, "Here, one sense of hope is, I'm a Buddhist. Although a not very good practitioner. But still I try to be a practitioner. One of my main practices is to make one's existence something useful and helpful to others. That's my prayer." (His prayer, I notice, is his practice. His practice is his prayer). "That really gives me inner strength. So, generally, when there is some challenge, there is better opportunity to make some contribution." Again, it sounds so simple, but it is as real and complex an idea as his beloved Shantideva's reminder that your seeming enemy is your best teacher, moving you to call upon your native clear-sightedness and patience and compassion.

When asked what advice he can give to Japan, he stresses at the outset, "Of course I have no direct responsibility." But then he responds with typical pragmatism. "But I feel—just one small gesture: you young Japanese have great potential to serve, to help humanity, particularly in Asia. Now, maybe here one obstacle is language. Perhaps learning English more widely may be one factor: you have the knowledge, you have the ability, but language sometimes becomes an obstacle. In order to utilize your abilities widely, perhaps more attention to learning English may be a good thing."

I notice those favorite words of his—"utilize," "widely," "perhaps"—but I also notice how he's speaking about communication, dialogue, the search for common ground, not in the lofty words of the Golden Rule, but in terms of concrete, everyday practices. "Even this poor English, broken English, quite useful in communicating with other people," he says, and the girls relax and laugh again.

And so it goes. Someone asks him what has touched him most in his life, and he says, "I don't know" (which always draws a laugh—

of surprise blending into relief: he doesn't claim to have all the answers). "Usually, one is Buddha's teaching," he goes on (as he did once in telling me how tears come to his eyes when thinking of the Buddha, or any act of kindness). "Infinite altruism. That shows us the purpose of our life." That applies even to the media, he goes on, as it can "make clear to the people what reality is" (and I recall how, the previous year, in Japan, he'd said that he thinks of the Buddha as a scientist, whose main aim is to show us reality, objectively, empirically, precisely). "The media should have a long nose, as long as an elephant's nose. Smell, in front and behind, make clear what's happening. Media people have great potential to help humanity."

Throughout the trip, he's been asking people—scientists, politicians, journalists, and now schoolgirls—to go to Tibet, if they have the chance, just to tell the world what's happening there. Don't listen to Tibetan propaganda, he says; don't listen to Chinese. Just give us a neutral, factual account of how people are living there since the area was blocked from media investigation in March 2008. A doctor who can't see his patients, or even hear what's happening with them, is at a loss.

And asked once more what he does when he can't succeed, he reminds his audience of some of the brighter sides of impermanence. "This present situation has to change. Change will not come from the sky. We, as individuals, must make some effort, no matter one simple, insignificant case. One person leads, ten people join, a thousand people join, then the media . . ."

I hear, as I listen, the vision of incremental, soul-by-soul change he'd outlined to me the day after he'd been awarded the Nobel Prize. He really wondered if his efforts were enough, he'd told me on the very day when others were celebrating what they hoped would mark a new future for Tibet. But all one could do was try one's best, and know that the effort might reach to others, and then still others, and then more. Two days before Fukuoka, speaking to more than three hundred journalists crammed into Tokyo's Foreign Correspondents' Club, he'd suddenly offered, "Blessings come from yourself," in telling the story of a wealthy Indian family who had come to him to ask for his blessing. Your wealth is itself a blessing, he'd told them; don't ask me to give you anything. The kind acts you do, the way you share the blessing of your money, is what generates blessings for you. And don't just give it out, but use it wisely and practically, for education, hospitals, clinics.

And then, as the event begins to draw to a close, I notice, as listeners always do, how much of his instruction comes just in the way he walks through the world. He much appreciates the questions, he says; they were very good (practical, honest, unqualified). He asks all the young ladies brave enough to stand up in front of their classmates and ask him something to come up onstage, so he can greet them personally and be photographed with them. (I remember when my daughter, seeing him as a schoolgirl in Kyoto, was most moved after another girl asked him an anguished question about her life and he said, "I don't know the answer," but asked her to come onstage so he could just hold her at least.)

Then one of the students, a smiling girl of about sixteen from Bangladesh, the winner of a contest, I'm assuming, is asked to deliver a short essay on behalf of the school to its visitor. As she stands on the stage and reads, in fluent Japanese (translated for the Dalai Lama by an assistant), about her feelings returning to her very poor home country and then coming back to affluent Japan, where it's so easy to take everything for granted, the Dalai Lama watches her intently, never taking his eyes off her, as if he were listening to a teacher of his expound a lesson about the Buddha.

He embraces her and gives her a ceremonial white silk scarf. The next day, after we fly back to Tokyo, when he addresses a large audience in a sumo stadium, his biggest public event of the tour, equivalent to a talk in Madison Square Garden, he starts, to my surprise, speaking about the student from Bangladesh he'd just met and the story she'd shared with him. Lessons and precepts and stories and practical counsel are filling every moment of his day, as he stops to shake the hand of every waiter after lunch, or suddenly tells me, eyes moistening, how moved he is that Tibetans have brought something of Buddhism back to the country of its birth. I transcribe every moment. But from this particular morning, one thing I take away is how ready he is to learn from a teenage girl and to distill everything he knows for even the smallest and least elevated of settings.

When his talk is over and he's finished going down to shake hands with students in the front rows, posing for photographs with the questioners, draping the head teachers with silk scarves, he's asked if he'd like to take his lunch in peace, alone. Oh no, no, he says, with absolute conviction. We must all eat together.

We go back out into the bright November sunshine, after lunch is over, to the next appointment, and I suspect that this small event on his schedule is as important to him as any meeting with a head of state or billionaire. I remember, twelve years earlier, his telling me that the press inevitably makes a big deal out of whether he meets a president or prime minister. But for him the much more important thing is just meeting a single soul, sincere, who may look on her life with a little more confidence and clarity after their talk. That is where the possibility of transformation is most great. "Then I really feel I've made some contribution," he had said. Change, again, comes not all at once, but with one turning heart and then another. All that's needed, he might be saying, is attention.

This Is Getting Old

Susan Moon

It was the generation that thought it would stay young forever. Now the adjective most often applied to it is "aging." As baby boomer Susan Moon contemplates her impending old age, she learns from her mother and her circle of elderly friends that a youthful spirit and zest for life have nothing to do with how old you are.

I was having Cheerios and milk with my mother at the little table beside the window, in her retirement building in Chicago. Her sixth-floor apartment overlooked Lake Michigan, and one of my mother's greatest pleasures was to sit in her favorite chair and watch the passing of ore boats and clouds.

This was the first morning of my visit, and my mother turned her attention from her lake to her daughter, saying, "Your hair is so wild! Can't you do something to get it out of your face?"

"Why don't you ever tell me when you *like* my hair?" I asked.

She tried to redeem herself that evening, lavishing compliments upon me when I put barrettes in my hair before we went downstairs to dinner. But again the next morning she looked at me over her bowl of cereal with her head cocked, and I felt it coming.

"You looked so beautiful last night," she said, trying to be diplomatic. "I could hardly take my eyes off you." I knew that was just the prelude. "But this morning . . . can't you just brush it back?"

"Mom," I said, "I'm sixty-three years old. I'm too old for you to be telling me how to wear my hair." Apparently I wasn't too old to mind.

"I just want you to know how nice it looks when you brush it back."

"I know how you like it, Mom."

"No, you don't! That's why I'm telling you."

I thought: You've been talking to me about my hair for sixty years. Do you think I don't know what pleases you? But I didn't say it out loud. Anyway, I wasn't in an entirely blameless position. A couple of years before, when my mother's hair had been down to her shoulders and she sometimes wore it in pigtails, she asked me if I liked it that way. I said I didn't think it was "age appropriate." (If she hadn't been my mother, I probably would have been charmed by her braids.) She pretended she thought that was a great witticism, and a couple of times I heard her say to friends, "Susan thinks my braids are not age appropriate!" But it hurt her feelings. Not long after, she cut her hair short, so that it floated soft and white around her face. And did I mention to her the next time I saw her how nice her hair looked? No, not until she asked me outright whether I thought her new haircut was age appropriate.

My mother was a generous woman, and she loved her children and grandchildren with unconditional love—almost. As the Zen teacher Suzuki Roshi said to his students as he was trying to explain buddhanature: "You're all perfect exactly as you are, and you could use a little improvement."

I rented a car for my weeklong visit so I could take my mother places. She had given up driving a couple of years before, after she drove into a parked car for no particular reason. Not driving was hard for her. And she couldn't walk far because of her bad back, so the bus stop two blocks away was beyond her reach. A van from the building took residents shopping, but she found that walking around the enormous supermarket, even with a shopping cart to lean on, was a strain. And she hated not being able to choose when to go.

I did errands for her: I was glad to be able to take her to the eye doctor to get her cataracts looked at. Doctors' appointments were an emotional issue for her, and the older she got the more of them there were. In a phone conversation not long before my visit she had spoken to me enviously of a friend in her retirement building.

"Janet's daughter drives her to every doctor's appointment. Oh, I wish one of you lived in Chicago!" My siblings and I tried to coordinate our visits with her doctors' appointments, but we all lived far away and couldn't be counted on on a regular basis. She went to most of them by taxi, and it was a long wait for a taxi.

One day that week I took her to an exhibit of Japanese prints at the Art Institute and pushed her through the galleries in the folding wheelchair she used for such excursions. Several times, when she wanted to look at a different picture than the one I was aiming for, she quite literally put her foot down, and suddenly the wheelchair wouldn't go, like a locked shopping cart. It was annoying until I looked at it from her point of view and realized it was her way of reclaiming a little control over her own experience.

I tried to be helpful in other ways as well. My mother's culinary needs were simple; the system in her building was that she ate her dinners downstairs in the community dining room and prepared her own breakfasts and lunches, which were minimal, in her tiny kitchen. So I cleaned out her refrigerator, bought cold cereals and little yogurts, and made a big pot of leek and potato soup and put some of it away in the freezer for future lunches.

Then there was her computer. I showed her a couple of things she always forgot between visits: how to change the margins in her word-processing program and how to send an e-mail. This was rewarding for me, because my mother was the only person in the world who considered me a computer expert.

I admired my mother's life. Chicago was her city; she had grown up there. She still had old friends whom she saw now and then, and she had a rich life in her building. This time I visited the weekly poetry class she had been leading there for many years. One of the residents, a descendant of the African American poet Paul Laurence

Dunbar, brought several editions of his books to the class, and the assembled group, a mix of whites and African Americans, had a challenging discussion about writing in African American vernacular English.

I was impressed. I could almost imagine myself in a group like this, but I would have hated to be as cooped up as my mother was. Sometimes she didn't leave the building for days and she only knew the temperature outside by how the people were dressed as they walked their dogs along the lakefront. She spent hours at her post by the window, swiveling her chair through the one hundred and eighty degrees of her view, looking through her binoculars at the ducks on the lake. I think she preferred to look at the weather—whatever it was—from her comfortable chair rather than to be out in it. I got restless in the small apartment, in spite of my years of Buddhist practice, but my mother, having to stay put, was getting good at staying still.

The day before I went back to California, it was snowing when I woke up. I slipped out of the apartment while my mother was still asleep. I took the pedestrian tunnel under the outer drive and walked in the little lakefront park right across from her building. There was no one else there; mine were the first footprints in the fresh snow. I could have been in the country, with the little white peaks on top of the fence posts, and the lake beside me that had no end because the falling snow blocked out the smokestacks of Indiana, and the squirrels dropping things from the branches. I could have been in the country except for the roar of traffic behind me.

I thought: I'll visit her when it's spring, when the snow is gone and the sun is out, and I'll push her in her wheelchair through the park so she'll be able to hear the birds and smell the willows. I turned to walk back and saw my mother's building on the other side of the river of cars. I counted up six floors to pick out her window in the brick façade, and waved, just in case she'd gotten up and happened to be looking out.

That evening, my last, my mother had a party before dinner for a group of friends she called "the mothers of daughters." All of the women had faraway daughters who visited them there—like me, from Berkeley. Before the party, I brushed my hair and clipped it back as neatly as I could.

Six women traveled by elevator to my mother's apartment for wine and those little goldfish-shaped crackers. I didn't have to take their coats when they arrived, because they had all come from inside the building, but I took two walkers and put them aside. My mother was happy to see them—she always said she liked to show off her children to her friends. They settled in a semicircle facing the big window. The day's light was fading to gray over the lake, and the snow was already dirty at the edge of the road below.

The only woman I hadn't met before said, "You look just like your mother!" Even in old age my mother was an attractive woman, but does any daughter want to be told she looks just like her mother? It wasn't so much that I minded if there was a resemblance, but I did want to look younger than my mother. In fact, whenever I rode in the elevator without her, I had a horror of being mistaken for one of the residents. I was almost sixty-five—officially old enough to live there.

I was moved by this group of women—all of them lively and warmhearted, all of them dealing with the ruinations of old age. Betty, the eldest of the group, was in her nineties. The others were in their eighties. Betty was robust and always laughing. A few years before, she and my mother had ridden the trans-Siberian railroad together, but after that she had begun to suffer from dizzy spells and had had to give up traveling. One of the guests couldn't hear a thing, and another, whether she was sitting or standing, was bent into the letter C. Jane, who had been my mother's friend since childhood, had advanced mouth cancer. She had lost her teeth and had an artificial palate. She didn't go down to the dining room for dinner because, as she told my mother, she was afraid it would spoil her tablemates' appetites to see her eating. It even hurt to talk, and her speech was slightly impaired, but she was a woman of remarkable fortitude and she still joined in the conversation.

When it turned to the popular topic of visits from adult children, she remarked wryly, "A son is a son till he gets him a wife, but a daughter's a daughter the rest of her life."

All these women were widows, including my mother. I couldn't know how hard it was to become a widow after sharing your life with another person for fifty years. Nor could I know what a relief it might be, after the last long years of caretaking.

When you look at old women from the outside, not identifying with them, you don't think how lonely they might be, or how much patience it takes to get the walker in and out of the elevator. You forget that they didn't used to be like that, that they used to go canoeing in the Minnesota woods or waltz until the wee hours, that they knew another kind of life outside this building. You think they came into the world wrinkled and deaf.

I passed the crackers, like a good daughter. I offered wine, red or white, in my mother's pretty blue Mexican glasses. Her youthful cat, Sigo (for Significant Other: my mother adopted her after my stepfather died), lay on her back and pawed the air, wanting to be played with. My mother held a wire with a fluff ball on the end and dangled it in front of Sigo, who hunkered down, moving nothing but the tip of her tail, and then leapt straight up so suddenly that we all laughed.

Betty said to me, "I hear you were just on a long Zen meditation retreat. Did it make you calm?"

As a Buddhist, I was slightly exotic there. That afternoon my mother had introduced me to two of her fellow residents in the elevator, where a lot of her social interactions took place. "This is my Buddhist daughter from California!" she had said proudly. They wanted to know all about Buddhism, and whether I believed in reincarnation, but I didn't really have time to explain between the sixth floor and the first.

Now I responded to Betty's question. "You're not supposed to try to accomplish anything at all, not even calmness," I said. "The idea is to let go of gaining mind. Let go of your attachments."

"Well, I can see that I don't need Zen meditation," said Betty. "Getting old forces you to let go of one damn thing after another!" The others laughed in agreement.

"I like Zen," my mother said, "because it says you should be in the present. That's important in old age. I'm losing interest in my past—it was so long ago! And it's pointless to think about the future—what future? But the present! There's plenty going on right now, I tell myself."

I offered more wine but there was only one taker, and I wondered if they had always practiced such moderation.

The conversation moved on to the new cook in the kitchen downstairs and a dangerously creamy mushroom sauce he had used on the chicken. As the women talked and laughed, as they passed around the bowl of crackers with shaky hands, I studied them. I saw how they paid attention to each other. They were accomplished people: scholars, artists, social workers, poets, raisers of families. Now in old age, they were accomplishing friendship, accomplishing community.

My mother was only twenty years ahead of me, and at the rate things were going, I would be her age in no time. She was scouting the territory for me, and it behooved me to observe carefully.

It was 5:30 p.m.—time, in that establishment, to go down to dinner. After I fetched the two walkers from the corner of the room, the seven mothers of daughters and the one daughter—me—started down the long hall to the elevator.

My mother rode in her wheelchair, making it go by walking her feet along the floor in front of her, like a toddler on a riding toy. This was how she liked to do it when she was on her home turf. She said she got her best exercise in her wheelchair. People assumed she was in a wheelchair because her legs didn't work, but it was her back that hurt if she walked more than about fifty paces.

Sometimes, on a good back day, she walked to the elevator with a cane. Her cane had a handle that flipped down sideways and became a tiny seat, allowing her to stop and rest. She ordered those canes from England. If you were looking at her from the front and she was sitting on her cane, it was startling, because you couldn't see the cane and she appeared to be doing a strenuous yoga posture—her knees partly bent, pretending to sit in a chair that wasn't there. But today was a wheelchair day.

Our ragtag band moved down the corridor, and I had to make a conscious effort to go slow. Betty, walking beside me, said, "You have such beautiful hair, Susan." My mother looked up at me from her wheelchair and we grinned at each other.

Another Black Mark

Karen Connelly

*Some teachers say that the fast track to enlightenment is not found
in some Japanese monastery or cave high in the Himalayas; it's right
here in the life of marriage and family, that tumultuous training ground
of love and conflict. Here novelist Karen Connelly works with the* lojong
*(mind training) slogans as she duels with her rambunctious young master
of the universe, Timo.*

Timo, will you please give that to me?"

"No."

"That isn't your toy, Timo. That belongs to Mama. It's not a good idea to make a mess, okay?" I purse my lips and shudder, wondering why on earth I would say that it isn't a good idea to make a mess. That's just fanning the fire.

Timo, a three-year-old master of the universe, stands on the other side of the sofa, an open challenge animating his small face. His dark eyes sparkle with pleasure. From his point of view this is a game we've played many times before, chasing each other around the sofa. Naturally, he knows that he has something he's not supposed to have, something that I want, but that only adds to the excitement. Like many parents, I'm often distracted as I engage with my child; the phone needs to be answered, the rice on the floor needs to be cleaned up, this one newspaper article has grabbed my attention—*just this one, please, just a minute, just a minute!*—as he stands beside me at the table or crawls on my lap or shouts for me to come *now* and I pretend to engage with him while simultaneously ignoring him. He always knows when I am ignoring him.

Ha! Now he knows I am genuinely involved. No wonder he's thrilled.

I've followed him from the kitchen to the living room, a distance of twenty feet. We are just steps apart now, but I don't want to make another wrong move. His left hand is outstretched, like a runner about to sprint; his right hand clutches an extra-thick permanent black marker, which is poised above the tawny back of the sofa.

This is a moment for practical as well as philosophical parenting concerns. Why is that leather sofa dark yellow? What were we thinking when we bought it? Why was that permanent marker left in the kitchen drawer, among the washable kiddy felts and crayons? Why must I care so much?

Because Timo has wrecked the CD player, dug up the houseplants with his bulldozer, and ruined every lipstick I own. He searches out the lipsticks, crawls up bathroom shelves, hunts for them in my overnight bag, ferrets them out no matter where he goes. After drawing all over his face, the walls, the stairs, or, most recently, the bedspread, he smushes them to a pulp.

"Timo!" Unconsciously, I have raised and sharpened my voice. The effect of my harsh tone is instantaneous. The game look on my son's face hardens into anger. It's always like this. He gives me back the emotion I have just sent out to him. My reactions set the tone of the conflict that is to come; I am the adult, after all. *Drive all blames into oneself,* says one version of the *lojong* slogan for mind-training, which isn't a recipe for more mother-guilt but an admonishment to examine the nature of power and responsibility. I have power over my child. Yet I so easily misuse it. I do the precise opposite of that other Buddhist meditation practice, *tonglen.* Instead of sending out calm breath, I shoot a javelin from my mouth. We love each other, this boy and I, out of necessity, so that javelin always finds its mark.

He responds, equally sharply, "No, Mama, no! I going draw on the couch!"

"Please don't do that Timo, or Mama will be very . . ." What will I be? I want to say *angry*, a word he knows well. And I will be angry. But beneath the anger is usually a feeling of disappointment, even defeat, especially when the disagreement turns into a protracted battle. The threats may turn into reality—he will be hauled up to his room, have his toy taken away, or not go for the walk at all—but the tears come and the mood is unhappy for both of us. *Don't bring things to a painful point* suggests another *lojong* slogan. I am increasingly conscious of the times when I could have done it differently, and arrived at a happier outcome.

It's true that day-to-day parenting is full of snap decisions; sometimes we're in a hurry. Modern life requires an adherence to schedules, a tremendous degree of organization. Because my husband and I are self-employed, we are much freer with our time than many others, but we still need to manage busy timetables and juggle responsibilities. Children have to learn about that, with parents who encourage their participation but also train them in the difficult quality of patience. The big choices rarely involve children at all, at least not while they are small; the parents decide where to live, what to eat, what school the child will attend, when to go to the doctor, what morality to instill. What example to set.

All our lives, we learn about being human by watching what other people do, but during childhood, it is our first and deepest form of education. Children want to do what their caregivers do; they want to be like us. Very little escapes their sensibilities. Our actions pass through them like electrical impulses, subtly or overtly influencing their behavior, flavoring their essence. In everyday conflicts with my child, I know that slowing down will add lightness to the air, a moment of breath for both of us. This black-haired boy resembles me in so many ways; he has the same quick temper, the same readiness to laugh. When I remember to play more, even through my anger, he responds in kind. But I often forget to play. I tighten up, clamp down. I want my will to be done, like the old

Christian God. I, too, want to be a master of the universe, and of my child. But I am not. And he knows it.

We all know it. None of us can rightly cling to the arrogant notion of our dominion over the earth, not with the plethora of intractable wars, abusive governments, environmental and economic crises, injustices committed with impunity even in democratic countries. The only hope for our complex, fragile world is human consensus and negotiation, forms of dialogue that continue to be unpopular because they are unwieldy, time-consuming, and often dull. I know, because I try to employ them on a regular basis with my kid, and often we don't get to the end of the conversation. I just pull a dictatorship on him, throw him over my shoulder, and let him scream.

But he's getting too big and too smart for me to do that anymore, and I am too aware of how my tyrannical methods are doomed to failure because they poison our little society with bad feelings. When arguments escalate, especially around dinnertime, Timo will refuse to sit or eat; then my husband and I will fight over the right way to socialize a three-year-old while the meal gets cold and we lose our appetites.

Viewed from a distance, these moments can be funny, and instructive, but when I'm in the moment, anger holds me in a vise grip. Other negative emotions are there, too, but anger is the heaviest. It keeps me from moving freely; it keeps my mind from loosening up enough to understand that the boy likes it when we are utterly focused on him. It's what he craves. We've usually been away from him all day; dinnertime is a perfect opportunity for him to arrange his starring role in a big drama. If we take fifteen minutes to play and chat with him before one of us disappears into dinner-making mode, he is usually ready to come and sit down with us again by the time the food is ready to eat.

Even though I understand this mechanism, I forget it. My anger fills the space quickly, like a brush fire, igniting whatever it touches. Anger is an important emotion; it can be the flame that wakes us to injustice and the need to speak out, inspiring us to be brave. But when I'm angry at my young child, I am usually stuck in old patterns of reaction, which is a form of laziness. In Thailand, where I've lived and meditated in the Theravada Buddhist tradition, the expression for quick-tempered anger is *jai-raan* (hot heart). Likewise, when someone tells you to calm down, they say, *Jai yen-yen* (cool your heart).

Jai yen-yen. Like most wise advice, it's hard to implement in the heat of the moment. "Angry! I will be really mad, Timo, if you draw on the couch! So give me the marker!" With that, I lunge over the cushions and try to grab the felt pen out of his hand. But with reflexes quicker than mine, he easily eludes me and hops into a run, clearing the corner of the sofa and dashing back into the dining room. Where there are white walls all around (albeit much fingerprinted).

He stands beside the antique blue china cabinet, holding up the black marker like a knife. His face teeters between a frown and a laugh. "Come on, Timo. Please don't draw on the cabinet. Mama will be very sad. Let's get *your* markers out. We'll draw something together." With that, I turn my back on him and go into the kitchen, where I noisily rummage through the kiddy drawer, praying he will follow my lead.

Beside the kiddy drawer is a glassed-in shelf lined with bottles of liquor and wine. What will happen when my spectacularly willful and charming child is fifteen, curious about alcohol and drugs, surrounded by other teenagers who have never heard stories about the Dalai Lama and the importance of loving-kindness? It's just a black marker now, a stain on the furniture, a line on the wall, but who will he become when his own peers make him furious, or when a girl doesn't want to have sex with him?

I don't know who he will become. I only know who is he now. Pure in impulse, pure in power, perfectly honest in his response to the world and to me. I am still so much of his world. That will change swiftly—is already changing.

"Mama, are you sad?" He sidles around the edge of the fridge, with the marker flush against his chest. He's wearing his favorite

Thomas the Tank Engine shirt; a black stain, already two inches wide, spreads like blood below his sternum.

Another *lojong* slogan: *Abandon all hope of fruition.* "I am a little sad."

"Why are you sad?" His voice is like a flute, high and silver, bright with concern.

"Because I don't like it when you don't listen to me. And because your shirt is all dirty now. Lift up the marker."

He holds it away from himself and awkwardly peers down at his chest. I expect him to burst into tears but he smiles. "Look, Mama! What a mess!" He does a spontaneous little jig of delight and offers me the marker, which I take quickly, lest he change his mind. "Thank you, Timo." He pulls the shirt away from his skin so he can see the damage better, and laughs.

Taming the Mind

Khenchen Palden Sherab Rinpoche and Khenpo
Tsewang Dongyal Rinpoche

*If you were to summarize all of Buddhism in one phrase it would be this:
taming the mind. When wild and out of control, the mind is self-centered,
deluded, unskillful, and full of suffering. Calm and disciplined, it is wise,
peaceful, loving, and brings joy to ourselves and others. We can achieve
this, say Khenchen Palden Sherab Rinpoche and Khenpo Tsewang Dongyal
Rinpoche, because the tamed mind is the enlightened mind, and the
enlightened mind is the true mind. This truth is Buddhism's great gift to us.*

Like all sentient beings in this world, we have problems and fears. If
we try to find the cause of our unhappiness, we may think that there
are various things and people in the world that cause our suffering,
but this is not so. The external factors that bring sorrow at one time
can bring joy at another time. We have to look inward to find the
source of our problems. Everything we experience, whether pleasant
or unpleasant, is the result of causes and conditions related to our
state of mind.

The mind produces all our experiences and perceptions. When
we tame the mind so that it rests calmly and clearly, then all our
experiences are open and relaxed. When the mind is peaceful, then
simultaneously the speech and body become peaceful. But if the

mind is uncontrolled, then our words and actions are also out of control. Until we tame the mind, experiences of joy do not last more than a short time, no matter how many external supports we use. It is only by taming the mind that we can truly understand ourselves and others and find ultimate peace and joy.

People do many things in this life to become famous, rich, or successful. These things may provide momentary excitement, but they will not bring lasting happiness. For example, when you die you have to leave your wealth and power behind. No matter how famous you have been, sooner or later you are forgotten. Fame is like a thunderbolt that makes a loud noise but soon becomes silent. This lifetime is very precious because of the unique opportunity we now have to practice the dharma, to remove our ignorance and reveal our inner wisdom. If we do this, it will definitely benefit ourselves and others in this and future lives.

Dharma practice means taming the mind so that its true nature or essence is revealed. When you tame your mind, you find joy in this life and guidance for the *bardo* state after death. Controlling the mind brings peace and confidence and the ability to act with authority to accomplish your goals.

An important point about disciplining the mind is that it is something that we must do for ourselves. We cannot depend on someone else to do it for us. Buddha Shakyamuni taught that you are your own protector and savior. It is through controlling the mind that you will achieve realization and develop inner wisdom.

Taming the mind does not mean eliminating outer objects or suppressing inner thoughts. It means revealing and maintaining the natural state of the mind. Taming the mind has nothing to do with cultivating certain thoughts; it is simply keeping the mind in its fundamental state, where its clarity and wisdom are revealed. The true nature of the mind is calm and clear and full of compassion and love and wisdom.

We do not always experience the mind in this way because ignorance obscures our awareness of the mind's true nature. However, the wisdom nature is always there, and it can shine through and guide us in our lives. Even foolish people have wisdom and can exhibit beautiful qualities because this basic goodness is found equally in all beings. Not only human beings, but all sentient beings have the same nature and potential for enlightenment. The problem is that temporary obscurations cover and distort the essential nature of the mind. When we completely remove the ignorance and reveal the mind's true nature, we are enlightened.

It is important to remember that our true nature is only temporarily hidden. When we know that, we can work with courage and joy to remove the ignorance and let the essence of the mind shine forth. It is important for our diligence to be based on a joyful attitude, because without joyful effort we cannot reveal this true nature.

We need to exert ourselves now because this opportunity will not last forever. We must remember impermanence and the changing stages of life and death. Thinking about death and impermanence is often unpleasant—we usually do not like to acknowledge that everything, including ourselves, is subject to the law of incessant change. But change has good aspects as well, because without change there is no growth or improvement. With the right techniques, skills, and effort, we can learn and make positive changes. By understanding impermanence and causality we can work toward enlightenment and make the most of this human life.

As sentient beings we are constantly searching outside ourselves for happiness; but external causes of happiness never last. Eventually the happiness turns into suffering. After the suffering more happiness may arise, but we never seem to rest in ultimate peace. By reading history or by examining our own experiences we can see that external conditions never bring permanent joy.

This means that we have been looking in the wrong place, like thirsty people digging for water in rocky ground. They know water comes from the earth, so they dig and dig, but they are digging in the wrong place. Likewise, we should not look outward for the source of peace and happiness; it can only be found by looking inward and experiencing the natural state of the mind. The nature of the mind is not hollow or blank; it is profound and blissful and full of wonderful qualities. The mind is the source of both worldly existence and enlightenment, samsara and nirvana. Everything needed to find liberation from suffering is contained within the mind.

All the levels of the teachings by Buddha Shakyamuni are dedicated to subduing the mind and bringing out inner wisdom. Once we are able to tame our wild thoughts, then everlasting inner peace and joy will manifest. This is not a fairy tale—this can be demonstrated by personal experience. Once you have this realization, your mind will be unshakable like a mountain, always calm and peaceful.

Right Concentration

Ringu Tulku

The unique practice that defines Buddhism is insight: deep penetration into the true nature of reality that cuts through the ignorance that causes our suffering and brings us wisdom. But insight is not possible without a calm and concentrated mind, for a mind that constantly flits from thought to thought and perception to perception sees only the illusory surface of reality. The Tibetan Buddhist teacher Ringu Tulku offers us this outstanding instruction in shamatha, or mindfulness practice, the essential starting place of enlightenment.

All the different kinds of Buddhist meditation can be categorized into either of two techniques. In Sanskrit these are called *shamatha* (concentration) and *vipashyana* (insight); in Tibetan they are called *shiné* and *lhakthong*. *Shi* means "peace" or "tranquillity," and also "subsiding." *Né* means "stable abiding." Thus, *shiné* can be translated as "calm abiding." *Lhak* means "extraordinary," and can also mean "clear" and "vivid," or "without any obstruction." *Thong* means "seeing." *Lhakthong* therefore is "clear seeing" or "special insight." Of the two aspects of meditation, shiné is the means to make the mind calm, stable, and peaceful, and lhakthong will lead us to clearly see the truth, the true nature of everything. All meditations are included in these two.

There are different traditions regarding the order in which these should be practiced. Some say that shiné has to come first, otherwise, it will not be possible to see the true nature of mind. Normally our mind is in too much turmoil, too confused, rough like a wild churning sea. First, the mind has to become calm and thereby eventually clear. When the mind is calm and clear, this forms the condition to see its true nature.

Then again, it is said that there is a danger in just letting the mind dwell in calmness and clarity for too long. The ego can get attached to this state, which is experienced as being so nice that it can result in falling into the extreme of tranquillity. If this happens, no further progress will be possible. Thus a second tradition says that one should not try to completely attain shiné before beginning to practice lhakthong. Once a certain level of shiné is reached, it is advised to take a break and proceed to lhakthong meditation. According to a third tradition, one should train in lhakthong first, since a certain amount of understanding is needed as a prerequisite to any practice.

In my view these differences in approach are not that important at the moment. It is vital for all of us to make our mind calm and clear, not only as a means to see the truth, but to enable us to deal with our emotions and to be more relaxed in our everyday lives. Furthermore, once the mind is calm, there is a greater chance of seeing clearly. How much is then seen depends upon the extent to which we look and know how to look. Both aspects are necessary, and in the end they should be in union.

As for shiné meditation, the main idea can be described as follows. If water is clouded by dirt, an easy method to clarify it is to leave it undisturbed and to let the dirt settle by itself. Similarly, if the mind is left to itself without interference, its waves, confusions, and bubblings will slowly subside, and it will become calm and clear. The technique, therefore, is very simple. Nothing at all is done. Then again, not doing anything is not that easy. So we have to start by doing something to occupy our mind very lightly, occupying it only to the extent that not too many things can take place within it.

For shiné meditation it is traditionally said that the physical posture is very important, since body and mind have a very deep relationship. The posture of the body affects the mind in many ways. Once the physical posture is correct, its effect on the mind will be very positive. There is a story in the sutras in which a group of monkeys watch some arhats meditating in the woods. Later these monkeys were seen sitting in the same posture. Through this, they actually attained the state of shiné.

The correct posture for shiné meditation is called "the seven-point posture." Once one is used to it, it is very comfortable and meditation can be sustained for long periods without feeling physical pain or discomfort. Of the seven points, the first is most important: the back should be as straight as possible. The other six points are just aids to facilitate this. If we are able to do so, we should sit cross-legged, ideally in the full vajra-position. If we find it too difficult, we should just sit on a chair and not worry—Maitreya himself, the future Buddha, sits on a chair.

The hands should be in the so-called *dhyana* mudra, the right hand on top of the left and the thumbs slightly touching each other. This helps to balance the shoulders. The shoulders should not lean to the right or to the left, since the first will promote the arising of desire and the second the arising of anger. The hands can also sometimes rest on the knees. The chest and the shoulders should be expanded to allow the breath to flow in and out as deeply as possible. The neck should neither be held to the back nor to the front too much; it should just slightly bend forward so that the Adam's apple is not seen. The teeth should be a bit apart and the lips slightly parted as well, so that it is possible to breathe through them if wanted. The tongue should touch the upper palate and be placed flatly against it. This is a very good way to prevent having to swallow saliva too often.

The central point is to relax the eyes. As soon as the eyes are relaxed, the body and mind are relaxed as well. Without relaxing the eyes, there is no way to relax the body and mind. Some people prefer to close their eyes, but according to the Tibetan Buddhist tradition, the eyes should not be completely closed. They should be left slightly open, neither looking too far away nor too close, and not getting cross-eyed either. This can be seen from buddha images or from the photographs of great masters. Though the eyes are not closed, the gaze should not be tense or focused on anything in particular. The eyes should be just lightly open. Again, this is a general rule, so it does not always apply. Sometimes, when the mind is very active, it can be better to close the eyes. At other times, the mind may get so sleepy that the eyes will close involuntarily. In this case, it may be advisable to open them quite wide and even look up high into the sky or into the far distance.

In shiné meditation, the posture of the mind is what is truly essential. The mind should be completely relaxed. To achieve this relaxation, we should first try to feel our body being totally relaxed. Although we sit in this posture, which is slightly tense, within it there should be looseness and spaciousness. When the string tying a bundle of straw is cut, the tension is released and the pieces of straw immediately fall into a perfect circle: there is total release and total order at the same time. Similarly, we should feel this relaxation from the core of our being, and then let the mind be. That is the main point. As long as we are in the present moment, we are relaxed. In shiné meditation a widely used practice is to be just lightly aware of breathing. This is a very suitable method, since breathing happens automatically and we are never without it. Being aware of our breathing we will be here and now, aware of the present moment. That is the central issue. Not being involved in the past or future, we should take a vacation from our hard work and just relax. We should allow ourselves to think, "For fifteen minutes I will be off duty, away from my usual routine of being immersed in my past and future worries." This is possible in all kinds of situations, while sitting in our room or in a railway station, wherever we have a bit of time. There are many methods to just sit and relax. The essential point is to be here and now, in the present moment, neither in the past nor in the future. When using the "breathing method," we should not concentrate on the breath in the literal sense. Our concentration should be very light, since the aim is to loosen our tension while trying to be calm and clear. If we concentrate too much, we will counteract this and build up tension. For this reason, there should be just a light awareness. The mind is allowed to be aware of the process of breathing in and out. This only forms a kind of basis for the mind to settle upon. The eyes and ears are not closed. We are not trying to cut off or avoid anything. When, for instance, a car passes by, this is all right. We should not pursue the event thinking, "This car disturbed me." The passing of the car is just one moment, and then it is over. There is no need to think about it. We should just be with our breathing without wondering, "How do I breathe in and out?" We could occupy our mind with anything in this way, not only with breathing. The aim is to be aware of the present moment and not to think about it. Thinking means to bring something that already happened back through our memory and to analyze it. As soon as we think, we are no longer here but elsewhere. We should let it flow. Whenever we hold on to something, we interrupt the flow.

In learning how to do shiné meditation or any other meditation practice, mere struggle and deliberate trial are of little use. Too much trying is not very helpful. Although a great amount of effort is needed, this effort should consist merely of the willingness to do the practice again and again. There is no real technique, in the sense of something being taught and learned and then applied accordingly. We learn through doing. This can be compared to the way swimming or riding a bicycle is learned. Someone who knows how to do it will say, "Just be flexible and relaxed and don't forget to pedal." Then you sit on your bike and tell yourself, "I have to be flexible and relaxed." But this will not prevent you from falling off. If you keep at it, though, a point will be reached when you find, to your astonishment, that you do not fall down any longer. You have learned how to do it, but do not know how it happened. Once it has happened, there is no more struggle. Almost the same process is true of meditation.

In the Tibetan tradition, the experience of meditation is sometimes described through three characteristics: *dé*, *lhö*, and *yang*. *Dé* means "comfortable" and refers to just sitting comfortably at ease without any pain or discomfort. *Lhö* is the opposite of tightness, and describes a state of total relaxation. *Yang* means "spacious," and it is saying that we should be very open and wide. Meditation is not equivalent to controlling our mind, to putting it into a small box or narrow canal. There is no need to shut our eyes and other senses. We should be open to such an extent that we almost dissolve into and merge with everything. This is not brought about through deliberate trial. Thus these three important features of meditation—feeling comfortably at ease, relaxed, and spacious—may not be achieved very easily. They have to come one by one.

Just in order to learn how to relax, a lot of exercise is needed. We will not find it easy. Just letting go, letting everything be, not doing anything is totally opposite to our usual way of behavior. Once we are able to give in a bit, to relax our muscles, our stomach, our shoulders, and finally our eyes, that in itself is already meditation. Doing a yoga exercise can be helpful. First one feels the total relaxation of the trunk and then gradually the relaxation of the feet, ankles, calves, knees, and thighs. From here, one slowly feels the intestines relax, the kidneys, liver, and so forth. Then one proceeds to the hands and shoulders, to the face and mouth, until one finally arrives at the eyes. The relaxation of the eyes is most vital. According to Buddhism the eyes are directly related to our heart. They are said to be the doors to the mind. Once we can relax our eyes, we can really relax. This is quite difficult, since almost all our tensions are channeled through the heart. In order to learn how to relax the eyes, we should neither fully close nor fully open them. This point is very important.

So, shiné meditation in its actual sense means not doing anything, just letting ourselves be. For this reason, even though a focal point—such as breathing, an image, a light, or a letter—is used to settle the mind, these things are not necessary as such. They are just used when one finds that the mind is too turbulent or distracted. In this situation, it is sometimes helpful to have something that allows the mind to settle down, something that lightly occupies it. This is the only reason why these means are applied, and one could make use of anything that serves this purpose, not just breathing, an image, and so on. In Tibet, pebbles or sticks were sometimes taken as a focus in meditation. The main thing is to know when we are distracted. As soon as this happens, the mind should be lightly settled back on whichever focus is used. Whenever we find that the mind is not really there, we simply bring it back. Meditation is just a means to make ourselves calm, relaxed, and spacious, and thereby eventually clear.

In this context, two faults can arise. One is distraction, a state in which the mind is not present. The other is sleepiness or dullness. Both are not meditation. When distracted, one should apply a bit of introspection. One should either be more alert or more relaxed, whichever proves necessary to bring the mind back to focus. When having fallen into dullness, we should be more alert. We should look up or make ourselves slightly tense. Machig Labdrönma described the right balance in meditation with the example of how to produce thread from yarn by twining the yarn, alternately tightening and loosening it. Similarly, when meditating, there should be a certain tension and a certain softness as well.

As was mentioned before, we have to learn how to meditate by ourselves through trial and error. We have to fall down and get up and do it again. Recently I learned how to swim. In Tibet the opportunity did not arise, and there is no chance to do that in Sikkim where I live. The rivers come down like swords. Last year, I spent some time in Barcelona and was taken to a very nice beach where I was taught how to swim. I did not do very well. I was told that I had to do this and that. Yet, whatever I tried did not work. I always went down head first. Then the people teaching me said, "If you just lie on your back, you will float." That did not work either. At last, I was a bit frustrated and said, "Let it be whatever happens." Then somehow, my ears went in but the rest did not. I floated. It was the most wonderful feeling. And it was actually fear that was preventing it. When there is no fear, we can float. As soon as it comes back, I will go under again. I can float when I know I am in touch.

This captures the way we learn how to meditate. In the beginning, we will often find that we cannot completely relax, we cannot be totally tranquil and peaceful. Sometimes we may even feel that during meditation more disturbances occur than when we are not meditating. Then we may think we are getting worse and worse, but actually this is said to be a good sign. It does not mean that we are more distracted; rather it means that we are more aware of how busy our mind usually is. If we have the feeling that more things come up in our mind, that it is more agitated and unable to be peaceful, this does not mean that meditation is not taking place. During this time many people give up, thinking, "This is too hard. I can't get any peace!" In this situation, patience is needed to be able to carry on. If we patiently continue, we will find it gets much better.

One may wonder whether it is possible to reach enlightenment solely through shiné meditation. Though this is not possible, shiné is indispensable. We may not get enlightened just by being peaceful and clear, but the other part, the part that brings about enlightenment, will almost arise spontaneously once a good and strong state of shiné is reached. This other part is *lhakthong*, or insight, seeing the truth. Once the mind is calm and clear, and we do not get stuck in the experience of calmness and clarity, all we need to do is to look. This is called the union of shiné and lhakthong. This union will result in enlightenment. Shantideva has said in this context, "Insight born from strong shamatha is what totally destroys all the negative emotions." For this reason, shiné is the foremost practice.

Stars of Wisdom

Khenpo Tsultrim Gyamtso

Milarepa was one of the great yogis of ancient Tibet, traveling from place to place, singing his famous spontaneous songs of realization, and spreading the teachings of the Kagyu (Practice) lineage of Vajrayana Buddhism. Khenpo Tsultrim Gyamtso Rinpoche is one of the great yogis of our time, who traveled for decades from country to country, imparting the joy and realization he had gained through deep philosophical study and long solitary practice. Surely it is no coincidence that he often taught, as he does here, from the literary and spiritual treasures that are the songs of Milarepa.

Outside the three realms are shining in freedom
Inside the wisdom, self-arisen, shines
And in between is the confidence of realizing basic being
I've got no fear of the true meaning—that's all I've got!

In this verse from the song "Seven Things That Shine," Milarepa sings about his realization of the true nature of reality. To realize the true nature of reality, the necessary outer condition is for the "three realms" to be "shining in freedom." The three realms refer to the universe and all of the sentient beings within it. Sentient beings inhabit the desire realm, the form realm, and the formless realm, so these three realms include all the experiences that one could possibly have, and they are shining in freedom—they are

self-liberated. (Most sentient beings, including animals and humans, inhabit the desire realm, so named because desire for physical and mental pleasure and happiness is the overriding mental
experience of beings in this realm. The form realm and the formless
realm are populated by gods in various meditative states who are
very attached to meditative experiences of clarity and the total absence of thoughts, respectively.)

"Self-liberation" in one sense means that appearances of the
three realms do not require an outside liberator to come and set
them free, because freedom and purity are their very nature. This is
because appearances of the three realms are not real. They are like
appearances in dreams. They are the mere coming together of interdependent causes and conditions; they have no essence of their own,
no inherent nature. This means that the appearances of the three
realms are appearance-emptiness inseparable, and therefore, the
three realms are free right where they are. Freedom is their basic
reality. However, whether our experience of life in the three realms
is one of freedom or bondage depends upon whether we realize their
self-liberated true nature or not. It is like dreaming of being impris-
oned: If you do not know you are dreaming, you will believe that
your captivity is truly existent, and you will long to be liberated from
it. But if you know you are dreaming, you will recognize that your
captivity is a mere appearance, and that there is really no captivity at
all—the captivity is self-liberated. Realizing that feels very good.

The term "self-liberation" is also used in the Mahamudra and
Dzogchen teachings, which describe appearances as "self-arisen and
self-liberated." This means that phenomena have no truly existent
causes. For example, with a car that appears in a dream, you cannot
say in which factory that car was made. Or with the person who appears in the mirror when you stand in front of it, you cannot say
where that person was born. Since the dream car and the person in
the mirror have no real causes for arising, all we can say about them
is that they are self-arisen, and therefore they are also self-liberated.

When we apply this to an experience of suffering, we find that
since our suffering has no real causes, it does not truly arise, like suf-

fering in a dream. So, it is self-arisen, and therefore it is self-liberated. Since the suffering is not really there in the first place, it is pure and free all by itself. Apart from knowing self-liberation is suffering's essential nature and resting within that, we do not need to do anything to alleviate it.

Thus, Milarepa sings that what one needs on the inside is to realize self-arisen original wisdom. This wisdom is the basic nature of mind, the basic nature of reality, and all outer appearances are this wisdom's own energy and play. Original wisdom is self-arisen in the sense that it is not something created; it does not come from causes and conditions; it does not arise anew, because it has been present since beginningless time as the basic nature of what we are. We just have to realize it. The realization of original wisdom, however, transcends there being anything to realize and anyone who realizes something, because original wisdom transcends duality.

How can we gain certainty about this wisdom and cultivate our experience of it? Since wisdom is the true nature of mind, begin by looking at your mind. When you look at your mind, you do not see anything. You do not see any shape or color, or anything that you could identify as a "thing." When you try to locate where your mind is, you cannot find it inside your body, outside your body, nor anywhere in between. So mind is unidentifiable and unfindable. If you then rest in this unfindability, you experience mind's natural luminous clarity. That is the beginning of the experience of original wisdom. For Milarepa, original wisdom is shining. It is manifesting brightly through his realization of the nature of the three realms and of his own mind.

In the third line, Milarepa sings of his confidence of realizing the true nature of reality, the true meaning. There are the expressions and words that we use to describe things, and the meaning that these words refer to—here Milarepa is singing about the latter. He is certain about the basic nature of reality, and as he sings in the fourth line, he has no fear of or doubts about what it is. He is also not afraid of the truth and reality of emptiness. When he sings, "That's all I've got," he is saying, "I am not somebody great. I do not have a high realization. All I have got is this much." This is Milarepa's way of being humble.

One can easily be frightened by teachings on emptiness. It is easy to think, "Everything is empty, so I am all alone in an infinite vacuum of empty space." If you have that thought, it is a sign that you need to meditate more on the selflessness of the individual. If you think of yourself as something while everything else is nothing, it is easy to get a feeling of being alone in empty space. However, if you remember that all phenomena, including you yourself, are equally of the nature of emptiness, beyond the concepts of "something" and "nothing," then you will not be lonely. You will be open, spacious, and relaxed.

In the context of this verse, it is helpful to consider a stanza from the *Song of Mahamudra* by Jamgon Kongtrul Lodro Thaye:

From mind itself, so difficult to describe,
Samsara and nirvana's magical variety shines.
Knowing it is self-liberated is view supreme.

"Mind itself," the true nature of mind, original wisdom, is difficult to describe—it is inexpressible. And from this inexpressible true nature of mind come all the appearances of samsara and nirvana. Appearances do not exist separately from the mind. What appears has no nature of its own. Appearances are merely of mind's own energy, mind's own radiance, mind's own light. And so appearances are a magical display. To describe the appearances of samsara and nirvana as a magical variety means that they are not real—they are magic, like a magician's illusions. Appearances are the magical display of the energy of the inexpressible true nature of mind. When we know this, we know that appearances are self-arisen and self-liberated, and that is the supreme view we can have.

Outside the five sense pleasures are shining
Inside the wisdom, free of clinging, shines
And in between is conduct where everything tastes the same

I am not thinking joy and pain are different things—that's all
I am!

In this verse Milarepa sings of the conduct of equal taste and how to
practice it. What we need on the outside to practice equal taste are
the five objects of sense experience: pleasant and unpleasant forms
that appear to our eyes; sounds that we think are pleasant and unpleasant; smells that we enjoy and that we find revolting; tastes that
we like and do not like; and finally inner and outer bodily sensations
that feel good and bad.

The conduct of equal taste sees all of these experiences to be
equal, in the sense that they all equally lack inherent existence. They
are all equally appearance-emptiness. Because Milarepa realizes
this, he sings that on the inside he abides in wisdom—wisdom that
realizes emptiness. This wisdom is therefore free of clinging, free
from attachment to sense experiences as being real. When we think
that good experiences are real, we get attached to them and want
more; when we think bad experiences are real, we are averse to them
and want them to disappear. That way of adopting what we fancy
and rejecting what we do not is completely opposite to the conduct
of equal taste. On the other hand, when we realize that none of these
experiences is truly existent, the conduct of equal taste naturally follows from that realization.

The conduct of equal taste is very similar to the conduct one
performs in a dream when one knows one is dreaming. When we
dream and do not recognize it, although the sensory objects that appear are not truly existent, we do not know that and we cling to
them as being real. However, when we recognize that we are dreaming, we abide in the wisdom that realizes sense objects are dependently arisen mere appearances, appearance-emptiness inseparable,
and we are free of clinging and attachment. When that happens,
whatever sensory objects appear, they do not cause us suffering.

As a result of realizing sense experiences are appearance-emptiness and performing the conduct of equal taste, Milarepa does not
think joy and pain are different things. He is neither attached to

being happy nor afraid of being in pain. He knows that in genuine reality, joy and pain are equal. Milarepa does not differentiate between joy and pain like ordinary people do, because he realizes their basic nature. Milarepa demonstrated this many times, and it is good to look at Milarepa's life story to see how he practiced equal taste and realized the equality of joy and pain. At the end of the verse, Milarepa sings, as a way of preventing himself from being arrogant, that realization of joy and pain's equality is "all I've got!"

> Outside creations are shining in ruins
> Inside the freedom from hope and fear shines
> And in between, I'm not sick with striving or straining, no, no, no!
> I am not thinking right and wrong are two different things—
>   that's all I am!

How is Milarepa able to achieve freedom from the fixations that produce hope and fear? First, he sees that on the outside, "creations are shining in ruins." This means that Milarepa knows that whatever appears on the outside is impermanent, because all things are creations or composites of causes and conditions. When a particular thing's causes and conditions change, that thing will fall apart. Sentient beings make problems for themselves when they think that appearances will last, that the situations they find themselves in are permanent and unchanging. In fact, whatever we do or create, whatever situation we are in, and even we ourselves have no power to remain. Everything is subject to decay.

Realizing that, on the inside Milarepa is free from hope and fear. He is not attached to outer appearances as being permanent, so he has no hope that things will remain nor fear that they will not, no hope that things will come out one way nor fear that they will not.

Then in between, Milarepa sings of how it is a sickness when, while meditating on the genuine nature of reality, one tries to make something happen or tries to change or improve things. The true nature of reality transcends all concepts of what it might be; it is inexpressible and inconceivable. Therefore, the true nature transcends improvement and degradation. So the way to meditate on it is to simply relax within it, free from striving and straining. That is how Milarepa is—he is able to rest in the basic nature of reality in a spacious, uncontrived, natural way.

These first three lines reveal how Milarepa practiced dharma at the end of his life. When it was time for Milarepa to pass away he did not suffer, because he knew that his body and life were subject to decay. Therefore, he had no hope to live forever and no fear of dying. He did not strive or strain to avoid death. He meditated on death's true nature, which transcends even the concept of death, and so he experienced his death as simply another manifestation of the true nature of mind's energy and play. Unlike ordinary beings, for Milarepa death was not frightening. It was blissful.

At the end of the verse, Milarepa sings, "I am not thinking right and wrong are two different things—that's all I am!" Milarepa does not deny that there is any difference between right and wrong, between positive actions and negative ones. Rather, he is free of thinking that right and wrong truly exist. He is free of attachment to right and wrong as having any inherent nature—he knows they are dependently arisen mere appearances.

The way that ordinary people relate to right and wrong, good and bad, and virtue and nonvirtue is to believe that they are real. This is just how someone would relate to a dream of good and bad actions when they did not know that they were dreaming. However, when one realizes the nature of emptiness, one relates to virtue and nonvirtue in a different way, understanding them to be mere appearances that do not truly exist, just as one would during a dream when one knew that one was dreaming. That is Milarepa's perspective.

That is why karma, right, wrong, virtue, and nonvirtue only exist for ordinary sentient beings who have not directly realized the true nature of reality. In contrast, the noble ones, who directly realize the true nature of reality, transcend all concepts of right and wrong. As the Buddha taught in the sutras: "For those belonging to the family of the noble ones, karmic actions do not exist, and results of karmic actions do not exist, either." Since the noble ones have purified themselves of clinging to true existence, they transcend the concepts of virtue and nonvirtue.

The Indian master Aryadeva explained that there are three levels of teachings about virtue and nonvirtue:

> First, the lack of virtue is counteracted,
> Second, the self is counteracted, and,
> Finally, all views are counteracted.

The first level's purpose is to reverse the tendency beginning students have to do things that are negative. In order to accomplish this, students are taught the benefits of performing good actions that are helpful to others, and the suffering that comes from doing bad things that are harmful to others.

At this stage, virtue and nonvirtue's true nature—emptiness—is not taught. Furthermore, in order to have a basis for the explanation that there is an actor who performs actions and experiences their results, the self is described as if it exists. The self is the one who performs actions, good or bad, and then experiences happiness or suffering respectively as a result.

Once students have gained confidence that it is important to perform positive actions and refrain from negative ones, they are introduced to the second level, whose purpose is to reverse the students' clinging to a truly existent self. Students are taught how to analyze the self and determine that the self does not exist in genuine reality. From this, they understand that there cannot be any truly existent virtuous or nonvirtuous actions either, because there is no truly existent actor to perform them. At this stage, virtue and nonvirtue are taught to be nonexistent in genuine reality.

Then, when students have gained certainty in selflessness and emptiness, they are introduced to the third level, whose function is to reverse clinging to any view or reference point at all, even the views of emptiness and selflessness. This level leads students to the realization that reality transcends all of our concepts about what it might be, whether they be concepts of existence, nonexistence, emptiness, or anything else. At this point, we are taught that even the more subtle understanding that we had at the second stage, of things not truly existing, cannot accurately describe the true nature of reality, which lies beyond all concepts. So we transcend even the idea of nonexistence, even the idea of emptiness.

Something from Nothing

Ken McLeod

*What's the most beneficial—and threatening—thing we can do? Nothing.
From ego's point of view, doing nothing is the biggest threat of all, because
we stop cranking out all those story lines and occupations that confirm our
illusory sense of self. But from enlightenment's point of view, doing nothing
is the most beneficial practice of all, because we discover that things are
perfect exactly as they are, with no need for all that painful struggle.
Here's what the Western lama Ken McLeod found when he spent three
weeks doing exactly nothing.*

What is it like to do nothing? I mean, really do nothing, nothing at
all—no recalling what has happened, no imagining what might happen, no reflecting on what is happening, no analyzing or explaining
or controlling what you experience. Nothing!

Why would you even try? We struggle in life because of a tena-
cious habit of wanting life to be different from what it is: The room
you are in is too warm, you don't like your job, or your partner
isn't quite the person of your dreams. You adjust the thermostat,
get a new job, or tell your partner what you need. Now it's too cool,
you are earning less money, or your partner has found some flaws

in you. The more we try to make life conform to our desires, the more we struggle, and the more we suffer. The only way out of this vicious cycle is to accept what arises, completely: in other words, do nothing.

Paradoxically, such radical acceptance opens a way of living that we could hardly have imagined.

Years ago, I attended a three-week retreat in Colorado. I had done many retreats, including seven years in France during which I had no communication with the outside world. There the days were full. We started meditation sessions well before sunrise and ended late in the evening. We had daily and weekly rituals and much preparatory work and cleanup. We practiced different meditation methods, with set periods for practice, set periods for study, and a set number of days on each method. With so much to do and to learn, there was no free time.

This retreat was different. The only meditation instruction was "Do nothing." "That's it?" I thought. "I came here to do nothing for three weeks?" We met for meals, one teaching session in the morning, and one group practice session in the evening. We had a meditation interview every few days. The rest of the time was our own. E-mail, cell phone, text messages, all the usual means of communication weren't available. With no practices to learn, no commentaries to study, no preparations for rituals, I had quite literally nothing to do except sit, lie down, or go for a walk.

My cabin was on a hillside that looked over a magnificent view of tree-covered hills, with a range of mountains just visible on the horizon. The silence was highlighted by the songs of birds, the wind in the trees, rain and thunderstorms, and the grunts, scuffles, or calls of animals in the dark. Every day the sun rose, crossed the sky, and set, with the moon and stars dancing in the night.

"What a relief," I thought, "plenty of time to rest and practice." But I soon found that doing absolutely nothing, not even entertaining myself, wasn't so easy.

Ajahn Chah, one of the great Thai teachers of the twentieth century, gave the following practice instruction:

Put a chair in the middle of a room.
Sit in the chair.
See who comes to visit.

One has to be careful with such instructions. I once gave this to a woman who came to see me and was surprised to learn that she put a chair in the center of her living room, sat in it, and waited for people to visit. When nobody knocked on her door, she decided that meditation wasn't for her. Ajahn Chah was, of course, speaking poetically. Nevertheless, in some sense, all of us are like this woman, waiting for something to happen.

No shortage of visitors for me! Relief, peace, a deep sense of relaxation, joy, and happiness all paid their respects. "Good," I thought. "All this will deepen, and wisdom or insight will come." After all, I had read in many texts that as the mind rests, it naturally becomes clear.

Instead, the visitors continued, but with a difference. The more deeply I relaxed, the more I became aware of stuff inside me, stuff stored in rusting boxes in mildewed basements. Along came memories, pleasant and unpleasant, stories about my life, old desires, boredom, and a sense of futility. I kept pushing these visitors away, or analyzing them, trying to understand them so I could be free of them. I was back in the old struggle, trying to control my experience. The visitors became more disturbing, more demanding of attention. Some harbored hatred and a desire for revenge. Others cried with unfulfilled longing and yearning. Still others drugged me into a dull lethargy. They had no awareness of the beauty and peace around me. I began to lose hope that I would achieve anything in this retreat.

Hope is the one quality left in Pandora's box, and it is not clear whether it is a blessing or a curse. T. S. Eliot, in *Four Quartets*, writes:

I said to my soul, be still, and wait without hope
For hope would be hope for the wrong thing; wait without love
For love would be love of the wrong thing; there is yet faith

But the faith and the love and the hope are all in the waiting.

Wait without hope? The prospect seemed unimaginable. A chill crept down my spine, and I found myself slipping into hope's counterpart, fear. Was I going to sit on the side of this mountain and have nothing to show for it? A consistent theme in the many texts I had read and translated was "No hope, no fear." I had never thought of applying that instruction to my concern about achievement.

For most of us, the demands of each day keep us busy. Hope and fear come as reactions to specific situations—rumors about possible promotions or layoffs, our child's first competition or performance, illness in a parent, and so on. The deeper hopes and fears remain, untended, forgotten perhaps, but there all the same. Again, from *Four Quartets*:

And the ragged rock in the restless waters,
Waves wash over it, fogs conceal it;
On a halcyon day it is merely a monument,
In navigable weather it is always a seamark
To lay a course by: but in the sombre season
Or the sudden fury, is what it always was.

One of my ragged rocks was hope for achievement. I feared an acute disappointment if, at the end of the retreat, all I had done was sit on a mountain and contemplate my navel. Slowly, I realized that to do nothing meant I had to let go of deeply cherished beliefs that I was just beginning to sense—the belief, for instance, that I had to achieve something.

Most of us are quite happy to do nothing for a few minutes, perhaps an hour or two, or, if we have had a particularly demanding stretch, for a day or two, a few days at the most. But to do nothing, to produce nothing, to achieve nothing for a month, a year, six years or more, is quite a different kettle of fish.

I thought of my own teacher, who had spent years in mountain retreats in Tibet. As he had told me himself, he would quite happily have stayed in the mountains, but his teacher had demanded (in the strongest terms possible) that he return to the monastery and teach training retreats. What was it like, I wondered, to be at peace with doing nothing day after day, month after month, year after year?

Then I thought about Longchenpa, the fourteenth-century teacher, whose text was the basis for this retreat. He had spent fourteen years in a cave near Lhasa. What had it been like for him to sit day after day doing nothing?

The depth to which these teachers, and many others like them, had let go of any concern with success or failure was like a knife in my heart. Here I was, practicing for a mere three weeks, worrying about whether I was going to achieve anything. Only now did I appreciate what letting go of hope, ambition, or achievement meant, and I found myself feeling a quite different kind of respect and appreciation for these teachers.

The classical texts have relatively little to say about the emotional turmoil that intensive practice often uncovers. Here, too, these lines from Eliot apply, even though he was writing about old age:

> And last, the rending pain of re-enactment
> Of all that you have done, and been; the shame
> Of motives late revealed, and the awareness
> Of things ill done and done to others' harm
> Which once you took for exercise of virtue.
> Then fools' approval stings, and honour stains.
> From wrong to wrong the exasperated spirit
> Proceeds, unless restored by that refining fire
> Where you must move in measure, like a dancer.

From the beginning of the retreat, space surrounded and permeated my experience, but I had been unable to relate to it. I had been completely caught up in trying to control my experience. Now I stopped ignoring it and just stared into space. My relationship with the emotional turmoil changed, subtly.

Space, I realized, has many dimensions. In front of me was the vast space of the sky. It didn't depend on anything, and nothing depended on it. I watched the play of light and colors as the day passed. When the sun set and the sky lit up with shades of rose and yellow and blue, the space that let me see the sunset didn't take on any color, yet it was not something apart. At night, it became an empty blackness, punctuated by a thousand points of light, but the panorama of stars was not separate from space. Likewise, thoughts, feelings, and sensations are not different from the space that is mind.

Silence is another kind of space. When everything is quiet and suddenly there is a noise, we ordinarily say the silence was shattered. But it's more accurate to say that we forget the silence and listen only to the sound. I started to listen to the silence, around me and inside me.

Time is another dimension. Kant once said that time is the medium in which we perceive thoughts, just as space is the medium in which we perceive objects. Hopes and fears, projections into the future, regrets and joys are all thoughts that come and go in time. Because there was nothing to do with any of them, I began to experience them as comings and goings, like the mists that rose from the ground in the early morning, only to vanish as the day progressed. Some days, what arose was more of a thunderstorm, but, like the thunderstorms in the mountains, the turmoil came and went on its own, leaving the space as it was before and the ground and trees refreshed and rich with life.

I became aware of another dimension, an infinite internal space that had to do with my ability to experience my body. This dimension had more the quality of depth: it seemed to go down forever. There was no bottom. There was no me there. It was like looking into a bottomless abyss, except that sometimes I became the abyss. Years later, when I was discussing this experience with an aging teacher, he used the Tibetan phrase *zhi me tsa tral,* or "No ground, no root."

Two young boys were playing together. One asked the other, "We stand on the ground and the ground holds us up. What does the ground stand on?"

"Oh, my father explained that to me," the second boy said. "The ground is supported by four giant elephants."

"What do the elephants stand on, then?"

"They stand on the shell of a huge turtle."

"What does the turtle stand on?"

The second boy thought for a long time and then said, "I think it's turtles all the way down."

Like the woman in the chair who waited for someone to knock on her door, I had been waiting for something to happen, some experience or insight that would make sense of everything, put all the ghosts to rest and silence the "thousand voices in the night." For decades, I had held the belief deeply embedded in our culture: Ye shall know the truth, and the truth shall make you free.

"You have to be kidding," I thought. "I have to let go of belief in truth?" Slowly, it was becoming clear to me that there is no truth out there—or in there, for that matter. There is only the way we experience things. To let go of this belief required a very different effort. Again, from Eliot:

Wait without thought, for you are not ready for thought:
So the darkness shall be the light, and the stillness the dancing.

Here is where faith and devotion come into the picture. Devotion, whether to a tradition, a practice, a teacher, or an ideal, is the fuel for faith. I had practiced with devotion before, in the form of guru yoga, or union with the teacher. It's a powerful practice, greatly valued in the Tibetan tradition, where there are numerous prayers with titles such as "Devotion Pierces the Heart." The teacher at this retreat exemplified this. He felt such devotion for his own teacher that he could not talk about him without crying.

Faith and devotion do not come easily to me. Now, here, at this retreat, I felt a different kind of devotion for my teachers, and with that understood that there was nothing to do but to experience whatever came through the door.

We have a choice between two very different ways to meet what arises in experience.

The first is to rely on explanation. We interpret our experiences in life according to a set of deeply held assumptions. We may or may not be conscious of the assumptions, but they are there. Even when we explore our experience, we are usually looking for evidence that supports or confirms them. These assumptions are never questioned. They are taken as fundamental. A self-reinforcing dynamic develops that results in a closed system in which everything is explained, the mystery of life is dismissed, new ideas, perspectives, or approaches to life cannot enter and certain questions can never be asked. This I call belief.

The other way is to open and be willing to receive, not control, whatever arises—that is, not only allow but embrace every sensation, feeling, and thought, everything we experience. In this approach, we allow our experience to challenge our assumptions. Here, there are no fundamental or eternal truths, and some things cannot be explained; they can only be experienced. This willingness to open to whatever arises internally or externally I call faith.

This being human is a guest house.
Every morning a new arrival.

A joy, a depression, a meanness,
some momentary awareness
comes as an unexpected visitor.

Welcome and entertain them all!
—RUMI

Early in the retreat, when difficult experiences arose, I would analyze them, trying to understand what had happened and why. I thought this would help to resolve them and then I wouldn't have to be bothered by them. Sometimes I would be completely swallowed by emotions and sensations and only come to my senses a few minutes—or a few hours—later. Frequently, I just couldn't face what was arising. I shut it down, or went for a walk. In short, if what arose didn't fit my picture of what I wanted or needed, I would start doing something.

Gradually, I learned just to stare into space, in any of its dimensions—the sky, the silence, time, or the infinite depth in my own body. I recognized that the only way I could do nothing was, well, to do nothing. I had to receive whatever arose, experience it, and not do anything with it. I needed faith to experience powerful feelings of loneliness, worthlessness, despair, or shame, because I often felt I would die in the process. I recalled how many times my teacher had said this, albeit in different words: "Rest in just recognizing." But no one had said that "just recognizing" might lead to pain so intense that I wouldn't wish it on my worst enemy. And I came to appreciate that all my efforts in previous practice had built the capacity so that I could now rest and just recognize.

When I did open to everything, there was no opposition—there was no enemy. I didn't have to struggle with experience. At the same time, there was no truth, no state of perfection, no ideal, no final achievement. Years later, in a conversation I had with another teacher about this experience, he said, "Don't worry about truth. Just develop devotion so strongly that thinking stops, and rest right there."

Any concept of higher truth creates hierarchy, and with that, authority, boundaries, dualism, and opposition. What various religious traditions, including Buddhism, call truth is better described as a way of experiencing things. Such phrases as "All experience is empty" or "Everything is an illusion" are better viewed as descriptions of experiences: stories, in effect, not statements about reality.

What, then, do we make of all the teachings of various spiritual traditions and other forms of human knowledge? For me, God, karma, rebirth, emptiness, brahman, atman, heaven, hell, all of these are stories that people use to understand, explain, or give direction to their lives. The same holds for scientific views, astronomy, biology, quantum mechanics, or neurology. If we wish to be free of suffering, to be free of struggle, then the way to look at experience is to know "There is no enemy" and stop opposing what arises in experience. Is it difficult and challenging? Yes, but it's possible. And the way to learn to do that is to simply do nothing.

"How strange!" I thought, as the retreat came to a close. "Who would have thought you could find a way of freedom simply by doing nothing?"

Undivided Mind

Rodney Smith

While genuine Buddhist dharma helps us to realize the truth of nonself,
ego tempts us to corrupt the teachings by using them to further solidify our
sense of self. In his memorable phrase, the late Chögyam Trungpa described
this as "spiritual materialism." Rodney Smith looks at the special chal-
lenges as Buddhism enters a society in which politics, economics, culture,
psychology, and, yes, sometimes our spiritual practice, all conspire to
celebrate the self.

Over the last half-century, Buddhist practices in the West have
grown in popularity. Mindfulness has become associated with stress
reduction, enhanced immunological protection, psychological well-
being, and profound states of happiness. In many cases, mindfulness has been uncoupled from the Buddha's teaching altogether and
is a stand-alone cognitive therapy for the treatment of various mental difficulties, from depression to obsessive-compulsive disorder.

The term *anatta*, which means "no [permanently abiding] self
or soul," is at the heart of the Buddha's teaching, but with our Western emphasis on psychological health it is perhaps inevitable that
this essential aspect of the teaching is downplayed or even avoided.
Emptiness, after all, stands in opposition to many of our most important values, such as self-reliance, individual initiative, and the

pursuit of pleasure. We want the contentment and happiness promised by the Buddha, but with "me" fully stabilized and intact.

This selective approach to Buddhism would seem to allow the best of both the Eastern and Western worlds. We can use the techniques and practices that serve our immediate purpose without asking the deeper spiritual questions concerning our very existence. Best of all, the methods work, and the benefits of greater mindfulness dramatically affect both our mental health and the ease of our life.

The story would end happily here, except that there is a rub when we pare back the dharma, the Buddha's teaching. Externally we see the Earth's environment eroding before our eyes, the population soaring, and our natural resources diminishing. We see unparalleled greed and anger forming greater divisions within an ever-shrinking planet. At a time when the world pleads for kindness and compassion, we see cultures continuing their ancient bickering while forgetting their shared heritage.

Internally our problems continue as well. We hurt, and we do not understand why. Fear, desire, and grief fill our life. Our psychological sophistication should solve our problems, but therapies and self-improvement methods do not seem to diminish our isolation and separation. We would like to feel compassion for all beings, but our own problems are so demanding that we have little time to include others in our heart. We try to compensate for these shortcomings with more socially engaged activities, but we find that our motivation is often based in righteousness, which further divides the world.

Through all our techniques and procedures, the sense-of-I remains the cornerstone of our existence. When we look at our experience, we appear to be the center of the universe. All experiences seem to confirm our central place in life, and every input is interpreted through the lens of self. We hear about the corrupted power of the ego but seem unable to shake off this ever-present sense-of-me. Its authority seems absolute; most of us eventually acquiesce to its rule, and we engage our dharma practice carrying the sense-of-me along within our spiritual development.

Many of us incorporate a gentler and kinder spiritual "me" into our practice, which is in opposition to the worldly "me," the trouble-making twin that needs a resolution. We then play the familiar theme of divide and conquer, pitting our spiritual ideals against our worldly reactions. Eventually we see that calling the ego different names serves to strengthen its overall grip and control, which inevitably leads to greater pain and ill will.

Some of us pursue the path of wisdom to weaken the ego's influence, and we have genuine insights into the ego's insubstantiality, but we may return from those revelations with the power and force of "me" very much intact. The ego has a way of claiming reference to its own demise by saying, "Oh, I just had an experience of my own emptiness." No matter what we do, no matter how many revelations we have regarding our true nature, we still seem to organize the world around the basic premise that "I" am in here looking out at everything else.

At some point the sincere dharma practitioner realizes that as long as the "I" is the governing force behind thoughts and emotions, then our internal world will be filled with abstract arguments and the external world will be laden with conflict and struggle. We begin to further understand that the cause of our suffering is not what we do but the way we perceive, and until this obstacle is addressed, all actions of body, speech, and mind will predictably reinforce our old perceptions of self and other, problem and solution, and limitation and freedom.

Spiritual practice is stepping out of the assumed reality of "me" by understanding what the "me" is and withdrawing energy from its perceptual fixations. The Buddha made the realization and integration of anatta central to his teaching—we are without separate existence; that is a fact. When we align all our practices and efforts with this fact, the spiritual path becomes quite simple and transforms everything we do. All the monasteries, renunciations, restraints, skillful means, full-lotus posture, and nose-tip awareness, all of it, has only this intended purpose. We must be very careful not to carry the assumption of separation to the practices that have the intended purpose of stepping out of self-deception. If we do, we will be reinforcing our egoic conditioning and move in the opposite direction from the freedom of the Buddha.

Much of my early practice carried this contradiction. My heart genuinely sought the truth, but I conceived of freedom as a very long and arduous process that needed focused determination and hard work. My efforts were directed toward surmounting myself. "I" was the problem, and "I" would apply effort toward resolving the difficulty of "me." Often my teachers spoke of lifetimes necessary to achieve awakening and the long cultivation of mental qualities that freedom depended on. I thought of freedom as something that I was working toward but that was not accessible now.

After a few years of strenuous retreating, I ordained as a Buddhist monk and went on a pilgrimage to Bombay in January 1980, to visit the renowned sage Nisargadatta Maharaj. I had known of him years earlier through his book *I Am That*. After a few days of bantering back and forth about my attachment to being a monk, he said, "You are like a man holding a flashlight, trying to run beyond its beam. The view you are holding . . . is undermining your intent."

"You don't understand Buddhism," I retorted. "You do not understand the truth," he replied. I was righteous, but he was right, and his message stuck. As the days unfolded, I lost my arrogance and my identification with the Buddhist robes, leaving me naked and exposed. By directly pointing to the truth, Nisargadatta destroyed my spiritual structure, purpose, and frame of reference. In their absence, something awoke with an upsurge of energy that seemed impossible to contain. It exploded with the revelation of what the Buddha was pointing to: The path that Nisargadatta revealed was not a search but a find, not a struggle but an abiding, not a cultivation but something intrinsic to all. I had been committed to the long-enduring mind of practice but not the essence, not the inherent freedom that was immediately available. From this vantage point, there seemed far too much methodology in the Buddhism I had been practicing and not enough release.

The Buddha's Eightfold Path can either build upon or dismantle the sense-of-self, depending upon how we use it. When aligned
within its proper orientation, the path appears like a perfectly
formed diamond, each facet complimenting the beauty of the whole.
After my meeting with Nisargadatta, the Buddha's teaching became
breathtaking in its simplicity and elegance. The entire path was, and
had always been, accessible. Prolonged retreats in silence or conversations over dinner had the same reference point. Nothing was ever
at odds with its opposite. Every practice and action had its place and
appropriate time, but never contradicted or enhanced what was already there. Everything was perfectly together, and every movement
arose from that perfection.

This was the beginning of my understanding of lay Buddhism.
A lay Buddhist is one who fully embodies his or her entire life of
work, family, and relationships without spiritually prioritizing any
activity. From this perspective all moments are equally precious,
and whether we are practicing formal meditation on retreat or
showing up for ordinary moments of our lay life, freedom is never
diminished. The unequivocal resolve not to move away from where
we are is essential. Once we abandon the belief that there is a more
spiritually useful moment than the one we are in, we have embraced
our life and infused it with the energy for awakening.

There are three impediments to lay Buddhist practice. The first is
the belief that monasticism and long retreats are the only way to
realize one's true nature. In Asia monasteries have served as the central training ground for aspiring Buddhist practitioners, and because of this strong history within a monastic tradition, much of
Buddhism is derived from that formal culture. Now, as the Buddhist
tradition settles in the West, monasteries have played a diminishing
role in the training and teaching of Buddhism, and in their place
residential retreat centers have formed as substitute monasteries.
The lay Western Buddhist often undertakes intensive training during residential retreats, which last from a few days to several months,
much as their predecessors did within monasteries in previous cen-

turies. All of this has given rise to an emphasis on a silent, secluded life as being central to Buddhist training.

For a few people, a full lifetime as a monastic or living many years on retreat is a wise direction. Each of us has a unique spiritual design that pulls us toward freedom. The problem arises when we listen to others for our direction, or think we "should" do something because others have done it in the past. Spiritual growth is a fine-tuning of our ear to the needs of our heart.

What obscures this understanding in many of us is the belief that the silent retreat is a priority over other expressions of life. When we believe we are not where we need to be for spiritual growth, we relegate our daily life to a secondary tier. We energetically pull out of our spiritual life and wait for the appropriate secluded moment in order to fully engage. Leaning toward or away from any experience creates an anticipation of fulfillment in the future, and the sacred that exists here and now is lost. Discovering the sacred within all moments is the hallmark of awakening.

We often feel our everyday existence is a distraction from our spiritual intention. When this happens, life is divided between the sacred and mundane, and the mind pits one concept against the other. But belief shapes reality, and if the belief is maintained that the sacred lies somewhere else other than Now, our spiritual life will be governed by that limitation. The truth is that the sense-of-self is not separate from the moment in which it is arising, any more than the sense-of-self is outside the mind that it thinks it possesses. In fact, realizing the undivided mind also heals the dualistic notion of "me" being outside the moment.

We cannot delay fully embracing the moment. To do so maintains the divisions within the mind, the division between the mind and the body, and the division between the organism and its environment. All divisions are attempts to keep us from the truth of what is right here. When this is understood by the sincere practitioner, there can be no more hesitation, no more postponement, and no more pulling back and waiting for a more opportune time. It is literally now or never.

Suddenly the Buddha is found in the middle of relationships, work, and family, within all activities, reactions, thoughts, and emotional responses. Nothing is outside Now, because no boundary is drawn to separate Now from then. The message of the Buddha is equally relevant in all locations and at all times. Until this is fully realized and until there is no movement to escape this environment for a better spiritual setting, we will continue to suffer.

The second way in which lay Buddhist practice is impeded is through misunderstanding the teaching of the long-enduring mind. Buddhism is full of metaphors of time that disarm us. "You have cried more tears than the waters of the great oceans," says the Buddha, speaking of our endless lifetimes in terms of inconceivable numbers.

I have heard some students express hopelessness with these numbers. They interpret the metaphors to mean that it takes endless reincarnations to achieve freedom. I believe the Buddha uses these analogies to point toward patience. The numbers he uses are so vast that he seems to be taking time away, but he certainly is not discouraging our efforts. When time is removed, so is the future expectation of what and when something might occur. Anticipation is actually counterproductive to the practice, because by waiting to be fulfilled in the future, we drift away from what is immediately present.

Perhaps the Buddha's use of time is also an attempt to motivate us out of complacency. Through these analogies he seems to be pointing out that if we do nothing, nothing will change, and we will spend endless lifetimes lost in our divided mind. These examples are a call toward urgency—but it is an urgency moderated with patience. Patience is essential on the spiritual path, but delay is not. Patience invites the timeless back in, and practicing becomes a waking game, not a waiting game, because patience is the state of full wakefulness.

The most important understanding for a lay Buddhist is the immediate availability of awakening. Awakening need not arrive after a long, protracted practice history unless we believe that this is necessary. We deliberately delay our readiness because we are divided about what we really want. We practice until we are tired of preparing for what has always existed here and now, then we become quiet and surrender.

The question of readiness is really a question of intentionality. Do we want this or not? If we do, we have to look squarely at our competing interests. We can use our time most skillfully by observing the value and limitation of our opposing desires. A fully engaged lay life allows continuous feedback regarding those interests. Most of us indulge our desires rather than learn about their limitations, but that learning opportunity is always present. Again, it is the sincerity of the student that will determine whether her life is a hindrance or a support to her spiritual growth.

A third way a lay approach to spiritual fulfillment can be impeded is by investing the sacred within particular practices and conditions. When I was younger, I followed the example of an experiment once performed by Krishnamurti: I placed a rock that held no special significance on my mantel and bowed to it each day. I did this deliberately to see whether I could infuse a unique quality into something completely ordinary, simply by incorporating the rock within a morning ritual. At the end of a month, the rock held a special, holy place in my perception.

The Buddha statue, the *zafu* (cushion) we sit upon, the saintly picture or poem, the states of mind accessed in meditation, solitude, or even nature itself, can all become accentuated beyond the ordinary by infusing them with special attention. When we invest the sacred into specific conditions, we feel spiritual only when we are having those experiences. The rest of life goes spiritually unnoticed.

Spiritual forms and rituals can be very helpful in focusing our intention and providing a doorway to the sacredness of all life. They can awaken a sensitivity of heart and allow our mind to become quiet. Forms and rituals become a problem when they stop representing a gateway into oneself and become an exclusive presentation of the sacred, such as the belief that the only way to commune with God is by going to church or taking a walk in nature, or that the only way to meditate is to be alone in quiet surroundings. When we think of rituals and forms as the only way to access the sacred, the rest of our life is placed on spiritual hold.

The lay Buddhist begins to recover the sacred in the most remote areas of life, in the midst of difficulty and dissatisfaction, loneliness and despair. The reality of problems is challenged and investigated, and life begins to thrive free of circumstances and conditions. The heart takes over and is resurrected from the conditioned habits of mind.

The lay Buddhist harbors no defense, seeks no shelter, and avoids no conflict for the resolution of wholeness. It is here in the middle of our total involvement that this alchemy of spirit can best be engaged. Our life becomes focused around this transformation as our primary intention for living. We find everything we need immediately before us within the circumstances and conditions we long begrudged ourselves. Spiritual growth becomes abundantly available and is no longer associated exclusively with any particular presentation of form.

Rustbelt Dharma

Richard Eskow

Richard Eskow goes back to his childhood home of Utica, New York, to report on an unlikely community of Burmese Buddhists there. What he finds in the memories of then and realities of now are impermanence, change, and suffering, the Buddhist teachings he's been studying made real. He rediscovers the place he was from, the place we are all from.

Utica, New York, was a factory town when I was born here, famous for corruption and violence, for the vanished Mohawk tribe, for white bread and cheap beer and the Erie Canal. That city's gone, dying like the rest of the Rust Belt: Utica's population is down 40 percent. Incomes are less than half the national average. Nearly half the buildings downtown have been torn down.

I left Utica forty-seven years ago, age ten, and never returned. The day I left, John Kennedy had four months to live. They were advertising a new TV show called *The Fugitive*. Radios played "Surf City," "Memphis," and bad-girl group The Angels promising a "beating" in "My Boyfriend's Back." "You're gonna be sorry you were ever born," they sneered. "If I were you I'd take a permanent vacation."

And now, instead of The Angels, devas. Refugees, including Buddhists from war-torn regions in Asia, have arrived in Utica. The monks who led Burma's "Saffron Revolution" came here, along with Cambodian and Vietnamese exiles. Their presence gave me a reason to return. There was something I didn't want to face here, some reason I never came back. I'd first engaged with Buddhism as something exotic, another form of escape like many I'd tried. Impermanence, interconnectedness, *dukkha* (suffering), the nature of self—they had been abstract ideas to me. Maybe seeing this place again and meeting these people would make them more real. For years I'd run away from the frightened kid I'd been. Maybe now I was ready to face this place, and whatever remained of this place in me.

"Sin City USA!" screamed the cover of a 1959 magazine about Utica. "Corrupt Policemen, Racketeers Laughing at The Law . . . An Empire of Vice and Drugs." A few years later the town's prosperity began to fade, until finally even the hit men left for more promising territory. The house where I spent my first few months of life is now boarded up, abandoned like most on the block. Drug deals go down on the street outside. But three blocks away, kindly monks encouraged me to eat an apple and sip a Thai energy drink. "I spent ten years in prison for pro-democracy activities," said U Pyinya Zawta, executive director-in-exile of the All Burma Monks' Alliance. "There I suffered the pain of torture."

The Burmese monks were brought here by the Mohawk Valley Resource Center for Refugees, the hub of a thirteen-thousand-person immigrant community that makes up roughly 20 percent of the city's population. Most of Utica's two thousand Burmese are ethnically Karen Christians, along with some Muslim families and two or three hundred Buddhists.

Some Buddhists speak of karmic residue, *vasana*, as "perfume." "After you scream," said the Zen teacher Dainin Katagiri, "something is still there . . . not as a shadow, but as something in your body and mind." At the age of eight I was held in our family's garage for hours by a gang of older kids, stabbed nineteen times with a rusty hatpin. U Pyinya offers no specifics about his ten-year ordeal. Instead, he told me how his experience with HIV-infected prisoners led him to build the first HIV facility in Burma.

Peeling paint and crayon scribblings marked the walls of the tiny house he shared with three other monks. I asked him if monasticism and political activism are in conflict. "The Buddha taught us that we need to work for the whole universe," he answered, "and for all living beings to be peaceful and happy." Burmese visitors wandered in and out of the house, but activity stopped when the BBC's Burmese-language news broadcast came on, and the monks huddled around the radio.

"Do you meditate?" U Pyinya Zawta asked me. "You seem like that. Calm." I thanked him, thinking my wife might disagree. What does he expect now for Burma? "Things will get worse," he said. "Soldiers are raiding villages, raping and robbing the people there. There will be more poverty. They'll keep recruiting younger and younger child soldiers. We hear they are recruiting them at fourteen and fifteen now. Burma was very rich in jade, sapphire, natural gas, tea . . . but the military doesn't share it with the people. In a country rich with natural gas, people can't get electricity more than a couple of days a week."

Poppies are a natural resource there, too. Burma reportedly supplies more than half of the United States' heroin. How's this for interconnectedness? Americans who die from overdoses in cities like Utica are victims of Burma's generals, too. A question I hesitated to ask: Do they feel their uprising failed? "We're satisfied that more people know about Burma now. The world community is much more aware of the brutality of the military regime." He pauses. "We will continue to make people aware of Burma's problems."

U Gawsita, the public face of the Saffron Revolution, wandered in and out of the room with what seemed like indifference. Later I heard him say in a taped interview that life in Utica was difficult because he couldn't understand the language. I asked his fellow monk U Agga how they handled loneliness. "We meditate and pray and develop our loving-kindness. We can't call or e-mail our families, because the regime controls all communications. If we miss them, we meditate more."

Utica's Burmese have adapted their folk traditions, moving

their annual Thingyan Water Festival from April to July to accommodate the long winters. The number nine—*ko*—is considered good fortune in Burmese tradition. Traveling parties of eight sometimes brought along a symbolic "ninth member" for luck, and traditionally nine monks would perform the ritual that dispels restless ghosts.

Those ghosts may have to linger now. All but eight Burmese monks in the United States have been forced into lay life, working at meatpacking plants and other blue-collar jobs. In response, the Utica monks have formed the All Burma Monks' Alliance to build a monastery and publicize Burma's struggle.

"Young Girls Led into Lives of Degradation," headlines shouted in 1959. "Joy Houses Ran the Gamut from Tawdry to Posh Pleasure Palaces for the Well-Heeled." I left Utica before puberty, a presexual being as celibate as a monk. The erotic images I saw here were brutal or tawdry: the nude Marilyn Monroe calendar in the gas station, the sordid sex-and-violence covers of *Police Gazette* and *True Detective* ("No Mercy for Mary! Pretty Chicago Brunette Loses Her Fight against a Killer") in the neighborhood barbershop.

Others have sensed a degraded sexual perfume here, too: "Most corrupt, vial [sic] city in New York state," one online comment reads. "Hey, remember when the Mayor said Utica doesn't have $2 hookers, it has $20 hookers?" reads another. Utica has several strip joints but no bookstores.

The city was a "processing hub" for Vietnamese refugees, four or five hundred of whom stayed and built a temple. A photo of their monks' induction ceremony shows women marching single file down Miller Street, baskets on their heads and children in costumes at their feet. The temple's erecting a statue of Quan Am, Bodhisattva of Compassion. Perhaps her intercession will help the city's Amerasians, mixed-race children of U.S. soldiers and Vietnamese mothers, brought here after Congress granted them citizenship. As small children some of them lived on Vietnam's streets, bearing the poetic-sounding but heartless name *bui doi* ("dust of life"). Some, their fathers unknown, say they don't know their true names. Others wonder where they're "from."

The night I returned, I found a pharmacy in an unfamiliar industrial area. Inside, loudspeakers played only the oldies of my childhood. I remembered an old *Twilight Zone* episode: a man returns to the poor neighborhood where bullies once tormented him, only to become a trapped child again. I wondered how far we were from my old home and keyed the address into my iPhone: "Driving time: One minute."

The pharmacy was built on the site of a White Tower burger joint. The ice cream parlor had been replaced by a body shop. They'd torn down the Pontiac dealership where a salesman once lifted a tarp to show me the taillights on the new Bonneville—a "company secret"—and then said, "Son, promise me you'll never sell cars for a living."

Walking toward our old home, I saw a friend's house, where his drunken mother once said, "Shut up or I'll smash your lips." I passed the corner where kids from another block threw rocks at me just for the hell of it. In contrast to the now-abandoned house my parents brought me home to after I was born, the gray-and-white house we moved into a few months later was well maintained. The garage was gone.

My earliest memory: I'm sitting on the floor of this house, playing with blocks as the babysitter leaves. I can still see her clearly, smiling as she kneels down to spell my nickname with the blocks. I see that, too, red letters on cream-colored blocks: "R-I-C-K-Y." Some might say her act bound me to my identity, my ego, *samsara*. But she showed me what words are. She gave me my name. I miss her.

A transistor radio upstairs once played a saxophone instrumental called "Stranger on the Shore," making me sad in a way I wanted to feel over and over. Outside, when I was four, a factory whistle sounded in the distance and the sky seemed to turn gold. I felt completely alone in the universe. I tried to find that feeling again for a long time.

I set off for my school, John F. Hughes, a third of a mile away, and found I still knew every turn of a walk I hadn't taken for nearly half a century. Approaching the building, I remembered something I'd heard decades later in a support group for alcoholics and addicts: "The minute I walked into kindergarten, I needed a goddamned drink."

The Thai teacher Ajahn Chah once spoke about dukkha and rebirth, using the Utica-friendly metaphor of a boxer who only ducks after his teeth have been knocked out. "You have to duck before they slug you," he said. *Dukkha* is usually translated as "suffering," but some say it means "craving" or even "addiction." Ajahn Chah said, "Dukkha sticks on the skin and goes into the flesh."

Happy memories return, too: Oneida Avenue, at the hill's summit, limning the farthest reaches of my childhood. The cemetery, with knobbed stone gates like a troll's gateway. Train tracks, now gone, where I'd look down the line and imagine I was seeing California.

The barbershop's gone. In 1962, I was getting a haircut there when an air-raid drill sounded. It was illegal to be outside during a drill, but the barber sprayed me with hair tonic to drive me away. "Get the fuck outta here," he said. Reeking of Vitalis, I walked home through deserted streets as sirens wailed. Now I cut through the same vacant lots, behind the same brick buildings, which today also stood vacant. Two bikers drank beer on their porch, motorcycles gleaming at the curb. On my block an old woman watched me suspiciously until I introduced myself. Everyone you knew is gone, she said, listing one family name after another. Dead, or moved to New Hartford, a nicer town up the road.

A small boy stared at me. He was dark-skinned, something unimaginable on this street in my segregated childhood. My Utica's as ancient for him as the Wright Brothers were for me. There's a picture of me using my cell phone outside the monks' house. It shows a man in black clothes of no known 1950s fashion. A headset flashes in his ear. The object in his hand links him to the entire world. He's an emissary from my childhood's future visiting refugees from its agrarian past.

The next day I joined the monks for lunch. As Burmese women served food and shared the meal, two refugee children lingered outside. Where do you guys go to school? "Hughes." Me too, I said—fifty years ago. They laughed. It is funny, though I once longed for adulthood and escape from its playground. How do they like Hughes? An American answer: "It's okay."

U Agga described a shootout outside their front door last winter. "Bang! Bang!" he says. "Two bodies. Many police came, with flashing lights. Scary." These monks faced down an entire army, but nothing prepared them for a shootout in the darkness and blood in the dirty white snow. Outside the house was a garden, its fence and gate made of woven branches in the traditional way. Once I had a garden in Utica, too, with carrots and morning glories. I could never wake up early enough to see the flowers' blossoms, which only appear at daybreak. Finally my father carried me outside to look at them. I only saw them that one time, but they were beautiful.

From the monks' garden I saw this on the street outside: An African woman in hijab trailed by two burly teenagers, watched by blond kids inside a house draped with a giant American flag. Villagers from Vietnam and Cambodia passing each other in the midday sun. A fat, shirtless, ponytailed white man driving down the center of the street on a tractor, pulling a trailer filled with junk.

A tattooed Burmese man sees our rental car. "Where are you from?" he asks. "I'm from *here*," I say. The words feel alien in my mouth. He rolls up his T-shirt for the photographer, a cigarette dangling from his lip like James Dean. His tattoo shows a dove flying over a "Mother Hen," which either represents his mother country or the entire world. It's not clear which. "Peace for the people," he says.

Utica's Cambodian temple is a few short blocks away. The seventy-five families who built it wrote their wishes on pieces of paper that are buried beneath its cornerstone. A beaming monk lets us in. An old man in his undershorts is watching TV in the kitchen, but he slips away as we enter. A researcher found that many Cambodian refugees watching American television thought that the special effects were real. "We used to see that same kind of spirit in

Cambodia, shooting through the air at night," one said of a ghostly fireball. "You have them here, too . . . I've seen them in back of the apartment building."

A Cambodian-American whose name sounds like "Phil" wears a sparkly T-shirt and jeans and speaks at a street vendor's clip. He shows us the altar, rich with offerings. Shrines outside face the eight directions. The eaves are draped with Christmas tree lights. Admiring the temple's fine woodwork, I'm told the refugees did it themselves. The sign over the gate reads "Wat Satheatak Uticaram." I know that *wat* means "temple" and the last word means "of Utica." Is that other word Pali, I ask? "You know a lot," says Phil. After conferring, they translate *satheatak* as "opening of the heart."

The house next door's for sale, and the monk wants the community to buy it. Phil thinks people are afraid to sleep near a temple. "Ghosts?" I ask. "I *knew* you know a lot!" Phil says, but the monk shakes his head in disagreement. Tradition says the fiercest *khmoc*— ghosts—are the spirits of people who died violent deaths. These refugees, survivors of the killing fields, know about ghosts. I leave an offering at the altar.

At dusk I stumble upon the hospital where I was born, framed in the sunset like a B-movie image. A giant banner is draped across it: "The Birthplace." It reminds me of the Philip K. Dick novel in which the protagonist finds the landmarks in his life replaced with signs bearing their names. But the hospital's just advertising its new maternity ward. I was a newborn infant once, right here, tiny and speechless. That idea has never felt real to me before.

The air force base whose B-52s once flew over our house is closed. Sometimes I'd look up to make sure the bomber overhead was "one of ours." During the Cuban Missile Crisis I dreamed an H-bomb exploded. No fire or noise, just the world turning yellowish-brown and crumbling away like old parchment. But Utica's still here, fighting to reinvent itself. There are signs of attempted renewal: microbreweries, a still-thriving museum, a playhouse. There's even a haunted house in an abandoned factory called "Horror Realm," where make-believe ghouls enact freakish industrial experiments for paying visitors. Our childhood nightmares have become a tourist attraction.

I found myself straining to hear the soft-spoken monks. The gates of the senses, first opened here, have begun the long process of closing forever. My city's gone. The child who lived here is not the same person as the man I am. But there's a connection, an unbroken current. Utica will continue. Or it will die, and something else will take its place. Utica's Buddhists seem intent on staying. But the Mohawks, whose empire vanished centuries ago, probably thought they were staying, too. So did the families on my block. Two weeks after my visit, I learned that the Burmese monks had unexpectedly left town.

As I drive away, I see they haven't torn up the old trolley tracks in some older neighborhoods. The sign outside the Catholic church, "Fish Fry or Pirogis Every Friday," could've been there fifty years ago. The Cambodian kids in the takeout restaurant might have been the Irish or Italian or Polish teenagers of my childhood, as the girl behind the counter licks the overflow from a takeout cup and apologizes shyly, "It's for my boyfriend."

Most stories here won't be told, but then most stories never are. Angels become lovers. Memories fade, and other people create new ones. One person's Horror Realm becomes another person's refuge. Ghosts aren't real, or if they're real, then they too melt away. Stories can be rewritten. You can decide for yourself where you're from.

I'm from here.

Hugging Whoooole World ⊙⟩⟩

Shozan Jack Haubner

The pseudonymous Shozan Jack Haubner tells humorous, soul-baring tales of his missteps and mishaps as a Zen practitioner. He may be the funniest writer in American Buddhism, yet this story of life with his ancient, ailing, but still powerful Zen master asks a very important question: What happens when the great Asian teachers die and American Buddhists have to make do on their own?

It is the final evening of Rohatsu, the most intense retreat on the Zen monastic calendar (the "monk killer," Japanese practitioners call it), and we are taking a drive down to the sutra hall, where the following morning we would perform the traditional Jodo-e ceremony in honor of the Buddha's enlightenment. For the first time in anyone's recollection, our teacher would not be attending.

"I coming diiiiiiiificult," he'd said in his broken English. "My body ooooold." His face, ancient yet lineless, bloomed into one of those buoyant expressions that the elderly and infants have in common.

Body old, check. Going to the sutra hall difficult, check. And yet here we were at 11 p.m., loading him into the old Lexus. *He should be resting at this late hour,* I thought. *What does he want to show us?*

Exhausted and ornery, I was in no mood for a lesson. Which is to say, I was ripe for the kind my teacher excels in providing.

I crouched on the driver's seat and a nun guided our teacher from his wheelchair down onto my upturned palm. Not five feet tall, this man is nonetheless profoundly dense. I heaved and strained until he was comfortably positioned in the passenger seat. Have you ever felt the butt of an impossibly old man? Well, there's not much of it to feel. It was as pliant and yielding as overchewed bubble gum, and my fingers went straight to the bone. I could feel his skeleton. He is that exposed to the world. "There is just the thinnest membrane separating him from death," my priest-mentor told me recently.

"Okay, Roshi?" I asked, using his honorific.

"Yeahhh," he sighed. He was cocooned in two cashmere blankets and a massive scarf that went around his tiny yet rotund body three times. He wore an enormous fur hat that towered on the top of his head. He looked like a Mongolian warlord. He pursed his lips and blew through them. "Ooooook."

I carefully drove the length of camp through fog that becomes clouds when seen from below the mountain. We passed two cooks heaving steaming silver cauldrons up the driveway. It was time for *tempatsu*, the tradition of eating *udon* noodles in a thin broth on the last night of Rohatsu.

"Tempatsu, Roshi," I said, and was overjoyed when he seemed unconcerned that we would be missing it. The Japanese like to slurp their noodles; apparently it is a culturally accepted way of expressing culinary approval. And so naturally all forty of us Americans sit there in our Pacific Northwestern zendo, pucker our lips, and inhale our noodles as noisily as possible, looking for all the world like delegates from the First Annual Japanophile convention. My first year here, the slurping apparently wasn't of a sufficient volume, and so one of the zendo officers felt compelled to break the silence and announce: "Slurping okay."

When my teacher dies I will have many such memories of Americans engaging in formal Zen practice. Fortunately, I will have other memories, too.

I wheeled Roshi through the double doors of the sutra hall, which was in various states of preparation for the following day's ceremony. Roshi's eyes slowly traveled right, then left, taking in the scene. One of the priests produced her Blackberry and began recording our teacher on video. I watched this old master on her high-tech screen as she dictated the date, the time, and the people present. Most of what our teacher does now is accompanied by this kind of hullabaloo. We can't take for granted that he'll be around much longer.

In many ways this ancient man has become like a child whose every breath and bowel movement we must monitor. This isn't sycophantic hero-worship: the guy is a living relic, as if someone performed incantations over a classical koan text and out he crawled, flinging teacups and shouting non sequiturs. He is literally the last of his kind, a pre–World War Two–trained Rinzai Zen monk with core Buddhist principles hardwired into the very marrow of his bones. Every teaching he gives is like a piece of fruit fallen from a tree that is about to go extinct from this planet.

Be that as it may, I was exhausted and, frankly, annoyed by the proceedings. Let me ask you something: How many times do you think a Zen monk bows during an average morning of full-on formal practice? I once counted. We're talking forty to sixty bows here, and that's not including the nine full prostrations you perform variously in sets of threes. You bow when you enter the zendo, bow to the tea server, bow to get up and sling the *kesa* portion of your robes over your shoulder, bow to the "zendo guardian" on the way out to your private meeting with Roshi, whom you will then bow four times to, twice before you even say howdy.

"If you're ever in doubt about what to do," I tell new students, "just bow. You can't go wrong."

Earlier that day I had taken a controversial bathroom break at a time not normally allowed for such bodily functions. I entered a stall and slumped on the toilet seat in my underrobes, only to discover that in fact I didn't have to go at all. I guess I simply wanted a moment away from formal Zen practice and subconsciously drifted to the only place on camp where I was assured one.

Hell, I think I just wanted to escape all those bows—the bows, and the punctilious and heavily policed *oryoki*-style meals, and the cloying and ubiquitous *kyo-nishiki* incense, and the weighty forced silences of the zendo, and our American mispronunciation of the Japanese mispronunciation of the Chinese mispronunciation of the Sanskrit mispronunciation of the original Pali chants—and the googolplexian other contrivances that make monastic Zen life what Chögyam Trungpa Rinpoche once called "the biggest joke that has ever been played in the spiritual realm. But it is a practical joke, very practical."

Sitting on a toilet I had no intention of using, I whispered my sacred mantra, given to me by my very first teacher, which was pop culture, mostly MTV, mainly '80s new wave, specifically the Vapors' single hit: "*I'm turning Japanese I think I'm turning Japanese I really think so!*"

At eleven that evening, I was still sour on all things Zen. Roshi must have smelled the nastiness oozing from the bald pores of my febrile skull, because he immediately banished me to a tiny crawl space behind the altar. He did this in the name of choreographing tomorrow's ceremony. To reach this place of exile I had to climb over the white-sheet-draped altar with its ceremonial pound cake platters and towering tea and fruit stands, and I felt very foolish standing in this dark stuffy space in my elaborate "seven layered" robes. Though what I quickly discovered is that sometimes feeling foolish feels very very good. It breathes air into that dark stuffy crawl space between your ears.

Every time I tried to poke my head around the curtain Roshi would point at me and laugh. "Ha ha ha Shozan-san." I felt like the hapless protagonist in a Beckett play, consigned to some ridiculous fate by a mad taskmaster. "*A-hahahahahahaha!*" Roshi cried, jiggling askew that hat that looked like a small television made out of fur. "Shozan's in his little cage," said the nun I'd been fighting with all week.

Roshi turned next to the priest who would be pinch-hitting for him at the ceremony the next day. "More on floor!" he cried, gesturing for the priest to put his *hara*, or diaphragm, flat on the carpet while performing his great bows. This particular priest, with his egg-heady Ken Wilbur glasses and exhaustless penchant for mischief, knows Zen form inside and out, and has a unique talent for tweaking it just enough so that you know he's doing something wrong but you can't quite figure out what it is. He sprawled on the floor, looking like a gunshot victim, trying to mash his hara into the carpet, doing some abomination of the breakdance move "the Worm."

"No no no," Roshi cried, and began to rise up out of his wheelchair in that time-slowing way of his. Dealing with an extremely old person is like dealing with an extremely drunk person: they can tip in any direction at any time. People scrambled to box him in and grab a limb. The great thing about Roshi, I realized, as he stood, balanced, and then produced possibly the longest flatulence I have ever heard in my entire life, followed by, "*Ohhhhhh*, gas come out," is that he allows you to see both the "Great and Powerful Wizard of Oz" manifestation and the "wrinkled old man behind the curtain" manifestation. Both are equal. To favor the spiritual is to be "too in love with heaven," he claims. "And the problem with heaven is—no toilets and no restaurants there."

"*Oh no uh oh*," the nun murmured as Roshi descended to his knees before the bowing mat, his joints sounding off like confetti poppers and all of us gasping and groaning in sympathetic agony.

First he crunched into what's known as child's pose in yoga, his hands outstretched before him, his shins flat on the carpet—the most prostrate stage in a Zen great bow. But then he began to slowly, inexplicably, stretch his legs out behind him one nano—and much-argued-against—inch at a time, until he was lying flat on his stomach with his face pressed into the bowing mat. It was really quite extraordinary, like watching someone suddenly do a double backflip while waiting in line at McDonald's. He balanced on the fulcrum of his tight, rounded stomach, arms and legs outstretched like a kid pretending to fly.

From my confinement behind the altar I craned to catch a glimpse of "the Roshi show" over a votive candle and practically set my *koromo* sleeves ablaze. Surely some mind-blowing lesson awaited us at the end of all this significant effort! But then, maybe the effort itself was the lesson.

"This . . . how Tibetans do it," he grunted.

The priests looked at one another, pens paused over their notebooks. "What, Roshi?" someone asked. "This . . . how Tibetans do it," he repeated, his face muffled on the bowing mat.

"Apparently in the Tibetan tradition they go all the way down and lie flat like this when doing their full prostrations," the priest with the Ken Wilbur glasses explained.

That was the big lesson.

But already Roshi was rising, and the two priests and nun scrambling to help ease his rickety, tendon-trembling ascent. Now he was going to show us how full bows before the altar and Buddha statue were done in the Zen tradition. Whatever. I was over this little lesson, mentally downshifting as I often do when I privately figure that my teacher is having a senior moment.

I was studying the bloody end of a cuticle I'd been nervously gnawing all week when I looked up and saw my teacher staring straight at me—straight *through* me. He was at the top of the bowing mat, squared off in front of the altar, looking very samurai, his hands passing just over his heart, that invisible sword. Behind me was the Buddha statue he was ostensibly addressing with his momentum-gathering gestures. He looked ever so slightly past me to it. And so I saw how he sees the Buddha.

I have never been looked at this way in my entire life. It took me completely off guard. Have you ever been fixed with a gaze of total love that was not a smile? He was, in fact, utterly expressionless. *How do these Zen masters do it?* I thought. *Catch you so off guard with something so simple?*

I watched him find his balance at the top of the key; I watched him extend those tiny, withered hands, the fingerprints worn smooth, out in front of him; I watched him open his arms and widen them in a looping circle, hands meeting at the palms in a prayer gesture, or *gassho*.

"Taking whoooooooooooole world into your arms. Hugging *whole world*," he said.

For that's exactly what he did. He took the whole universe into his frail gray arms and brought it back into his chest like a great samurai sheathing his sword, unlocking for me in a single phrase and motion what had for six years been a largely meaningless gesture, repeated by rote, day upon day. "Turning Japanese"—aping the customs and rituals of a spiritual tradition so foreign to me—didn't seem like such a bad thing now. Watching my teacher in action, it hit me all at once what a tremendous container the rituals and customs are for a truly enlightened mind, and what a profound opportunity they afford for a cathartic gathering and releasing of group anxieties and energies.

"*Etai—etai!*" Roshi suddenly cried, Japanese for *ouch*. A few simple movements. The result—utter agony. The wheelchair appeared behind him, and as he collapsed into it my heart sank along with him, for I finally realized what I had witnessed that evening: certain crucial aspects of a tradition—and so, a whole way of life—literally dying before my eyes.

Rinzai Zen customs and rituals don't come naturally to us Westerners, but in our sangha, our community of practitioners, we heartily participate in them because in the context of this great teacher and his powerful manifestation, they make sense. But what, I wondered, will happen to these customs and rituals when he's gone? Will we have learned what's really behind them, or have we just been blindly participating in them, riding on the coattails of our teacher's understanding? I don't think most of us will truly know the answer to this until he's gone. A great teacher is what an old friend used to call a quality problem. Sometimes it's hard to get out from under his or her enlightenment and learn to think and practice for yourself. But we will all have to, and soon.

When he sighs deeply and stares out his window, past the snow-capped mountain peaks, retreating deep within himself, Roshi looks like a great mythical animal who knows its time has come, and who must soon go off into the forest to die alone. His tenuous health is like a bubble shifting under a carpet: one day his blue-veined feet are swollen but his back is okay; the next, his sciatica is on fire but he "came out"—got unconstipated—that morning; then his eyes are dried out and his mucus is green, but his energy is *genki*—good, strong.

Where his reach once extended to every aspect of sangha life, a gulf of responsibility now opens up behind him that we must fill. But the question on everyone's noodle-slurping lips is *how?* Change a tradition and you change its meaning: this is how traditions die. But follow it to the letter and you become its slave: who wants to be a spiritual company man, a bean counter of the cloth?

About a year ago Roshi got the flu, which can be lethal at his age. Three of us bore him down a flight of stairs to the Town Car, folded him into the front seat, and sped him to Cedars-Sinai, where I and his attendant stayed with him for a week, sleeping on the floor and in chairs upholstered with, it seemed, large slabs of granite.

I saw him naked for the first time. I helped him urinate and defecate. I spoke to nurses and doctors on his behalf, and he and I watched trashy medical dramas on the TV together. The standards of formality significantly lowered, and a new intimacy developed. We even joked around. "White rice, white flour, and white sugar," he proudly stated when I asked him his secret to living a long life. He reminded me of how my grandmother said she used to feel as we braved icy parking lots to her favorite diners: newly game for life with this whippersnapper at her side.

More important, watching Roshi in a nonmonastic setting gave me new insight into just how seamlessly he had made the Zen tradition his own—and vice versa. An uneasy tension had always existed between my free-spirited self and the hyper-disciplined, even militaristic conventions of formal Zen practice. But that week in the hospital I began to see that the proper relationship between an individual and a tradition *is* one of tension—healthy tension. This is what produces spiritual growth, both in the individual and the tradition itself: not the individual's solo efforts nor the tradition's overarching forms, but the two locked into a single struggle/dance, from which a new kind of person—and practice—emerges.

With the full force of the tradition behind him, my teacher searched within himself (the "backward step," as Dogen called it) and eventually broke through, turning himself inside out and taking the outside in. The tradition became personal and the personal universal. As the religious historian Karen Armstrong has pointed out, the tendency in our age is either to reject the traditional and remain isolated, secular individualists, or cling to religious forms and ideals and become fundamentalists. But the truth, like all truths, lies somewhere in between: We can't do it on our own, nor can the tradition do it for us. When the individual and the tradition are perfectly wed, intermingled and indistinguishable, a spiritual heavy hitter—a genuine master—is born, and an institution is revitalized.

In short, the tradition must be dissolved within the individual, and the individual must dissolve within the tradition. That's the middle way.

Toward the end of our strange, harrowing "vacation" in the hospital, I opened an Odwalla juice, poured it into a paper cup, delivered it to his bedside, and flat-out asked my teacher, who was swathed in a nest of blinking lights and wires and looked, with his soft pink skull and silvery hair net, like an alien life-form preparing to return to his home planet (the "space fetus," I dubbed him that day): "Roshi-sama: are you afraid of dying?"

It didn't take him long to answer: "Not afraid of dying. Afraid I die and no one understand my teaching!"

Over the next two days I watched him literally come back from the dead. "Hospitals where people go to die!" he shouted at us. "I not die till I one-hundred-twenty-eight!" *Resurrecting,* he calls it: "There is no true religion without resurrection." I have watched him do this time and time again. Get sick, slip into an exhaustion-coma, loiter on death's door—and then a day later he is reborn, fresh life rippling through him as he waves his gnarled manzanita stick in our private meeting. *This is why I stick around, don the robes, participate in the rituals,* I think, ducking. *Because some teachings transcend tradition.*

Roshi has often said that he will not die until true Buddhism is born in this country, but what will an American Buddhism look like? What *does* it look like? If my practice is the proverbial raft to the other shore, then which of the customs and rituals will I take with me when my teacher dies, and which will I throw overboard?

These questions were haunting me on the final evening of Rohatsu, as I drove Roshi from the sutra hall back to his cabin. But my worries cleared when the clouds briefly parted above and below, and a twinkling vista of stars and city lights opened up. I studied Roshi's one exposed hand, liver spot–marbled and gripping the handle above the door for support. Is there anything more beautiful than old, banged hands that have been put to good use over a lifetime? A tradition, I thought, is like an old man: it must be taken care of; taken with a grain of salt; taken for what it is—precious, limited, a window into the past and, properly plumbed, a door to the future. There we stand at the hinge, making it all happen—or not . . .

When the time comes, I decided, *I'll leave off noodle-slurping but bring with me every last one of my bows.* Noodle-slurping I can live without, but the practice of taking the cosmos above and the metropolis below—"the *whoooooooole* world"—into my arms, and sheathing them in my heart?

That is nonnegotiable.

Contributors

Rick Bass is the author of twenty-five books of fiction and nonfiction, including *Why I Came West*, a finalist for the 2008 National Book Critics Circle Award. He lives with his family in Yaak and Missoula, Montana, where he has long been active in efforts to protect the last roadless lands in the Yaak Valley, one of the wildest landscapes in the northern Rockies. His new book, *Nashville Chrome*, is a novel about music and the destructiveness of fame.

Misha Becker is an associate professor of linguistics at the University of North Carolina at Chapel Hill. She is a poet, a volunteer at the UNC hospice, and a mother of two.

Karen Connelly lives in Toronto with her family, surrounded by Buddhist texts and things-to-do lists. She is the author of *The Lizard Cage*, which won Britain's Orange Broadband Prize for New Novelists in 2007. Her most recent book is *Burmese Lessons*, a memoir of love and revolutionary politics.

His Holiness the Dalai Lama is the spiritual and temporal leader of the Tibetan people and winner of the Nobel Peace Prize. In talks and teachings throughout the world, he advocates a universal "religion of human kindness" that transcends sectarian differences.

Dzogchen Ponlop Rinpoche is a meditation master and scholar in the Kagyu and Nyingma schools of Vajrayana Buddhism. Fluent in the English language and well-versed in Western culture and technology, he is an accomplished calligrapher, visual artist, and poet. His books include *Mind Beyond Death; Penetrating Wisdom; Wild Awakening;* and, excerpted in this anthology, *Rebel Buddha.* Ponlop Rinpoche is the president of Nalandabodhi, a network of meditation centers, and he is also the founder of the Nitartha Institute, a course of Buddhist study for Western students.

RICHARD "RJ" ESKOW is a writer, blogger, and consultant who is active in the fields of public policy, health, communications, economics, and technology. He is a senior fellow with a Washington advocacy group, a frequent contributor to the *Huffington Post,* and a contributing editor for *Tricycle: The Buddhist Review.*

SHOZAN JACK HAUBNER is a pseudonym. He is a Zen practitioner living in the United States. He writes frequently for the *Shambhala Sun, Buddhadharma,* and *Tricycle.*

BRIAN HAYCOCK is a writer and former cabdriver living in Austin, Texas. He currently works for a nonprofit and secretly misses driving a cab. He is the author of *Dharma Road,* excerpted here, and writes noir fiction with a Buddhist bent.

PICO IYER is an essayist, travel writer, and novelist whose writing often addresses the theme of cultural identity in a global age. His books include *The Global Soul, Sun After Dark,* and *The Open Road: The Global Journey of the Fourteenth Dalai Lama,* a contemplation on his more than thirty years of talks and travels with His Holiness.

LIN JENSEN is the author of *Bad Dog!* and *Together Under One Roof: Making a Home of the Buddha's Household.* He is Senior Buddhist Chaplain at High Desert State Prison in Susanville, California, and founder of the Chico Zen Sangha, in Chico, California, where he lives with his wife, Karen. His most recent book is *Deep Down Things: The Earth in Celebration and Dismay*, excerpted here.

WENDY JOHNSON is a Buddhist meditation teacher and organic gardening mentor who lives in the San Francisco Bay Area. She is one of the founders of the organic Farm and Garden Program at Green Gulch Farm Zen Center in Marin County, where she lived with her family from 1975 to 2000. She has been teaching gardening and environmental education to the public since the early 1980s, and is an advisor to the Edible Schoolyard program of the Chez Panisse Foundation. She is a columnist for *Tricycle* magazine and the author of *Gardening at the Dragon's Gate*.

JACK KORNFIELD is one of America's best-known Buddhist teachers and authors. He trained as a Buddhist monk in Thailand, Burma, and India. He is cofounder of the Insight Meditation Society in Barre, Massachusetts, and Spirit Rock Meditation Center in Woodacre, California. He holds a PhD in clinical psychology. His books, which have been translated into twenty languages and have sold more than a million copies, include *A Path with Heart; After the Ecstasy, the Laundry;* and *The Wise Heart*.

GENINE LENTINE is the author of the chapbook *Mr. Worthington's Beautiful Experiments on Splashes*, and she collaborated with Stanley Kunitz and photographer Marnie Crawford Samuelson on the book *The Wild Braid: A Poet Reflects on a Century in the Garden*. She is a student of Roshi Enkyo O'Hara and is the artist-in-residence at the San Francisco Zen Center.

LEZA LOWITZ is an award-winning novelist, poet, translator, and yoga instructor. She has an MA in Creative Writing from San Francisco State, where she taught before moving to Japan. She is the owner of Sun and Moon Yoga studio in Tokyo; the author of fifteen books, including *Yoga Heart: Lines on the Six Perfections;* and has written about expatriate life and Japanese literature and art for international publications.

Eco-philosopher JOANNA MACY's wide-ranging work addresses psychological and spiritual issues of the nuclear age, the cultivation of ecological awareness, and the fruitful resonance between Buddhist thought and contemporary science. Her many books include *Despair and Personal Power in the Nuclear Age; Mutual Causality in Buddhism and General Systems Theory; Coming Back to Life; World as Lover, World as Self;* and *A Year With Rilke.* A respected voice in movements for peace, justice, and ecology, she interweaves her scholarship with four decades of activism.

ELIZABETH MATTIS-NAMGYEL is a Buddhist teacher who leads weekend retreats throughout the United States and Europe. The wife of Tibetan Buddhist master Dzigar Kongtrül Rinpoche, she was the editor of his books *It's Up to You* and *Light Comes Through.* Her first book, *The Power of an Open Question,* is excerpted in this anthology. She has studied and practiced in the Vajrayana Buddhist tradition for twenty-five years.

KATHLEEN MCDONALD (SANGYE KHANDRO) was ordained as a Buddhist nun in 1974. She is a teacher in the Foundation for the Preservation of the Mahayana Tradition and is the author of the bestselling *How to Meditate,* and *Awakening the Kind Heart,* excerpted here. She is the coauthor, with Lama Thubten Zopa Rinpoche, of *Wholesome Fear.*

KEN MCLEOD is the founder of Unfettered Mind, a Buddhist service organization that provides instruction, training programs, and guidance in Buddhist methods for being awake and present in one's life. He is a Buddhist teacher, translator, and the author of *Wake Up to Your Life.* Under the guidance of his principal teacher, the late Kalu Rinpoche, he completed two three-year retreats and is a qualified Tibetan lama.

KAREN MAEZEN MILLER is the author of *Momma Zen* and *Hand Wash Cold: Care Instructions for an Ordinary Life*, excerpted here. She is a priest in the Soto Zen lineage of Taizan Maezumi, Roshi and a student of Nyogen Yeo, Roshi. In daily life, as a mother to her young daughter, Georgia, and as a writer, she aims to resolve the enigmatic truth of Maezumi Roshi's teaching, "Your life is your practice."

SUSAN MOON is a writer and lay Buddhist teacher and was for many years the editor of *Turning Wheel*, the journal of socially engaged Buddhism. She is the author of *The Life and Letters of Tofu Roshi*, a humor book about an imaginary Zen master, and *This Is Getting Old: Zen Thoughts on Aging with Dignity and Humor*, excerpted in this anthology. Moon has been a Zen student since 1976 in the lineage of Shunryu Suzuki, Roshi and is now practicing with Zoketsu Norman Fischer's Everyday Zen sangha.

THICH NHAT HANH is one of the world's leading Buddhist teachers. He is a Zen master, poet, and founder of the Engaged Buddhist movement. A social and antiwar campaigner in his native Vietnam, he was nominated for the Nobel Peace Prize in 1967 by Martin Luther King Jr. He is the author of more than forty books, including *You Are Here*, *Answers from the Heart*, and *Reconciliation: Healing the Inner Child*, excerpted here. Still teaching actively at the age of eighty-five, Thich Nhat Hanh resides at practice centers in France and the United States.

Brothers and renowned Dzogchen teachers, KHENCHEN PALDEN SHERAB RINPOCHE and KHENPO TSEWANG DONGYAL RINPOCHE established the Padmasambhava Buddhist Center, with branches in the U.S., Europe, and Asia, to present the teachings of the Nyingma school of Vajrayana Buddhism. They jointly published a number of works in English, including *The Light of the Dharma, Door to Inconceivable Wisdom and Compassion*, and *The Buddhist Path*, excerpted in this anthology. Khenchen Palden Sherab Rinpoche passed away in June of 2010.

Roshi Pat Enkyo O'Hara received dharma transmission in both the Soto and Rinzai lines of Zen Buddhism and is abbot of the Village Zendo in New York City. Her focus is on the expression of Zen through caring, service, and creative response. She is the guiding spiritual teacher for the New York Center for Contemplative Care and also serves as cospiritual director of the Zen Peacemaker Family.

Susan Piver writes the relationships column for *Body + Soul* magazine and is a frequent guest on network television, including the *Oprah Winfrey Show, Today,* and the *Tyra Banks Show.* Her books include *The Hard Questions: 100 Essential Questions to Ask Before You Say "I Do,"* a *New York Times* bestseller; *How Not to Be Afraid of Your Own Life,* chosen as the best spiritual book of 2007 by Books for a Better Life; and *The Wisdom of a Broken Heart,* excerpted in this anthology. Piver teaches workshops on creativity, relationships, and spirituality and is a graduate of the Shambhala Buddhist Seminary.

Matthieu Ricard is a Buddhist monk who left a career in cellular genetics to study Buddhism in the Himalayas. A close student of the late Dilgo Khyentse Rinpoche, one of the great Buddhist teachers of the twentieth century, Ricard is an author, translator, photographer, and leading participant in scientific research on the effects of meditation on the brain. Two of his books—*The Monk and the Philosopher,* a dialogue with his father, the philosopher Jean-Francois Revel, and *The Quantum and the Lotus*—were best-sellers in France. His most recent book, *Why Meditate?: Working with Thoughts and Emotions,* is excerpted in this anthology.

Ringu Tulku Rinpoche, a teacher in the Kagyu tradition, was trained in all schools of Tibetan Buddhism under great masters such as the Sixteenth Gyalwang Karmapa and His Holiness Dilgo Khyentse Rinpoche. Since 1990 he has been traveling and teaching Buddhism and meditation at universities, institutes, and Buddhist centers in Europe, North America, Australia, and Asia. He is the author of *Mind Training, Path to Buddhahood,* and *Daring Steps,* excerpted here.

RODNEY SMITH is the founder of the Seattle Insight Meditation Society and a guiding teacher at the Insight Meditation Society in Barre, Massachusetts. He leads classes and retreats throughout the United States and is the author of *Lessons from the Dying,* a book that grew out of his many years in hospice work.

IRA SUKRUNGRUANG teaches creative writing at the University of South Florida. He is the author of the memoir *Talk Thai: The Adventures of Buddhist Boy,* and the co-editor of *What Are You Looking At? The First Fat Fiction Anthology;* and *Scoot Over, Skinny: The Fat Nonfiction Anthology.*

JOAN SUTHERLAND, ROSHI is founder of The Open Source, a network of practice communities emphasizing the confluence of Zen koans, creativity, and companionship. Before becoming a Zen teacher, she worked as a scholar and teacher in the field of archaeo-mythology and for nonprofit organizations in the feminist antiviolence and environmental movements.

BONNIE MYOTAI TREACE, SENSEI is the founder of Hermitage Heart and Bodies of Water Zen and teaches at Gristmill Hermitage in Garrison, New York. A student of Zen for more than thirty years, she is a dharma heir of the late John Daido Loori, Roshi and was abbess of the Zen Center of New York City. In addition to her literary studies, Treace had a career in hydromechanics prior to monastic training, and her work in recent years has been dedicated to bringing environmental protection and celebration into contemplative depth.

KHENPO TSULTRIM GYAMTSO RINPOCHE is a meditation master in the Kagyu tradition of Tibetan Buddhism. He taught extensively in the West for many years and now resides in Boudhanath, Nepal. He is well known for his teachings on the songs of the great yogi Milarepa, and for his own spontaneous songs of realization that offer insight into the nature of genuine reality. He is the author of *Progressive Stages of Meditation on Emptiness; The Sun of Wisdom: Teachings on the Noble Nagarjuna's Fundamental Wisdom of the Middle Way;* and *Stars of Wisdom: Analytical Meditation, Songs of Yogic Joy, and Prayers of Aspiration,* excerpted in this anthology.

Credits

rangement with Shambhala Publications Inc., Boston, MA. www
.shambhala.com.

Kathleen McDonald, "Awakening the Kind Heart." From *Awakening the Kind Heart: How to Meditate on Compassion*, by Kathleen McDonald. Copyright © 2010 by Kathleen McDonald. With permission from Wisdom Publications. wisdompubs.org

Ken McLeod, "Something from Nothing." From the Winter, 2010 issue of *Tricycle: The Buddhist Review*.

Karen Maezen Miller, "Hand Wash Cold." Excerpted from *Hand Wash Cold: Care Instructions for an Ordinary Life*, by Karen Maezen Miller. Copyright © 2010 by Karen Maezen Miller. Printed with permission of New World Library, Novato, CA. www.newworldlibrary.com

Susan Moon, "This Is Getting Old." From *This is Getting Old*, by Susan Moon. Copyright © 2010 by Susan Moon. Reprinted by arrangement with Shambhala Publications Inc., Boston, MA. www
.shambhala.com.

Thich Nhat Hanh, "The Child Within." From *Reconciliation: Healing the Inner Child*, by Thich Nhat Hanh. Copyright © 2010 by Unified Buddhist Church. With permission from Parallax Press. www
.parallax.org.

Pat Enkyo O'Hara, "Body And Mind Dropped Away." *From Freeing the Body, Freeing the Mind*, edited by Michael Stone. Copyright © 2010 by Michael Stone. "Body and Mind Dropped Away" is copyright © 2010 by Roshi Pat Enkyo O'Hara. Reprinted by arrangement with Shambhala Publications Inc., Boston, MA. www.shambhala.com.

Khenchen Palden Sherab Rinpoche and Khenpo Tsewang Dongyal Rinpoche, "Taming the Mind." From *The Buddhist Path: A Practical*

Guide from the Nyingma Tradition of Tibetan Buddhism, by Khenchen Palden Sherab Rinpoche and Khenpo Tsewang Dongyal Rinpoche. With permission of Snow Lion Publications, Ithaca, NY. www.snow lionpub.com

Susan Piver, "The Wisdom of a Broken Heart." From *The Wisdom of a Broken Heart: An Uncommon Guide to Healing, Insight and Love*, by Susan Piver. Copyright © 2010 by Susan Piver. Reprinted with the permission of Free Press, a Division of Simon & Schuster, Inc. All rights reserved.

Matthieu Ricard, "Why Meditate?" Adapted from *Why Meditate?: Working with Thoughts and Emotions*, by Matthieu Ricard. Copyright © 2010 by Matthieu Ricard. Published by Hay House. Available at www.hayhouse.com. Reprinted with permission.

Ringu Tulku Rinpoche, "Right Concentration." From *Daring Steps: Traversing the Path of the Buddha*, by Ringu Tulku Rinpoche. With permission of Snow Lion Publications, Ithaca, NY. www.snowlion pub.com

Rodney Smith, "Undivided Mind." From the Winter, 2010 issue of *Tricycle: The Buddhist Review*.

Ira Sukrungruang, "Dead Like Me." From the November, 2010 issue of the *Shambhala Sun*.

Joan Sutherland, "Through the Dharma Gate." From the November, 2010 issue of the *Shambhala Sun*.

Bonnie Myotai Treace, "The Sword Disappears in the Water." From the Spring, 2010 issue of *Tricycle: The Buddhist Review*.

Khenpo Tsultrim Gyamtso, "Stars of Wisdom." From *Stars of Wisdom*, by Khenpo Tsultrim Gyamtso, translated and edited by Ari